RIDICULOUS THEATRE:
SCOURGE

RIDICULOUS THEATRE:
SCOURGE
OF
HUMAN FOLLY

THE ESSAYS AND OPINIONS OF

CHARLES LUDLAM

EDITED BY
STEVEN SAMUELS

THEATRE COMMUNICATIONS GROUP

Ridiculous Theatre: Scourge of Human Folly is published by Theatre Communications Group, Inc., 520 Eighth Ave., 24th Fl., New York, NY 10018-4156.

This publication is made possible in part with public funds from the New York State Council on the Arts, a State Agency.

TCG books are exclusively distributed to the book trade by Consortium Book Sales and Distribution.

LIBRARY OF CONGRESS CATALOGING-IN-PUBLICATION DATA
Ludlam, Charles.
Ridiculous theatre : scourge of human folly : the essays and opinions of Charles Ludlam / edited by Steven Samuels. — 1st ed.
ISBN-13: 978-1-55936-041-8 (paper)
ISBN-13: 978-1-55936-042-5 (cloth)
ISBN-10: 1-55936-041-0 (paper)
ISBN-10: 1-55936-042-9 (cloth)
1. Ludlam, Charles—Aesthetics. 2. Ridiculous Theatrical Company. 3. Dramatists, American—20th century—Interviews. 4. Avant-garde (Aesthetics)—United States.
5. Aesthetics, Modern—20th century. 6. Experimental drama—Authorship.
7. Comedy—Authorship.
I. Samuels, Steven. II. Title.
PS3562.U258Z466 1992
812'.54—dc20   92-2944
                                                         CIP

Design and composition by The Sarabande Press

First Edition, April 1992
Second Printing, November 2007

Contents

CONTENTS

Introduction

Well-known, he would be famous. Influential, he would be unavoidable: onstage, on screen, over the airwaves or by whatever means late twentieth-century culture contrived. He had long labored Off-Off Broadway—obscurely and conspicuously in frequent alternation; honestly and valiantly always—but now he would bring one of his major works, *Der Ring Gott Farblonjet*, to the Great White Way (which moribund monstrosity, more than a few believed, he might help restore to former glory); now he would mount Shakespeare's *Titus Andronicus* audaciously (in the process possibly skewing our perception of the Bard); now, at last, he would achieve hard-won celebrity (pending the release of the first Hollywood feature to feature him, *The Big Easy*). Having previously portrayed figures historical and fictional, male and female both—Bluebeard, Camille, Hamlet and Maria Callas among the many—now this master illusionist would attempt his greatest feat: he would play Houdini.

But in 1987, at the height of his career, Charles Ludlam died, and little of this would be. Remarkably, his death made the front page of *The New York Times*. There was regret for the loss of all he promised, but respect for all he had achieved.

A mere forty-four when he escaped us, Charles had devoted two decades to leading New York's Ridiculous Theatrical Company from cult following to international acclaim. As artistic director, playwright, director, quondam designer and incomparable star, he had ransacked theatrical and literary history in an idiosyncratic, evolutionary quest for a modern art of stage comedy, essaying epic, farce, tragedy and assorted other genres (including several of his own devising) to create his twenty-nine *Complete Plays*—most prominently, *The Mystery of Irma Vep.*

His achievement was singular, if not unprecedented. Exploiting and surviving the aesthetic ferment of the sixties, he had sidestepped a lucrative commercial career, pursuing the unique circumstances which allowed him to create his plays without interference, *in* the theatre—scripting his comic dramas as he staged them. Who besides Charles could boast of a year-round repertory theatre devoted to his own writings exclusively, or of having introduced at least one new play and sometimes several in each of twenty consecutive New York seasons? Who could challenge his claim to have produced the most thought-provoking, liberating, *playable* entertainments available in the modern repertoire?

Over the years his audience grew, but few were aware of the rigorous framework Charles assembled for his theatrical explorations. Only two of his essays were well-distributed in his lifetime: "The Seven Levels of the Theatre," published in the short-lived *Performance* magazine in 1972, and "Manifesto: Ridiculous Theatre, Scourge of Human Folly," which appeared in *The Drama Review* in 1975. Unless you were among the small number of readers of New York's *Gay Power* newspaper in the early seventies, you would have missed his opinions of Mildred Dunnock and Zoe Caldwell ("*Colette*"), his celebration of the religious art of an obscure Lower East Side queen ("Mr. T. or El Pato in the Gilded Summer Palace of Czarina-Tatlina"), and his exaltation of the use of female impersonators traditionally and in his own early plays ("A Monograph and a Premature Memoir").

Prose puzzled him. He wrote little of it, in part because he was too busy writing, producing and performing his plays, but primarily because he understood the formal constraints of drama—the human, technical and temporal limitations of the theatre—and without them, how could he know when to stop?

After his death, a cache of fragmentary essays and notes was found amidst the notebooks and papers in his crowded, dusty study, together with significant statements written for grant applications to the National Endowment for the Arts and the New York State Council on the Arts, unusually provocative press releases, and the transcript of an illuminating talk he gave at New York University in 1979. Of these, I have chosen a half dozen to publish in full. "The Last Shall Be First" was printed as a program note for the revival of Charles' second staged play (the first produced under the aegis of the Ridiculous Theatrical Company), *Conquest of the Universe or When Queens Collide.* "Costume Fetishism or Clothes Make the Man," a paper he labored over in more sexually liberated days, reveals his intimate knowledge of the homosexual demimonde, and "Salomé" reflects the sexual and political ramifications he perceived in a role he never played but which absorbed his attention over many years. "From Pillar to Post Modern" recapitulates a theme to which he returned relentlessly—the fraudulence of most of what passed as "avant-garde" in the theatrical arena; a brief dialogue, "Ludlam Versus Critics," embodies his ambivalence towards one of the industry's more dubious necessities; and his abandoned "*Hedda* Journal," prompted by an independent production of *Hedda Gabler* with Charles in the title role, demonstrates how serious his comedy could be.

Engaging and insightful as these materials are, they only hint at the discoveries made throughout a life comprehensively focused on the theatre. Apart from the stage, the true outlet for the endless flow of ideas that bubbled up from Charles' superheated brain was conversation, talk which may have seemed an unstoppable stream of babble to the casual observer but which was, instead, the continual reprocessing of the endless supply of plot and dialogue preserved by a nearly photographic memory, combined with the vast, practical experience of a long and remarkable career.

Few of us privileged to have worked closely with Charles were blessed with his gift of total recall. Though we possess ineradicable memories, and have incorporated Charles' vision into our own lives and works, we cannot reproduce with any acceptable degree of accuracy his actual words.

Happily, Charles gave in-depth interviews frequently, and it is within these that the majority of his undramatized ideas reside. From the most detailed reports of the making and meaning of his plays to his more broad-based understanding of the purpose and place of comedy in modern life, Charles' thoughts were carefully formulated and cogently expressed.

Reprinting the interviews as they ran originally would make an impossibly long read, and significant pruning would gut the structure of these newspaper, magazine and radio pieces. In attempting to abide by Charles' intention someday to edit them into a book—keeping in mind that he learned early on to determine in advance what he wanted to say and to say it whatever he was asked—I have dispensed with questions, bringing Charles' "Opinions" together thematically ("Broadway," "Opera," "Film," etc.); and, in "Confessions of a Farceur," constructing a narrative derived from one of his many unrealized ambitions: an autobiography.

In the early eighties, Charles announced the writing of his memoirs much as he announced a new play: as an accomplished fact, once he'd written a few pages. His eyes lit up mischievously when he spoke of publishing his life story. Untruths and distortions had been perpetrated which he longed to set right. His autobiography was to be a gleeful act of revenge against all he felt had wronged him.

That project, too, died with him, but here Charles' assorted prose writings form the basis of an intellectual and aesthetic autobiography, which his interviews—edited discreetly—flesh out. The fragment which begins and lends its name to this section is among the most polished of Charles' prose statements: a forthright, deeply felt, well-considered exposition of the nature of his occupation as a maker of theatre.

He was not shy about explaining his plays, particularly since they provoked controversy and were, he felt, ill-understood. Charles had a preternaturally clear concept of what he was doing and he wanted to share it with his audience. He was his own best explicator, and if contradictions abound they expose not only Charles' ability to comprehend and represent opposing views, but also his admirable willingness to abandon a position or to alter course in accommodating circumstance and change.

The ultimate accommodation is addressed in a final dialogue I call "Envoi." This unusually autobiographical effort appears unexpectedly in Charles' *Houdini* notebook, amidst notes and drafts of scenes toward what was widely anticipated would be the culmination of his experiments with magic and illusion.

Early in 1987, when "Envoi" was written, Charles knew he had AIDS, but kept that knowledge close to home. He proceeded heroically with his myriad obligations: revising his comic take on Wagner's *Ring* for Broadway; preparing *Titus Andronicus* for the New York Shakespeare Festival in Central Park; editing his virtually handmade film, *The Sorrows of Dolores*, for its premiere at the Collective for Living Cinema; and embarking upon the writing, directing and portraying of *Houdini*, as well as the writing and directing of a documentary film about the making of the play.

When he was hospitalized on April 30 of that year, he refused to discuss or admit his illness. Even after the signing of his will, death was an unacknowledged subject. As the Ridiculous Theatrical Company's general manager, I had no idea of how Charles would like his company to continue without him.

That he wanted his company to proceed was inarguable. During a fall 1986 National Public Radio interview about his last play, *The Artificial Jungle*, the question was raised as to whether or not the Ridiculous could carry on without him. His fellow actors, as one, said no, which made him furious. Afterwards, he made it plain that he perceived himself to be building an enduring institution, and that he expected his work to flourish even after he was gone.

The company's decision to go on was made before we laid him in the ground. His co-star and lover, Everett Quinton, announced that Charles had named him his successor as artistic director; but, in his modesty, Everett felt keenly the burden of his position and joked self-deprecatingly on occasion of perhaps having fooled us all, since there was no witness other than himself to Charles' wishes.

As it happens, Charles bore his own witness. By the time I presented a transcript of "Envoi" to Everett, its points were moot anyway. While Charles lived, there was widespread doubt that anyone else would have the ability or nerve to mount or inhabit his plays. Five years after his passing, the persisting Ridiculous has repeatedly revived his works successfully, and they have been produced by numerous other companies around the world.

■

When I joined the Ridiculous twelve years into its history, I was fortunate enough to have half an hour each night to sit in Charles' dressing room and listen as he costumed himself, applied makeup, and talked. In structuring this book, I have thought often of that unintentional seminar in the Ridiculous, and of our thousands of subsequent artistic, business, political and personal conversations. In this volume, I have presented Charles in ways he could never have envisioned, but as I read and reread these words it is Charles' voice I hear, his wide-ranging considerations, his insatiable desire to reformulate and reform a debased culture, his endless effort to exceed his own extraordinary capabilities and to provide a vision—not of a better future, but of a better *present*.

Those who have mistaken Charles' theatre for the wild and meaningless antics of a gifted buffoon may be startled by this manifestation of a clear-eyed, hard-headed thinker who passionately believed in stage comedy as the best public forum for the discussion and dissemination of ideas. *Ridiculous Theatre: Scourge of Human Folly* belongs on that short shelf of books by master craftsmen. In these pages, too—as well as in his plays and on the stages that unfold them—the glory that was Ludlam lives on.

Steven Samuels
New York City
January 1992

Acknowledgments

I must express abiding gratitude to Everett Quinton and Walter Gidaly, literary executors of the Estate of Charles Ludlam, for entrusting Charles' papers to me.

Thanks are also due to those interviewers who provided a forum for Charles in publications as diverse as *The New York Times* and Paris *Vogue*. Without them this book would not exist: Ronald Argelander, Leslie Bennetts, Ruggero Bianchi, Ira Bilowit, Stefan Brecht, Ted Castle, Robert Chesley, Harrison Clark, Tish Dace, Gautam Dasgupta, T. G. Fiori, Sylviane Gold, Freeman Gunter, Mel Gussow, Robert Heide, Sylvia Heisel, William M. Hoffman, Michael Hoover, Joseph Hurley, Dan Isaac, Alvin Klein, Richard Laermer, Cole Mobley, Michael Musto, Don Nelsen, Mary Martin Niepold, Patricia O'Haire, Lola Pashalinski, Ron Pennington, Dennis Powers, Eva Saks, Curt Sanburn, Leo Seligsohn, David Shear, Don Shewey, Sam Shirakawa, Stephen M. Silverman, Jerry Slaff, Michael Smith, Alan Stern, David Sterritt, E. Donnell Stoneman, Robert Taylor, Teriananda, Calvin Tomkins, Joan E. Vadeboncoeur, Christopher Vaughn, George Vernadakis, Steve Warren, Andreas Weigelt, Ed Wetschler, Diane Wolff and Alan R. Yoffee. A special nod of thanks goes to Agnes Wilcox for transcribing and editing the original of Charles' 1979 talk at New York University.

Additional thanks to the staff of the Billy Rose Theatre Collection

1961

Founds the Students' Repertory Theatre in Northport, Long Island. Matriculates at Hofstra University with an acting scholarship.

1964

Writes first full-length play, *Edna Brown*, which he subsequently destroys.

1965

Graduates from Hofstra, moves to New York City.

1966

Makes his New York stage debut as Peeping Tom in Ronald Tavel's *The Life of Lady Godiva*, directed by John Vaccaro at the Play-House of the Ridiculous. Spontaneously creates the role of Norma Desmond in Tavel's *Screen Test*. Completes first extant play, *Big Hotel*, staged by Vaccaro under the aegis of the Ridiculous.

1967

During rehearsals for his second play, *Conquest of the Universe*, Ludlam is summarily fired by Vaccaro. Most of the actors walk out in protest, urge Ludlam to found his own troupe. He stages his own version of *Conquest of the Universe* as *When Queens Collide*, the first production by the Ridiculous Theatrical Company.

1968

Revives *Big Hotel* in midnight repertory with *When Queens Collide* at Tambellini's Gate on Second Avenue. Stages Bill Vehr's *Whores of Babylon* several times, once as a shadow-puppet presentation. Collaborates with Vehr on *Turds in Hell*, which is subsequently published in *The Drama Review*. Temporarily renames his company the Trockadero Gloxinia Magic Midnight Mind Theatre of Thrills and Spills.

1969

First version of *The Grand Tarot*, "A Masque." *Village Voice* Obie award to Ludlam and the Ridiculous for distinguished achievement in the Off-Broadway Theatre.

1970

Bluebeard, "A Melodrama in Three Acts," becomes the company's first critical success, originally staged at Christopher's End, then briefly at La MaMa ETC before an extended run at the Performing Garage. First college appearances. Guggenheim Fellowship in Playwriting awarded to Ludlam.

1971

First European tour. Second Prize awarded to *Bluebeard* at BITEF International Avant-Garde Theatre Festival in Belgrade, Yugoslavia. Premiere of *Eunuchs of the Forbidden City* in Germany, with subsequent publication in *Scripts* magazine. *Bluebeard* published in two Off-Off-Broadway play anthologies. First grants to the Ridiculous Theatrical Company from the New York State Council on the Arts and the National Endowment for the Arts. "The Seven Levels of the Theatre" published in *Performance* magazine.

1972

Corn, "A Country-Western Musical," with music and lyrics by Virgil Young, staged. Plans for a subsequent Broadway production fall through.

1973

Camille, "A Tearjerker," also called "A Travesty on *La Dame aux Camélias* by Alexandre Dumas *fils*," debuts with Ludlam in the title role. Obie for distinguished performance awarded to Ludlam for appearances in both *Corn* and *Camille.* Second European tour.

1974

Lease signed for the Evergreen Theater, the company's first "permanent" home. *Hot Ice* premiered, subsequently published in *The Drama Review.* Ludlam serves first of three terms on NYSCA's theatre panel.

1975

"Manifesto: Ridiculous Theatre, Scourge of Human Folly" published in *The Drama Review. Stage Blood* mounted, later published by Performing Arts Journal publications in volume of *Ridiculous Theatre*. First performances of *Professor Bedlam's Educational Punch and Judy Show*, which receives a special Obie award. NYSCA "Younger Audience" commission to Ludlam to write *Jack and the Beanstalk*. The Evergreen sold by owner Grove Press to the Baha'i Foundation.

1976

Commission from Adela Holzer to write book for *Isle of the Hermaphrodites, or The Murdered Minion*, an abortive Broadway musical concerning Catherine de' Medici and the Saint Bartholomew's Day massacre. Playwriting award from the Rockefeller Brothers Fund enables Ludlam to write *Caprice or Fashion Bound*, which marks the stage debut of Everett Quinton, with whom Ludlam will live and work for the rest of his life. Third European tour.

1977

CBS Fellowship to coach graduate students in playwriting at Yale University. Ludlam creates "Aphrodisiamania," a scenario for the Paul Taylor Dance Company, and writes *Der Ring Gott Farblonjet*, "A Masterwork," with a grant from the Ford Foundation's New American Plays program. Production wins Ludlam an Obie for design.

1978

The Ventriloquist's Wife, "A Psychodrama for Cabaret," plays several New York nightclubs and tours the country, including performances in the lounge of the MGM Grand in Las Vegas, earning enough money for the down payment on what becomes the company's permanent home at One Sheridan Square. Premiere of *Utopia, Incorporated*, "An Industrial." Award for Excellence and Originality in Comedy from the Association of Comedy Artists presented to Ludlam. Creation of *Anti-Galaxie Nebulae*, a sci-fi puppet serial written and performed in collaboration with Bill Vehr and Everett Quinton.

1979

Plays Chuckie in Mark Rappaport's film *Impostors*. Stages *The Enchanted Pig*, "A Fairy Tale for the Disenchanted." Revives *Conquest of the Universe or When Queens Collide.* Creates *The Elephant Woman,* a "midnight frolic." Adapts Charles Dickens' *A Christmas Carol* and stars as Ebenezer Scrooge. Teaches "Eccentric Comedy" in the Experimental Theatre Wing at New York University. Begins filming *The Sorrows of Dolores.*

1980

Company's final tour under Ludlam's leadership. *The Production of Mysteries,* a twenty-minute opera, written with composer-in-residence Peter Golub. Ludlam creates *Reverse Psychology,* "A Farce," and subsequently directs William Wycherly's *The Country Wife* for the drama department at Carnegie-Mellon University.

1981

Stages second farce, *Love's Tangled Web.* Films *Museum of Wax* in Coney Island.

1982

Receives NEA Fellowship in Playwriting. Produces *Secret Lives of the Sexists,* "The Farce of Modern Life," and *Exquisite Torture,* "A Romantic Ecstasy."

1983

Adapts *Le Bourgeois gentilhomme* into *Le Bourgeois Avant-Garde,* "A Comedy Ballet after Molière." Plays Maria Callas in *Galas,* "A Modern Tragedy," which is named among the year's best plays by *Time* magazine and *The New York Times.* A Drama Desk Special Award for Outstanding Achievement in the Theatre is presented "in recognition of fifteen years of Ridiculous productions." Ludlam receives an NEA Fellowship to teach playwriting at Yale University.

1984

The Mystery of Irma Vep, "A Penny Dreadful," starring Ludlam and Quinton, is named among the year's best plays by *Time* magazine and *The New York Times,* wins Drama Desk and Obie awards for the actors' performances and a Maharam Foundation Award for Excellence in

Design for Ludlam's sets. Ludlam guest stars with Madeline Kahn on network television's "Oh, Madeline." He writes but does not stage an adaptation of Euripides' *Medea*. His "Absolute Farce," *How to Write a Play*, is performed twice at the end of the season to fulfill contractual obligations before Ludlam leaves for Pittsburgh to appear with the American Ibsen Theater in the title role of *Hedda Gabler*.

1985

Adapts Gustave Flaubert's novel of the fall of Carthage, *Salammbô*, into "An Erotic Tragedy," playing the title role of the thirteen-year-old virgin priestess of the moon. Stages Hans Werner Henze's *The English Cat* for the Santa Fe Opera. Appears as a guest star on the season premiere of "Miami Vice." Receives another NEA Fellowship in Playwriting. Oversees performances of *The Production of Mysteries* by the Brooklyn Philharmonic Orchestra, Lukas Foss, conductor. Wins Rosamund Gilder Award for distinguished achievement in the theatre.

1986

Makes guest-star appearance on syndicated television show, "Tales from the Dark Side." Performs in two films: *Forever Lulu* and *The Big Easy*. Adapts and stages *Die Fledermaus* for the Santa Fe Opera. Stages his last play, *The Artificial Jungle*, "A Suspense Thriller." Begins work on *Titus Andronicus* for projected performances in the New York Shakespeare Festival's Central Park series. Negotiates a Broadway production of *Der Ring Gott Farblonjet*. Begins work on the never-completed *Houdini*, "A Piece of Pure Escapeism" [sic], as well as a film documentary of the making of the play. Is diagnosed with AIDS at Thanksgiving.

1987

Playscript publisher Samuel French, Inc., negotiates rights to represent *Bluebeard, Stage Blood, The Mystery of Irma Vep* and *The Artificial Jungle*. Ludlam is hospitalized on April 30, the same night *The Sorrows of Dolores* premieres at New York's Collective for Living Cinema. Ludlam receives an Obie Award for Sustained Achievement. He dies of complications from AIDS on May 28, at the age of forty-four. Everett

Quinton, at Ludlam's behest, assumes the artistic directorship of the Ridiculous Theatrical Company, produces the world premiere of *Medea*.

1988
New York City renames the street in front of the theatre at One Sheridan Square "Charles Ludlam Lane."

1989
The Complete Plays of Charles Ludlam published by Harper & Row.

1991
The Mystery of Irma Vep, already staged successfully nationally and internationally, becomes one of the most-produced plays in America.

CONFESSIONS
OF A
FARCEUR

I think of myself as an inventor of plays. The wright in playwright is worker, maker: one who works in wood such as a shipwright. My plays are wrought as much as written. I work in the theatre as well as the study. My literary efforts are concerned with drawing up plans and a recipe for an event. This event will take the form of a representation of a combat whose outcome is of some concern.

Playwrighting is based on the interplay of a fixed element and a variable. The fixed element is the architecture of the event as it will be brought to pass in time. The variable is the expressive element, the human element. My work is to organize the task of writing. My characters come from what I know of people, and my dialogue is my ongoing debate with my fellow beings.

Should I spectate? Should I perform? What is the best way to bring about an objective representation of images from an inner world? I like to give myself up to a role: enter a trancelike state, burn energy, aggrandize through influence, juggle, prestidigitate and ventriloquize. I like to feel redeemed by a lively tempo that leaps over obstacles and incongruities like the pulse of wholesome life!

I'm no good unless I'm doing three things at once. Diversity is incomprehensible in the Johnny-one-note atmosphere of contemporary art. This is a major misconception about my work. In the past my work was used by critics as a satiric cudgel to beat the last breath of life out of an expiring narrative-drama tradition. But secretly I reinseminated that tradition. All I ever wanted to do was to make anagrammatic use of the world's plot matrix. But still the Puritan taboo against cheerfulness would like to punish the Ridiculous. The debate over the value of farce rages on not, as one would expect, over morality but over causality, not over truth but over taste. Yes, I sometimes dispense with a purely rational connection between events, but never to replace it with a merely sentimental one. I prefer to advance the technology of dramatic literature.

Some plays have good audiences and bad audiences and some plays never have a bad audience. This interests me more than who the audience is. My plays are not for myself alone. I take seriously the responsibility of working in a public artform. I want to match my view of the world against that of the audience and leave myself vulnerable to their acceptance or denial.

I've taken the whole medium into my own hands because this is the most efficient way of realizing my ideas. I enjoy the whole ongoing enterprise. I work hard and walk in the virtue of my father, who built our house with his own hands.

1

History mystory I am going to tell my story because others have told it secondhand. It's not that they have not told it well, but none was able to tell what really happened. If I am going to end up a fictional character, as do all historical figures—which we all become sooner or later—I would prefer to be as much a character of my own creation in literature as I am in life. Others who have written about me have doubted the truth of what I told them or valued their own reputations as writers more than they did mine. Although I served as the excuse for them to write, I don't think anyone has been really fair.

Criticism is an ungrateful form of expression which gives little credit to the subject from which it draws its *raison d'être*. The critic wishes the end of the artist's creative life so that his criticism can be completed. Artists who continue to produce represent a chore.

∎

The Ludlam family is very old for this country. They came over in the sixteen hundreds and were the first settlers on Long Island. The first recorded Ludlam—William—was a miller who owned Southampton, and was probably the first white man buried on that island.

My mother's family were German. Her German father married an Irish girl. Both my grandmothers were Irish Catholic girls who converted their Protestant husbands to Catholicism.

A puritanical Protestant tradition with a *very* puritanical Catholicism glued on. . . . The whole imagery in my way of thinking is Catholic—icons, incense; sensual, theatrical; theatre as an essential part of life, which the Mass was; theatre as sacrifice, as a form of a ritual sacrifice; theatre as life, really integrated into the life.

■

When did my creative life begin?

In payment for a favor, a man who worked for Walt Disney gave my father free tickets to *Fantasia*. This my parents went to see while my mother was carrying me. It made a big impression on them and they told me about it for years before I actually saw the movie. When I finally did see it, I felt I knew it already.

My father was an eccentric with a great sense of humor, an extremely flamboyant man, a larger-than-life character to me. Once when I was little he brought me a stuffed panda bigger than myself, which I named Oscar. Oscar had a tiny bell in his ear.

We lived in an apartment over a drugstore. I slept for a time in a crib in my parents' room. The druggist's neon sign in red flashed outside the windows through the organdy curtains and created a fantasy effect. Birds used to nest in the sign and we fed them. I used to sit in the window of that room looking out on Jericho Turnpike and play with little tin soldiers with which I would stage battles . . . and watch the movie theatre across the street change its program and marquee twice a week.

My mother would take me every time the program changed. I didn't come from a theatre family, but I went to the movies two or three times every week and saw every film of the forties, every movie that came along. We ate Mason Mints, and my mother used to cry in the dark, which I found very painful. Often I cried too, in sympathy with her.

I remember when *The Thing* came out. They had squiggly letters on the marquee, and I was so terrified my mother wouldn't let me go see it. As a result, my imagination started to embroider what it was from every bit of evidence I could glean—reviews, tales from my friends. I became so frightened I couldn't sleep. I had nightmares. I lived in terror of *The Thing* because I didn't see it.

A couple of years ago, I was watching late-night TV and suddenly *The Thing* came on. I couldn't believe it was so much less than I had imagined as a child—not frightening at all; in fact, terribly funny. And all those terrors that were still there were dispelled.

It would have been better to let me see it than to be a victim of my imagination.

■

My mother never allowed me to see or read anything that might be frightening. Toy guns, *Keeper of the Crypt* comic books, horror movies and the freak show that always played the Mineola Fair were strictly forbidden.

On one occasion during our annual visit to this fair, my mother gave me two dollars to spend any way I wished. We visited a beehive behind glass and sampled various kinds of honey at one exhibit. Then I slipped away from my mother, assuming any way I wished meant *any* way I wished. I headed straight for the forbidden freak show.

Inside I saw the fat lady, a fire-eater, and for an extra fifty cents the thin man. I remember seeing armless black dwarfs painting people's portraits in pastels with their toes. I was enthralled.

But best of all was the Punch and Judy show performed in a booth high above my head. I remember looking up at the steep stage, hearing Mr. Punch's unearthly squeak, a voice produced through a reed balanced on the tongue—a swazzle.

> Mr. Punch: Who are you?
> Devil: I'm the devil.
> Mr. Punch: Well get the devil out of here!
> *(Whack with the stick)*

I remember Judy's tiny tin dishes came clattering out of the frame when she threw them at Mr. Punch.

After the show I drifted back outside sort of dazed, and found my mother beside herself with worry. She had the police looking for me. I was never aware that I was lost. I hadn't had a moment's insecurity.

Years later I met Al Flosso, a great magician and Punch-man. He taught me a lot. He even gave me a swazzle, just before he died. He told me he had played the Mineola Fair around that time. If it weren't for the stubborn memory of the little tin dishes—which he claimed never to have used in his performances—we would both have been convinced that it was he who gave me my first taste of live theatre.

Soon after this, I set up my own puppet theatre in the basement of our house. My younger brother Donald was the audience. Sometimes my mother came down, too; she's always been very supportive.

■

As a child, I was very withdrawn. I never liked other children. I never liked games. Animated cartoons and puppets shaped my life, along with movies. I learned to read from comic books.

I did plays with the little girls in a backyard next door. We used to put up a bedsheet for a curtain and I'd give them lines to say. Recently one of them wrote to me, "I can't believe you're still doing the same thing you were doing when you were seven years old."

■

One day my parents brought me a rolltop desk with drawers and pigeonholes in it—later it became my brother's, and now it belongs to my niece Rosalyn. This desk began my interest in writing. I wrote my first poem at it, about Halloween.

Halloween was my favorite holiday. I used to dress up as a girl and go trick or treating. I remember going to a school party in drag and causing a bit of a scandal. When I realized that such dressing up was forbidden, I began to practice it regularly in secret, using my mother's clothes. People frequently mistook me for a girl anyway.

■

I was always encouraged to pursue acting. It seemed the natural thing to do.

I really wanted to work in the theatre. As a kid, I liked Shakespeare and the classics and I read every play I could get my hands on. Classics seemed to be the alternative to theatre as "show business"—although I did have a kind of show business fantasy, too.

If I hadn't discovered theatre early on, I would almost certainly have become a juvenile delinquent. I think I was expected to settle down in Greenlawn, Long Island, marry a somewhat homely girl and produce lots of children. But if I had done that and not what I wanted to do, they would have found me hanging in the garage one day.

■

I saw summer stock productions on Long Island when I was in my early teens. I didn't get to Broadway until my late teens.

In 1958 I apprenticed to the Red Barn Theatre, Bill Hunt's summer stock theatre on Long Island, and met real actors and actresses. I started to realize there was a life beyond Greenlawn, and that this was what I wanted to do in life. It became more real, seeing them stage eight productions. They would do a play in two weeks, then they'd play while they rehearsed the next one. It was really a classical stock company. I learned all aspects of theatre.

■

Then I went to see the Living Theatre: Julian Beck and Judith Malina playing in New York, down on 14th Street, in the Village. I saw two productions on two different occasions: *Tonight We Improvise* and *The Connection*. That was really a big breakthrough for me, because I realized that it was possible to do something very different from commercial theatre—that theatre could be what you wanted it to be. It could be personal expression.

The Becks became idols. I wanted to be like them. At that time they hadn't taken the leap into the kind of nonnarrative theatre *The Brig* brought on. They were still into what they called poetry and symbol. They were doing Pirandello and Aeschylus. That's what I wanted to do at the time.

They did these very interesting plays using European theatrical techniques filtered through an American sensibility, with a lot of jazz and improvisation. It became very clear to me that the theatre could be more than just an entertainment medium.

The next year I opened my own place, with students, in North-port, Long Island. When I founded my theatre, it was up a steep flight of stairs, just like on 14th Street. I remember feeling I was just like my idols.

■

Every school has a drama department or drama club, and there are always one or two really good people. We got the best from several and had an incredible company. We even got reviewed.

We were precocious kids, but a lot of the parents got the idea some pretty sinister things were going on. We were really avant-garde. I'd always been interested in the literary byways of the theatre, really obscure plays. We did *Madman on the Roof* by a Japanese playwright, Kikuchi Kahn, and we did *Theatre of the Soul* by Nikolai Nikolaivich Yevreinov, a late-romantic, Russian avant-garde play that took place inside the human body, in the soul. And we did O'Neill's *Great God Brown* and August Strindberg's *Dream Play*.

It was a thirty-two-seat theatre in an abandoned Oddfellows meeting hall. We did a couple of seasons and then the theatre had to close, because I was going off to college.

■

I went to Hofstra, where I majored in drama, did the classics, staged and acted in them. I had a scholarship in acting. I thought acting was the priesthood of the theatre. But the teachers at Hofstra told me I should write and direct rather than act.

I had written plays before, but I took terrible offense at this. Now I realize I was just being silly. At the time I felt that my acting was being rejected.

Originally I was doing experiments with plotless drama. I was very influenced by Strindberg. Probably he is the most powerful influence in my development, especially his surrealistic work and expressionistic plays. You find in Strindberg's *Dream Play* lots of little modern master-pieces. Hidden there you'll find *Waiting for Godot, The Chairs* of Ionesco. You might find everything of Genet in the Hyacinth Room of *Ghost Sonata*.

I was very interested in the panoramic, baroque elements in his plays. From the beginning—even as a teenager, when I first became acquainted with him—his work struck a chord in me. The incredible somberness of it, the unrelenting sadness of it appealed to me at the time.

■

I started experimenting. I wrote a few plays that were expressionistic (a couple of one-acters) and a tragedy of courtly love (everything was in verse). By my senior year in college I wrote a full-length play about my family history, which I destroyed in a moment of desperation.

It was a sort of expressionistic, semiautobiographical play, seventy-eight pages long, called *Edna Brown*. I wanted to form a company of students to do it, but the school year was ending.

I can see now that it contained the seeds of many things I've done since. There was a character named Exotica A La Carte, who lived on the proceeds of a string of pay toilets. Another character spoke entirely in song titles.

■

Those four years at Hofstra were a very turbulent period for me. I was rebellious against my teachers, many of whose ideas I found offensive. I had an idea of the theatre that I wanted to create—I'd made a rough start on it with the Students' Repertory Theatre in high school.

Somehow, I felt I had to create a new theatre, but I didn't completely realize what that meant.

I was ten years ahead of my time.

2

I have worked with a lot of female impersonators, transvestites and drag queens since I first met Mario Montez in 1965 and discovered the dual nature of my own personality. I was on the set for the shooting of José Rodriguez-Soltero's epic underground movie, *The Life, Death and Assumption of Lupe Velez*, in which Mario played the title role. In one sequence José intended that Lupe's lover should discover her shooting up dope and break off their affair. Someone forgot to bring a set of works. Montez was applying layer after layer of lip gloss, patiently waiting until José got the idea to change the scene to Lupe's lover discovering her in bed with a lesbian. But who would play the lesbian? José looked at me. "You won't get in drag, will you?" he said. "Why not?" I said, "I identify with lesbians."

My love scene on the silver screen with Mario Montez caused something of a stir. At the time it was a breakthrough. Now it's history.

•

Later that year I walked into an improvisation called *Screen Test*, without rehearsal. Mario asked me to go on in drag to liven things up.

I'd been in drag once before, in a little film, but I'd never done it onstage and I was nervous. Other actors warned me I'd be ruining my career.

Suddenly the role of Norma Desmond, the fading silent-movie queen, came to me. It sprang from the head of Zeus full-blown.

Drag came naturally to me. I daresay female impersonators are born not made.

I went on as Norma Desmond with absolutely no preparation. Before that, I'd needed weeks of rehearsal for any part. It changed my life. The disguise, the costume, freed me, made me do things I could never have done myself. For me acting was always a chore—research, etc.—but with Norma I felt I could walk on with Hedda Gabler tomorrow. It would just come through.

The wig that I wore was given to Henry Geldzahler by Salvador Dali, and he had just given it to me before I went on. I put on the wig and—pow!—there was Norma.

It's that teetering on the edge of being a man and a woman that throws the audience. I believe that I am Norma.

And they recognize her. She's an archetype. Everyone thinks it's a different actress.

■

In a way John Vaccaro gave my whole theatrical life back to me. I had really given it up. In companies I had always stood out—not as a good actor, but as a sore thumb.

John has great instinct and is a brilliant actor. He gave me freedom. He allowed me to flip out all I wanted onstage. He never felt that I was too pasty, corny, mannered, campy. He let me do anything I wanted.

He is very primitive and very difficult for most actors to work with, because he's sort of savage. He gets you into doing things by rote. He criticizes ideas without giving any suggestions for improvements, and then makes you do it over and over again. It's psychological torture.

I felt John was too conservative. He didn't want homosexuality or nudity onstage because he was afraid of being arrested. I wanted to commit an outrage. For me, nothing was too far out.

■

In the Ridiculous theatre there was a highly competitive feeling among the practitioners, which did not encourage anybody new to do anything extraordinary. It was a lot of fighting. The Ridiculous is really about rugged individualism. It didn't come out of any communal, left-wing, sentimental, folksy thing. It was really just a bunch of egomaniacs fighting, demanding that their ideas were the greatest and most original. It was very chaotic.

We were working in a very volatile atmosphere. All those millions of ideas we had as a group became a problem. Everybody wanted to do this and that, and nobody wanted to agree.

I was just acting. I came to a nihilistic state where I wanted to do dadaist things. In my *Southern Fried Chekhov*, I put a copy of the complete works of Chekhov in a pan of hot fat and fried it. I wrote a play in Hungarian from a Hungarian menu. These were really minimalist things, four or five lines written on three-by-five cards, just for the amusement of myself and my friends.

Finally I started doing an experiment in collage which became *Big Hotel*, the first play of mine produced in New York. I was doing aleatoric writing then, cutting up other plays, scenes, things I'd hear on the radio or TV. The basic structure was that it took place in a hotel—all kinds of crazy things going on in this hotel.

■

There are a lot of ways of doing collage. One is mistranslation, a fabulous technique where you translate a language you don't understand by the way the words look. It's based on the idea of everything being a misconception. It isn't too far from Aristophanes' concept of the "happy idea"—the basic idiotic idea.

I would do mistranslation, then I would thumb through books and use a phrase. I would cut a play or have a friend read lines from one act while I would answer with lines from another act, and we'd jot them down. Or one character from one play could have a dialogue with a character from a completely different play. Something might come on the radio or you might hear something shouted in the street that would go in. I didn't think of all this stuff myself, mind you.

There's a story about *Finnegans Wake*: Joyce was having problems with his eyesight and needed to have Beckett, his secretary, taking dictation. At one point there was a knock at the door and Joyce said,

"Come in." When the text was being read back to him at the end of the session, he heard "Come in" and said, " 'Come in?' I didn't say that. It doesn't belong." Beckett said, "But I'm sure I heard it. Oh, there was a knock at the door!" Joyce said, "Leave it in."

Big Hotel was done in a little black-and-white notebook. When I got to the end—the last leaf—I just wrote "Curtain. The End." The last line is something like, "Then the fifth act of *Lady Windemere's Fan.*"

■

When Vaccaro fired me in 1967—from my own play—nearly everybody quit and left with me. We felt *we* were the company that had created this movement, the company that people wrote reviews about and admired. We had developed into an ensemble.

Vaccaro could be the Play-House, but we were the Ridiculous Theatrical *Company.* We decided to do my play the way we wanted to do it.

In a way I'm very divorced from the work of the others. Since there's an element of almost demented competition among the various branches of the Ridiculous—which is way out of proportion and totally inappropriate—I had basically to go and create the entire genre myself.

3

In 1967 it all came together for me. I found that I could shape the ongoing needs of my theatre by writing plays for myself. That's really how it evolved. I can't remember before then, except that it was depressing.

I started out as an actor. I had this company thrust upon me when the original Theatre of the Ridiculous broke to pieces and the actors were all kicked out. They decided I should direct the company. It was very much like a commedia dell'arte troupe. We had no theatre to play in, so it was really a troupe of actors taking matters into their own hands.

I had nothing to lose, so I threw my cards in the air and let them land where they would. I didn't really care what happened in those plays so long as I could put over my own scenes.

■

When I was in conventional theatre—even when I was going to school—people thought my acting was too broad, too pasty. So I had to create a theatre where I could exist. I had to create, for my own survival, a world where I could take advantage of my talents.

Naturalistic theatre is a very recent innovation, a corrective device. It wasn't the end of anything. It was a fashion to do things naturally. You can't really perform an unnatural act, unless you claim supernatural powers.

The idea of being natural becomes a very oppressive concept. It's shallow. Gradually, through training with Stanislavski teachers, I realized they wanted me to behave in a civilized manner in a room, not to do anything extraordinary. But everything I'm interested in is extraordinary.

In naturalism there is always the tendency to be less than you are, to be more specific and less. That was always a terrible danger. It certainly didn't work for me.

■

We began in 1967 with a freewheeling approach to the theatre. We did everything in a defiant way—radically wrong, you might say. It was a newfound freedom.

We felt that epic theatre had great expressive possibilities, and we used them without holding back. We threw out the idea of professionalism and cultivated something much more extreme than amateurism. Actors were chosen for their personalities, almost like "found objects"; the character fell somewhere between the intention of the script and the personality of the actor. The textures of meaning were amazingly rich. Everything contributed to the effect: the script; the performers; even the accidents which were always happening onstage.

These Off-Off-Broadway things were thrown together—casts were thrown together and busted apart. I wanted to create an ensemble. I found some like-minded people in the theatre, in underground movies. Friends, people I met on the street—I'd *invite* them. I created—invented—my own stars. I was building something by discovering people and creating a continuity for them.

Most actors don't get continuity. They get a job here and a job there. Their only continuity is in acting classes.

To create a company that performed all year round was a big challenge. We had no money—nothing. We lived like paupers on the Lower East Side, starving, but keeping the company working, trying to find places where we could perform. That took all my energy. That's what I did all the time.

We used to pay thirty-five dollars per night to play twice a week in a movie house after midnight. A lot of the Off-Off-Broadway people were playing in alternative spaces, church basements and so on. I wanted to play in a theatre, not in an art gallery or a loft, because we'd done that kind of thing. I had the idea that if you used a movie theatre after midnight, when there were no more movies, you'd have a theatre with regular seats and you could get a grander feeling of going to the theatre being an event.

■

Three years is a long time. We did *Big Hotel*, *When Queens Collide*, *Whores of Babylon* and *Turds in Hell*, all without funding. They were rather lavish productions, which we did entirely with volunteers and donated materials.

For years we had just five or ten minutes to set up the stage, and then we had to rush on and do it. We didn't have any time to prepare. We never rehearsed in a theatre. We rarely had any money to work with, to advertise it, to do anything. It is not fair to judge plays I did with no money and without any advantages.

At that time, all the actors, everyone, was in it for the adventure. There's a big difference between the times it was like a floating crap game and when it became a real theatre.

■

The first turning point came when I wrote a four-hour epic called *Big Hotel*, where we made a collage out of quotations, scenes, poems, one-liners—you name it—and put them together in different ways every night to see how they could work. We knew what the plot was, but I don't know if the audience did.

That wasn't really important. What was important for us was to break down that rote quality that you get in most theatre—the conventions, the blocking, the techniques used over and over to get points across. The creative process was *human*. We didn't focus on rote. It was about having ideas and developing something that was exciting.

I was very influenced then by the ideas of John Cage. I wanted to find ways of getting beyond my own personal taste and avoiding aesthetic decisions. I wanted to get rid of that "no," to say "yes" to everything.

I took the extra liberty of a great modernist, not caring whether any of it made sense or ever came to an ending. We tried anything that popped into anyone's head. It was very surrealistic. It was a wonderful play—you could do anything with it.

．

I had been gradually trying to bring the artistic policies closer to the physicalities of Artaud's theatre, as well as the verbal values. Costumes became more and more environmental. The costumes alone created the whole scene-value. The fans were gigantic.

At Hofstra they put on big epics, so I learned how to put one on. And my Catholic background influenced my theatre: we burned incense during the plays; there were many ritualistic things.

Our art was to bring everything in, to include everything until we finally admitted that the world was our work. We used banal counterbalanced with sublime. We used literature as the servant of the theatre. When the thing had to be said we said it.

Our goal was that the audience would become part of the theatre, that the theatre would expand to encompass the world. It was almost a religious idea.

A pure physical theatre from Artaud, with a verbal sound score. It was the solution for fitting dramatic literature into Artaud's theatre, since he condemned playwrights. The *mise en scène* comes into its own when the actors allow the theatre to admit its physicality.

．

Pornography is the highest development of naturalism. It was the seriousness of pornography that we were never into. It is not in depicting the sexual act that one becomes a pornographer; it is in demanding to be taken seriously. Depicting sexual things—nudity and all that —we were taking a satirical view, rather than trying to arouse the audience sexually. We weren't peddling our asses. We were celebrating physical love, or criticizing it, or commenting on it. We were never into that tedious seriousness that pornography always demands of its audience.

One night we had a fight with the audience. We started throwing fruit and vegetables at them. A dummy was thrown into the audience. They threw it back to us. It was war.

∎

In the course of this experimentation I was perhaps mistakenly credited—or credited fairly, I don't know—with getting rid of plot—out of the play, out of drama—and maybe I did. Stefan Brecht was writing about my work at the time, really studying it closely, keeping a journal of developments. One day he called and said, "I hear you're rehearsing. What are you rehearsing?" I said, "There used to be that number where Alexis Del'Lago came on in drag and sang 'Lady in Red.' I realized that just after that the Miraculous Mandarin was with Blondine Blondell in a scene of espionage, and I thought I'd put them together and have little tables, and when Alexis Del'Lago as Mata Hari came on and sang the song, it would be like he was doing it in a nightclub." Stefan shouted, "You're making it more of a play!" I said, "I *want* it to be more of a play," and he said, "Oh no! Don't do that!" I realized that I was being credited with being a figurehead, the creator of something others would do that I would not do, which was to throw out the baby with the bathwater, take it into formless, nonstructured drama.

A lot of this came from Jack Smith, who was a genius at doing things for no money. Jack Smith could take people and objects that everyone else considered worthless and transform them into the most exotic creations. Unfortunately, he was impossible to work with. He performed with us for a while in *Big Hotel*, but one day he got sore at Chris Scott and punched him in the eye, and then he quit.

∎

This was far from popular theatre, but we didn't intend to present popular theatre. We weren't chic enough, although we did have glamour and grandeur.

We developed a cult following, but we had to work for free. The audience was reportedly mostly gay, and that may have been true on certain nights. But the fact is the audience was small in those days. Since there were fewer people, the proportion of gay people may have been greater then.

■

I played three women's roles: Zabina, Queen of Mars in my play
Conquest of the Universe or When Queens Collide; Norma Desmond in
my play *Big Hotel*; and the Emerald Empress in Bill Vehr's *Whores of
Babylon*. Yet my male roles outnumbered the female ones. My flaw as a
female impersonator lay in this: I always played women who wished
they were men.

I always feel like a lesbian in drag. I am never content.

When I play female roles, they become collages of different
actresses. Bill wrote this line in *Whores of Babylon* in which his character
said to mine, "How well I understand that struggle in you between the
warrior artist and the woman"—this was a wonderful self-revelation—
and my line, that he wrote, was "*The* woman? Don't you know there are
a thousand women in me and I'm tormented by each one in turn?"

Since then I have never done a play in which I did not cast
someone in the role of the opposite sex. The drag is always supercharged with theatricality, and theatricality is the hallmark of the
Ridiculous Theatrical Company.

■

I knew a lot of drag queens who would go into Whelan's Drugstore on
Sixth Avenue for free makeup back then. They would go in and do their
whole face from the counter samples. I knew Candy Darling then, when
she was a street person. She was always out there on the corner, on the
avenue, everywhere. She had no apartment, no place to live.

Candy had emerged as a kind of underground celebrity. She was in
my *Turds in Hell* briefly, maybe one or two nights. I was playing a
priestess and she pulled my loincloth off. She exposed me and I was
stark naked. It wasn't in the play.

The main thing about Candy and Jackie Curtis was that they took
female impersonation into the street—off the stage and into their lives.
They tried to *live it*, twenty-four hours a day.

The Dionysian principle: you're drawing on your own personality;
you are committing an act of self-destruction, because you are obliterat-
ing your own identity to create another one. And so we have these

periods in which we must revive ourselves. You give a performance and come offstage, and you've got to get into yourself and rest, reconstruct your own true personality, indulge it. Only then can you go back and play the role again.

But once you start playing the fantasy twenty-four hours a day, you may have obliterated your personality on a more or less permanent basis. A mask can be a protection to preserve what's inside, but in the case of Jackie and Candy—particularly of Candy—they were always being overly generous with others, giving so much they didn't leave anything for themselves.

.

At a very early stage in our company's development, I was watching Bill Vehr's *Whores of Babylon* from the lighting booth. We had a lot of real people in it—not just actors, but people who were different, *strange*. They were acting the play and I was watching it from up there in this godlike perspective, and I found it terribly touching. I was so moved by it: those poor mortals down there on this stage of life, as fools. The play was very heroic, very highfalutin'—like a court masque, very elevated. I was very touched by this—*suddenly it was my cue!* I'd forgot. I leapt up and ran down, and I had to run up the stairs—suddenly I was on. I realized that I was one of those pitiful humans, one of those poor people I was so moved by.

I made stars of bizarre people. I used drag queens off the street as Fire Women in *When Queens Collide* if they had outré wardrobe. I interpolated an entire play around Crazy Arthur Kraft, *Turds in Hell*. It ran for ten months, and there were nights when it got up over four-and-a-half hours.

We never made a dime out of it, either. All the receipts went for the theatre rental and the weekly ad in the *Times*. Bill Vehr was working days then as a clerk in a bank near the theatre. He'd rush the weekend box-office receipts in on Monday morning to cover our weekend overdraft.

.

Eventually, I began to feel I was pouring everything into an abyss. I felt drained, and yet we went on and did *The Grand Tarot*, which was even more complex. It was sort of a medieval mystery play that took in the whole world.

That play never did get put together—it's still in fragments. It was great, but not aesthetically satisfying. I have plans to redo it. It's something I grow with.

It was performed in pieces in many places. It was like an opera, like a Wagnerian *Ring*. The twenty-two cards of the Tarot deck were like twenty-two plays.

The idea that it could be a finished play would be folly. It would always be a part of a play. It would never be complete. In its total journey through its existence, all its performances would be one performance, because it's a continuum.

Some people completely work that way. I personally feel that the endless drama—the infinite drama—is the negation of drama, because it's not isolated in time and space.

Here I come to my deadlock, my refutation of *The Grand Tarot*. It's infinite plot. The Tarot cards represent all of reality. Infinite plot is a negation of plot.

That was the period when I began to see everything falling apart. That's when I decided to abandon the epic form and write a well-made play.

4

Some of my discoveries gave startling performances. They blazed like meteors. But the initial impulses of self-exploitation and exhibitionism are not sufficient to produce an actor. When the work and working conditions got tough they fizzled out. Few of the performers were capable of making deep commitments.

It was clear that we couldn't continue in that direction indefinitely. I took a winter off—we couldn't find a place to perform, anyway—and wrote a play that was very traditional and formal, much more focused and carefully worked out than our previous ones. *Bluebeard* used melodrama, fantastic characters and exotic locations to comment on contemporary sexual mores. It inaugurated our period of experiments with concentric dramatic form.

Nobody could believe this, but in writing *Bluebeard* I was influenced very much by *The Seagull*. In *The Seagull*, every character is perversely attracted to someone who doesn't like him.

Bluebeard is an intellectual who really doesn't like either of the existing sexes, so he's trying to make a new one. To me, the third genital means the synthesis of the sexes. I like that speech Aristophanes makes in Plato's *Symposium*, where he says people were once shaped like spheres, but that the gods got angry and split them into male and female, and now each person goes through life looking for his or her other half.

On another level, *Bluebeard* is an attack on the idea of altering people's bodies to match their sexuality—"A man can't make love to a man; therefore we'll change one of you into a woman."

We were having a real down period. Sadie Kvetch came to me and asked if I would do something in a revue she was supposed to assemble for a sleazy bar. I told her I'd stage the whole thing. We put together *Tabu Tableaux*.

•

2/28/70 On the waterfront

Tonight we performed three scenes at Christopher's End. A Sleazy Gay Bar. Trilby, Svengali, the Venus Fucking scene and a blackout from *Bluebeard*. My concentration was lousy and after the performance I complained.

I must never complain again. About anything. I infect others with my discontent.

A week of diet for each complaint might cure me.

•

The owner of the bar was so impressed that he cleaned out his porno bookstore next door and turned it into a theatre for us. I called it the Trocadero because I'd always wanted to have a theatre with that name. Then I took the most dedicated and loyal performers and made *Bluebeard*, a production much smaller than our usual ones. It was a critical success—the first time the critics had even bothered to come.

There's a balance that has to be struck. For the artist to continue, he does have to find a public. Part of my survival, part of my job, has been to convince and develop my audience, to win converts.

They caught on in 1970, when I did *Bluebeard*. That was a hit.

•

April 14th, 1970

This weekend of *Bluebeard* performances at Christopher's End was noteworthy. Lotte Lenya came to Saturday night's performance and said to us after in the dressing room, "I've never seen anything like it. It was very pure. After this who could go to shitty Broadway—excuse me."

I was much struck by her lack of affectation, and her sexual aura. She must be in her late sixties.

That was Friday. On Saturday, as I entered with Black-Eyed Susan, who plays Sybil, through the laboratory door stage center, the door collapsed and I fell with her in my arms and rolled on over the door. The backstage area was revealed to the audience. Bill Vehr, who was pursuing me, leapt up and pretended to be about to enter. John Brockmeyer threw up the wall again just in time to stop him! Some acting! Anyway, later in the act, two set pieces fell off the stage almost simultaneously right and left. When I ran in blood-spattered from the operating room, panting the line, "The test tube! The test tube! Everything depends upon the sticky liquid now!" I saw audience members handing up the parts of the set that had fallen to Mrs. Maggot and Sheemish, played by John Brockmeyer and Eleven.

The other night a man came up to me on the street and said, "You're Charles Ludlam aren't you?" I said yes.

He said, "I'm just a fan. I've seen all your plays: *Big Hotel*, *When Queens Collide* at the Gate, *Whores of Babylon* at the Gate and as a shadow play on 42nd Street. You are the only thing that's happening in the theatre. I don't usually gush like this but I had to tell you. I saw *Coco* the other night on Broadway. A friend gave me some tickets. When we left the theatre after the show I said to my friends, 'Who needs this when we have Ludlam? Who can watch this shit when Ludlam has spoiled us?'"

∎

We went to Belgrade, Zagreb, Vienna, Berlin, Frankfurt, Copenhagen, London. That was one tour—1971. Everywhere we played we made friends and received glowing reviews.

The company was coming over on a phony charter flight. They were held up in some terrible motel at Kennedy airport for a week—five in one room with a color TV. I went on a ship with six hundred kilos of scenery and costumes. We were taking *Bluebeard*, *The Grand Tarot*, and *Eunuchs of the Forbidden City*, which we had rehearsed the previous summer.

When the company got to London they didn't have enough

money to fly to Yugoslavia. I was in Belgrade, and the head of the festival said, "Is your company coming or aren't they?"

John Brockmeyer called from London and said, "Don't worry, we're getting on a train, we'll be there for the opening." The head of the festival said, "Train is completely wrong! They must fly!"

Three trains were stopped at the Yugoslavian border. The actors were taken off the train and driven to the airport. They didn't know what was happening. They were told to put on their makeup on the plane. Some of them wear monster makeup.

I was at the theatre setting up all by myself. I worked with the lighting man in sign language. He said, "Do you want simple lighting or complicated?" I said complicated. We had thirty or forty minutes to go and no company, but I kept working.

All of a sudden I looked down and saw John Brockmeyer on the stage in complete costume and makeup, and I hadn't even started. He always was ready before I was—and I'd been there a week.

It was a unique performance. The cast hadn't slept for days. We hadn't seen each other since two months before in New York.

■

One of the most wonderful theatres was the one in Belgrade, a beautiful modern theatre that just had everything. The roof of the theatre opened up—a circular domed roof. Then stagehands came in and set the lights and went back through the roof. Then the roof came down again.

They have wonderful crews in Yugoslavia. In Zagreb they got inspired and built this fantastic gothic set for *Bluebeard*, with a cuckoo clock and candles burning. The prop woman kept bringing out different kinds of throws for the piano—it was beautiful.

Everything at the festival was Grotowski-oriented—Grotowski, Jr. It was disgusting. There was a Rumanian *King Lear* in plastic laundry bags. The front curtain hadn't been used at the festival in six years.

The second night, after word got around, they were standing in the aisles, and we got standing ovations. They were so relieved to laugh. Everything else was coming on like gangbusters, trying to reform the audience's terrible vices.

Bluebeard won second prize in the BITEF festival of avant-garde theatre in Belgrade. The first was a Serbo-Croatian *Hamlet*.

■

In Vienna they put us in a PTA meeting hall. There were fluorescent lights on the stage, linoleum on the floor of the theatre, folding chairs—it was just horrible.

We couldn't have any sex in the play. There was no advertising, just a poster on the door, and it was in a back alley. If we hadn't won the second prize in Belgrade, we'd still be in Vienna.

■

In Berlin there's a wonderful theatre called the Forum. It's the only avant-garde theatre in Berlin. All the young, beautiful, gifted people go to that theatre. It's all focused, just the opposite of here.

After the Forum we moved to the Reichskabaret in Berlin and opened *Eunuchs of the Forbidden City*, our Chinese history play. We'd been working on it for a year and a half. We had trouble getting it on because it had such an elaborate *mise en scène*. We needed a couple of dozen enormous wigs, gongs, music. It's epic style, and you have to have the palanquins and carts or you can't do it. It has long *tirades* like in French classical tragedy.

Chinese culture is far more advanced than Western culture. It was the most demanding play we'd done.

I played the Chief Eunuch. I was going to play the Empress, but Black-Eyed Susan did it much better.

The German press received it with gratitude and enthusiasm. Critics saw our style as a welcome alternative to the "Living Theatre approach," which dominated the European theatre scene then. Europeans appreciated our extensions of tradition—the habit of mining out, redefining and exploiting traditions rather than merely destroying them.

■

English critics are a nightmare. English critics are real old men. They came on crutches and in wheelchairs. Not a laugh the whole evening.

The critics in London seemed annoyed with me. All the plays on words were lost on the English. Then there'd be these incredibly lame lines from Trollope and they'd get a big resounding laugh every night. You felt like you were playing for a non-English-speaking audience.

In the reviews they praised the play but insulted our appearance. The phrase "these Americans" kept recurring. The reviews were admiring but grudging: "Americans Attempt Play."

At first the audience looked just like the critics—old farts, old fogies. But then the people that started coming—tsk, tsk, tsk! The second week people from the rock world began to come—younger people—and then the play took off.

We could have stayed in Europe indefinitely, but on tour we got tired very quickly. We'd been gone three months and were very tired. In New York we had done long runs, but we weren't performing eight times a week, which is inhuman. I didn't like to perform more than three or four times a week.

■

I communicate in universal terms. Any place we play, they understand us. When you have a plot, there is a story to tell, and people understand the story. Even the language ceases to be a big barrier, because they can understand the story.

We never really had problems . . . well, once or twice censorship problems, but that's all. Very rare.

We are more "different" in Europe. Here we live in a very rotten culture that is very primitive. We're still frontier people in America and we have those rough edges. You notice this when you go to Europe. The people in Europe are more civilized.

Europeans are more accepting, less amazed by the fact that we are just doing theatre. They understand that, but they don't catch all the little American things about the play. They like it that it's American, but they don't understand how expressly American it is.

■

Ridiculous is a very much more respectable word than our critics are aware. It's a sensibility.

29

People have said camp. They mean this. They're trying to grasp something. It's in the language. It's ancient. There are words for it, but they clutch desperately at the word "spoof." Spoof isn't a worthy word.

They say parody. It's a parody, but it's mock-heroic. Yes, it's serio-tragic, but I'm also committing an absurdity. I'm making a laughingstock of myself. Yes, it's a travesty but yes, it's prudish, yes, it's pedantic. It's stilted, it's obvious, it's a caricature. It's everything—all of those things.

The problem is that everyone fears ridicule because, as Camus said, "There is no defense against scorn," and that is basically what people fear. The critic is afraid to take us seriously: he may be made a fool of, drawn into the web.

This has always been the special power of the clown, because he can say serious things in a way that he cannot be punished for. A good fool, even in Shakespeare's day, got a kick in the ass occasionally, or thrown out. He would be flogged, perhaps, but he would endure. He was a social critic. The wise man could hear things in the prattling of the fool.

In Spain and Elizabethan England there were two kinds of fools: the natural and the artificial. The natural was a born fool. He might have been a hunchback with a dim wit or he might have been a sage people took for a fool—God knows they were usually mentally deranged people who often were also deformed or dwarfed. They were kept at court because they would constantly come out with weird things to say. They were kept around as pets.

Queen Elizabeth kept a girl fool known as Jane the Fool. There are court records of costumes being made for her. She's the only woman fool in recorded history.

In contrast to the natural fool, the artificial fool affects derangement in order to be comic. In theatre both sorts of fools can be utilized. In the Ridiculous Theatrical Company there has been a movement from the use of natural to artificial fools, perhaps because the latter are more predictable and artistic than the former.

We're like holy fools, in a way. We refused the idea of seriousness. And when you refuse to be taken seriously or refuse to take things seriously or you take an anti-serious attitude, it's very dangerous, because the fool can turn on anyone and make a fool of the person, jibe at anyone. No one feels safe with him around. The whim can attack anyone at any time, and it's been very hard for critics or theoreticians or whoever they are—philosophers—to line up behind us and say this is what it is or to support us, because they're afraid that that wit, that folly, will turn back on them.

There was a lashing back because it was obvious that we were against pretensions and certain kinds of bullshitting. That is the real value of a theatre of satyrs, a satirical theatre.

•

I had been struggling for a long time with the structure of plays. It hadn't been a terrible struggle, but I had given a tremendous amount of thought to this.

My problem had been to go beyond the circular, cyclical structure of the Absurdists, which represented a morbid philosophical position they had come to: they couldn't go forward, they couldn't go backward, and they couldn't remain where they are. They were sort of stuck. That was the only way they could structure those plays. They always went back to the beginning at the very end—or vice versa. I tried to break out of the structure of the Theatre of the Absurd, where the end is in the beginning.

The Theatre of the Absurd refused to take things seriously, sabotaging seriousness. Our slant was actually to take things *very* seriously, especially focusing on those things held in low esteem by society and revaluing them, giving them new meaning, new worth, by changing their context.

Even in high school I had rejected Beckett and Genet. I was looking for more arcane, more exotic material. Beckett and Genet were so minimal! There wasn't that richness of possibilities. They were already a generation past—they were twenty years before. To me, doing them was just admitting defeat. Even today, when I admire them as artists, I feel the same way.

Modern art up through Beckett is the reduction of form—the elimination of things. There's no way to go beyond Beckett, because you can't get any more minimal. You reduce and reduce until there's nothing. It's like being in a labyrinth with no exits: the only way to get out is to fly. I'm moving in the other direction, to a maximal, more baroque vision.

The Absurdists got bogged down in their own nihilism. We represent a positive nihilism, like the kind you find in Buddhism. Instead of negating anything we try to find its inherent value.

It's ecological theatre—we take the abandoned refuse, the used images, the shoes from abandoned shoe factories, the clichés, and search for their true meaning. We are recycling culture. If you learn to use the waste of society you can not only make yourself very prosperous but bring an era of prosperity for everyone.

I tried to come up with a revaluation of values based on a positive attitude toward *combat*. I was trying to revive the idea of certain things I think are essential in drama—very simple things.

■

I've always been interested in drama, which is quite specific. All show business isn't the same. You could be interested in films, revues with lots of different acts, burlesque. I've always exploited those techniques to make my plays available immediately, but I've always been committed to the idea of drama.

I might as well be pedantic and make a distinction. Theatre happens when a person or persons isolated in time and space present themselves to another or others. They are the receivers of the action of the actors presenting themselves. That is a very elemental definition— just to present yourself, isolated in space and time.

There are two men in the desert and one draws a circle in the sand and says, "For five minutes I am going to present myself to you." That's theatre. Our meeting in this room could be theatre if we said, "It will only happen at certain hours." I wasn't very punctual, but if I came on time and appeared and left, that would be theatre.

Now to distinguish between theatre and drama. Drama, to me, has to represent a conflict. It is a representation of an action; as Aristotle says, an imitation of an action. He was very open-ended about it, but I feel it must be *two* forces, personified and in conflict: either one overcomes the other, or they come to a stalemate, or they are both destroyed, *or* they could achieve harmony.

A boxing match is drama, but a person singing a song is theatre because there is no conflict in one person's single act. Until you add a conflict between two people, you don't have drama. It can be a conflict of ideas or a physical conflict.

All drama is theatre but all theatre is *not* drama. I am into drama, not just theatre. My dramas are very good theatre, in the sense that we present ourselves in a way that is very interesting.

I am a showman. Showmanship is something that every dramatist doesn't have. Some people may be interested in drama and have no desire to make a good show of it.

Drama is the playing out of a conflict. Drama is a battleground for ideas, characters, concepts. It's an *arena*, it's a *ring*—it's like a prize-fighting ring. Boxing and wrestling is the idea, the essence of drama, because human beings are in conflict in the most obvious and brutal way.

Boxing is the tragic form: it's serious; it's elevated; it's played by the rules; it's all very classical. In boxing you can't hit under one's belt. Wrestling is comic. They are like clowns—clown characters—and they cheat: they beat the people in the audience; they beat up the referee; they use weapons to beat the other person. Nobody cares, it keeps going on. In wrestling you can do anything because it's all faked.

A lot of avant-garde artists have embraced "the theatre" and thrown out the concept of drama. That's where we differ. Because to me the theatre is the necessary evil and the drama is what is great and eternal. It's an archetypal human situation with an outcome—somebody wins, somebody loses. Plays are combats—they have conflicts—which are a forum for debate and for the exploration of ideas . . . the intellectual function of the theatre, which must also be emotional and entertaining, of course.

Spectacle could produce only beauty, which is empty without subject matter. By combat one gets beyond spectacle, even beyond Buddhism, beyond the nausea of seeing through all things.

But the great thing is they are not mutually exclusive. You can have plot and you can have images. Or you can just have images. We realized that the images without the plot are not as good as the plot without images.

•

Tuesday, June 13th, 1972

I dreamed that I was Charlie Chaplin doing a dance pantomime of the dying swan on ice skates on a black mirror floor. The corps de ballet were like Larry Rée, huge ballerinas on ice skates, with huge ostrich-feather costumes. Charlie entered on a Chinese swan-boat sled which circled the stage in a "banking" movement; that is, tilted in. The actual dying-swan pantomime was done over the body of some woman who was also the narrator. I was actually dying and the effect was so sublime I was moved to tears. But toward the end she interrupted the highest moment by saying, "I think we had better take off my ZuZu rings." Apparently this was also in preparation for death.

•

I feel that there is always magic. The event itself has magic qualities but they're like a man trying to catch his shadow. When you're not focusing on magic, that's when it occurs. But when you think about it, it's like trying to say, "I will not think of a red cow." You can only think of a red cow. The more you try not to, the more you think of it.

If you just forget magic and don't try for it, mystical things occur. If you're striving after it, you're not in a receptive state and it eludes you.

When you get infinite you have nothing. It's like the black holes in space where a star burns out. There's a hole left supposedly even in space, and it's black, and anything that passes behind it can't be seen because it's a hole. On the other side everything is in negative. Where the star burns out in one reality it will have to appear in another reality because of the law of opposites.

Corn was the turning point, when I realized that the synthesis of opposites is the basic magic act. It's at the basis of all metaphysics. And I realized that this was what comedy had that tragedy didn't have.

5

We were overripe for funding. You had to be in existence two years at least, and have a consistent artistic policy, and have accomplished something. We had already done all that, and even then we got very modest amounts at first.

In 1972 the Ridiculous Theatrical Company received a grant of $10,000 from the National Endowment for the Arts and it made an enormous difference in the quality of our work. A little money made it possible for us to plan our work in advance with clarity of purpose. The years of struggle had made us strong. We had not forgotten our goal, which we came closer to fulfilling each season: to become America's great popular comic theatre, an instrument for social change.

The six leading actors of my company had, by then, performed together uninterrupted for five years, a record then unmatched in New York theatre annals. Why did we stay together? I used to think it was because we were crazy. Now I know it was because we were right. Each actor in the company became a master comedian. We honed our playing style and comic timing to the fineness of a razor's edge. Only an ensemble that has worked together year in and year out can achieve that kind of precision. The commercial theatre does not foster this kind of commitment and it shows.

During our first five years I staged eight completely new full-length plays, six of which I wrote myself, one by Bill Vehr, and one with

Bill Vehr. Like the classical playwrights, I fulfilled myself in the service of a company. The plays were collaborations, bigger in conception and richer in detail than a production of a single mind. The actors in the Ridiculous Theatrical Company were no puppets; they were whole artists who shaped the destiny of the work and—with their hard-earned skills and real feelings—communicated to an audience to whom we made no apologies for being avant-garde or precious. We upheld the idea of the Ridiculous and of ridicule as a weapon in defiance of theatrical pretension and class distinctions disguised as aesthetic criteria or pseudo-standards of professionalism. We molded the truth into a joke.

If they laughed they got it; if they didn't they didn't. It was as simple as that. We didn't explain ourselves. Our ethics and our aesthetics were built into our work. Our work was everything to us.

■

It had been seven years since we had gotten this company together, and all that time I'd been wanting to play Camille. Everybody said, "Oh yes. You should!" In my company we encouraged each other to do the roles we felt we must do. But we didn't have any money, and I knew I had to have fancy costumes for *Camille*.

I always wanted to play Camille. It had a lot to do with my feelings about love and the nature of love in one of its highest expressions. Is love, in fact, self-sacrifice, or is there another way of expressing love?

I saw the Garbo film when I was in college and was destroyed by it. It moved me to tears. I got riveted to it one night when I was very ill and too weak to turn off the television set. I developed such an identity with the role I began to think I *looked* like Garbo.

When I recovered, I read the Dumas novel, listened to *La Traviata* and heard recordings of actresses playing the part in a couple of languages. I didn't love it because it was awful. I loved it because it was so great.

One newspaper interview misquoted me terribly—that's the way they do it, isn't it? They said that I laughed at the Garbo death scene when I saw the film recently. *I* laughed? My God, I was right there with the rest of them, weeping my poor head off! How can you help it?

There was a snicker or two among the audience; but, after all, there may just be some ignorant fool who doesn't think this is one of the few great old death scenes left in the theatre. Laugh at Marguerite Gautier? At Garbo? Not this girl, I'll tell you!

Why is *Camille* the most successful play ever written? It reaches something. It strikes a chord in us. It's been a ballet, it's been an opera, it's been a play, it's been a film, it's been a novel . . . and in every form it hit home.

Camille is a melodrama that I adapted to my own interests. I kept thinking about doing it, and then, in 1973, I sat down and wrote the script in a month.

When I finished writing my adaptation, the comic and the tragic converged perfectly. It went through a lot of changes, but it never lost that balance.

■

I'm very interested in the structure of the play and the literary element. There is a way of crafting it—crafting a plot that makes it particularly work in the theatre the way it wouldn't in a novel or a movie or anything else. A way for the stage.

For instance, the novel begins after Marguerite's death, with the auction of *Manon Lescaut*, the book that Armand had given to her. You know she's dead on the first page of the book and the whole thing's flashbacks. The play has to start at the beginning, go through the middle and do the end. You couldn't do it the way it was in the novel.

The movie script of *Camille* was a brilliant piece of writing. It used film superbly. It established a great deal of the plot in the first short scene.

The film did things that could have been done on the stage, but they would have taken a lot more work and never really would have fit. Each person, too, has their own approach to the craft of it. Marguerite's very much a character study, but there's also the skill of revealing a character with a single bold stroke.

At first we thought of doing *Camille* in twenties style. We even thought of doing it ultramodern, just going over to Mays and picking up the clothes, because there were a lot of people in New York in the sixties who just went down the drain, all those underground movie stars, rock stars, groupies. But *Camille* is better from a distance.

We thought of doing an all-drag *Camille*, but then we decided not to. I had promised Bill Vehr the part of Armand.

The casting was made in heaven. Everybody looked surprisingly right.

We were doing *Camille*, *Camille* itself—the regular three-act play. I had gone into considerable research for the show—scripts, photos, reviews, playbills—everything I could get my hands on. Some of it was cut, of course—wonderful poetic monologues . . . marvelous, but not for us. Some of the lines had been largely or even completely invented— I did have to turn the 1850s into the 1970s. And we had the job of shaping an older play to suit our type of production.

Camille was our first production which was not built from scratch, on our stage. That time the poking around, feeling our way, consisted mostly of seeing how we and our view as a company might come through an established script. There was still the fun of playing with the character, *at* the character, before actually playing the character.

You have to be quick to work with me. I do a lot of rewriting and you get those changes real quickly. There's very little time. You have to be able to do precise things exactly the way I want them.

With *Camille*, it was only a week before opening that I wrote the last act. Of course, it was an adaptation—it wasn't like generating completely original material. On the other hand, we still hadn't had any experience playing the last act.

I felt we had to build to the last act. I didn't feel that it was something I could arbitrarily decide and then expect people, like automatons, to do. I felt I had to see the course of the characters, how they were developing, before drawing the last act.

Until two days before the opening I still hadn't decided whether Armand should come back alone or whether his father should apologize for him. I decided, finally, that the father should come back, because it postpones Marguerite and Armand's final meeting, and that makes it more romantic.

■

In the planning stage of any of our productions, we express ourselves, let ourselves go, so to speak, getting character and script together. It is a kind of creation by layers—ourselves, the parts, the company; the company, ourselves, the parts . . .

With all that, it was quite strictly *Camille*. We had a deep dedication to presenting something true—ridiculous but true to our subject; in this instance, true to the original *Camille*—but always from a ridiculous angle . . . an action toyed with, a line carried too far, etc. What we did in the show might have been outrageous—flamboyantly outrageous; that, shall we say, is the Ridiculous Theatrical Company!—but every gesture, every line, related directly to what was happening in the original, serious play.

Now to some people this may be burlesque, and it may be what they do in a burlesque show, but it isn't *meant* to be burlesque. We were not *burlesquing* anything or anybody. Most of the show did come out a howl—true—but that was not necessarily because we were camping it up, so to speak. I always fancied myself as a tragedian, but I found people always laughed when I came on stage no matter how tragic I was trying to act.

I just didn't see camp in our show. It was a play—very definitely *not* a drag show! One magazine referred to the show with that term, and it was a glowing tribute. But what did it mean? Terms have gotten out of hand, or into the wrong hands. People throw words around to feel *in*.

Only three members of the company—Jack Mallory as Nanine, Georg Osterman as Nichette, and myself—were dressed to play women. All the others in the show were women playing women and men playing men—perfectly straight.

The three of us were *not* males trying to be females. *That* is drag: regaling yourself in feminine folderol for the sheer antics of pretending to be a woman. *We* were out there on that stage the same as everyone else—hoping to give an honest, bona fide account of ourselves as characters in a play.

Our characters were female and we were male—there was that big difference. And I am not unaware of the fact—believe me—that I just might have looked a bit ridiculous, to say the least, all dressed up in high nineteenth-century "drag," shall we say, a plate right out of *Godey's*

Lady's Book! But the point is that that was *not* Georg Osterman up there in a frock, hosiery, patent-leather pumps, hat, pearls and purse; that was Nichette as played by Georg Osterman, Nanine as played by Jack Mallory, Marguerite as played by Charles Ludlam. It also worked out rather interestingly that real women were playing the more villainous roles, and the drags, instead of playing the usual monster violations of women, were very sympathetic.

Is it wrong to feel incensed, to think it silly or unkind that anyone considered our show a drag show? After all, that is what it must have looked like—to the inexperienced eye, anyway, with that sort of thing labeled "drag" all over the place in those days. How could the general public help making the comparison? Nevertheless, I insist we were nothing more than, nothing less than, nothing other than three actors trying to portray three characters in a play.

I see nothing wrong with a man playing a woman's role. In the Kabuki and in the Elizabethan theatre men played women's roles and no one blinked an eye. Originally, all women's roles in Shakespeare were played by men. And, in the reverse, Sarah Bernhardt played Hamlet.

Hamlet is traditionally a man's part, Marguerite is traditionally a woman's part. What ladies have been given to do in various male impersonations is just what I did in *Camille*. Women are Peter Pan and all the rest of it; I, a man, am Marguerite Gautier.

It's a matter of the part in the play, not the sex of the performer or the character. If it is suitable, anyone—any sex—can play it.

I pioneered the idea that female impersonation could be serious acting, an approach to character. I became known as the actor who does real acting in drag.

■

In the early days, with *Bluebeard*, we did at most four performances a week. By the time we did *Camille* we did an extended run with six a week.

Playing the leading lady was far from a cup of tea, shaving my face every night so as to look soft and seductive. After Sunday-night performances I usually let my beard grow, loving that relief until we were on again on Wednesday. On Wednesday nights *la dame aux camélias* was truly beautiful!

There is only one other man I know who had played Camille at the time (with the exception of Enrique Grou's abortive 8-millimeter film): F. J. Peschka, puppeteer of the Little Players, alias the Standwells. But he had an exquisite puppet through whom to pour his passion, Mademoiselle Garonce. I had only my own body.

I had to convince myself that I was beautiful before I went on. If I believed it. . . . Belief is the secret to reality. The Catholic Church understood that and made specific beliefs a virtue and thereby seized control of reality—"central reality control." Credibility is a big word in politics these days. My belief in what I was doing made me gullible, the ultimate dupe, as well as a hypnotist. Self-hypnosis . . . mass hypnosis.

When the audience laughed at my pain, the play seemed more tragic to me than when they took it seriously. A solemn audience trivialized the event. This play of *Camille* was the ultimate masochism. I went out there to try to have a happy ending every night and got knocked down by every peripeteia of the plot. How could I continue such a pessimistic enterprise? Even in a boxing match both sides have a chance to win, but not me. I had to pretend that I had a chance. No wonder I was mad and sought all kinds of sensation and ran away from the boredom of mediocrity.

I was not trying to kid anyone into thinking I was a woman. I was trying to wrench something artistic from the experience. It's more difficult to cast against type. You've got to stretch yourself.

I wanted the audience to keep in mind that I was a man playing the role. That's why I deliberately showed the hair on my chest through the open neck of Marguerite's gown in Act I. I was not trying, like the transvestite, to see how completely I could conceal my male identity. Wanting to look like a woman was not the point. Wanting to create the illusion of Dumas' heroine was.

It isn't any different from what anybody hopes to do on the stage. Ethel Barrymore—to take one of your illustrious ladies of the cough— must have hoped that the audience would not see Ethel Barrymore but Marguerite Gautier.

In my case it was an especially designed point of action in the play. That is, I felt I had a better chance at playing the part believably if I came to terms with the audience as early as possible, and let the actor fact be established once and for all; let them know it was me, a male, playing their Marguerite. If we could only get that first scene of meeting her—that *shock* of meeting her, if you will—over with, then that pre-curtain association with sex as such, of female impersonation as such, might go away, and we could all become involved with the part as a part and the play as a play. It is not a question, really, of what man is playing the hero today or what woman is playing the heroine, but simply what is being played.

We all knew that everyone had come to see a man play a woman. Let's not score the theatregoer for curiosity—there would be no more theatre. I just liked to make sure that what they did see they understood at the outset had nothing to do with this "drag queen" bit.

It was more than just doing away with the illusion; it was playing with the illusion, using it as an element, and also using de-illusionment. One had moments of being absorbed into the narrative, and moments when one was reminded that one was in a theatre. If I could persuade the audience to become involved with the character and the situation, to laugh but at the same time to feel the impact of this forbidden love, then it was not a trick, like the female impersonators who do their best to convince you they're really female and then, at the last minute, whip off the wig to remind you they're male.

I didn't want to engage in the kind of trickery that would make people think I was a real woman and then suddenly unmask at the end. I wanted to lure them gradually into forgetting, to make it more amazing later on.

Some nights I got so involved with it that I couldn't understand why the audience was laughing. Sometimes, at the farewell scene with Armand at the end of the play, just before I died in his arms, I became so totally wrapped up in Marguerite that my mascara ran down my cheeks in my own tears.

■

There is a fine line from either side of which one can view any play. By pushing it ever so slightly into the one direction or the other, you can make a sad play funny, a funny play sad—if it basically has that "give," of course. We have to thank the play itself for having the leverage for us to endow our *Camille* with comic values in order to make the male in a female role believable—acceptable—to the American audience.

It's not all that settled whether it's comedy or serious. In a sense I venerate the role—I love it—but it is a parody. I'm not so sure these things were ever taken so seriously. There were burlesque versions the minute the original was written.

The problem with period plays is that few actors are able to project themselves into the period—like Judith Anderson becoming Medea. There was the art nouveau Camille of Nazimova, then the art deco Camille of Garbo.

Certain women have tried to play Camille in modern times and failed because they were asking to be taken seriously. They were asking to be mistaken for the character in an everyday kind of way, so the audience thought they were being tricked. But if it's played in a manner that does not call for you to be a fool—if it's being created by, for and of the theatre—then they are able to appreciate and accept a much broader amount of material.

I think that I am the Camille of our era.

■

Sometimes people think it's sexism if you're in drag, but that's incredibly shallow. It's not easy to play a woman. I often think it must be hard for a woman to play a woman.

I think there is on the part of the audience an identification with the man who plays a woman that is very intense, because you have stepped out of your persona, you've gone out of your mind in a way. Men act like men, women act like women. For an actor to cross over and do it with intimate psychological truth becomes a very powerful image for the audience—because you're really both sexes.

Being an actor is about being a sexual object. Even if the audience is repelled by you, they're still dealing with that about you. It's fun to play with that. Dietrich used to say, "I got in drag because I wanted to attract both men and women."

■

Camille is a profoundly feminist work. There is a prejudice against a man dressing up as a woman because women are considered inferior beings. For a man to dress as a woman is a step down.

People are disturbed by female impersonation. They don't realize or understand its inner motive. They see something that is humorous. They don't understand what it means to play a woman.

There's an incredible cultural taboo against it, particularly in Anglo-American culture. It takes a lot of courage to open yourself up to those feelings.

Sexism motivates the prejudice against drag. A woman putting on pants has stepped up in the world. She's going to business. She's in a pantsuit. She's going to be an executive and this is a step up.

A man who gets into a flimsy negligee or evening gown has become a concubine. He's stepped down from his superior role. You're looked down on if you feel becoming a woman is something to be attained. To defiantly do that and say women are worthwhile creatures, and to put my whole soul and being into creating this woman and to give her everything I have, including my emotions (remembering that the greatest taboo is to experience feminine emotions), and to take myself seriously in the face of ridicule was the highest statement.

For *me* to play the diva is to step out of being a mere director to become a *goddess*: a step up. It's a reevaluation of these unfortunate sexual prejudices. I think it also validates the homosexual.

It's different than wanting to make women more like men. It allows audiences to experience the universality of emotion, rather than to believe that women are one species and men another, and that what one feels the other never does.

The women's movement is based on conflict and anger, but my *Camille* is synthesis, an altogether different tactic.

■

From my own point of view, there wouldn't be any Ridiculous if it weren't for me. There is a large extent of pain in my kind of Ridiculous, and there is a problem with pain. Aristotle defines ridiculous as the laughably ugly that does not give rise to pain. But pain has a lot to do with the significance of the work in our minds.

How lightly does it go by? How easy is it to take? To what extent are you asked to suffer, the way you are asked to suffer in opera or a piano concerto?

In my work there is both inner and outer direction. And the depth of involvement changes it from a mere spoof to something that transcends it. *Camille* could be taken as parody, but I perhaps have an ambiguous attitude towards these works.

I think it's a question of depth and complexity. *Camille*, on the one hand, *is Camille*—it's a totally legitimate interpretation of the original. The amount of personal anguish, how much of yourself you are going to reveal in it, is what makes it more powerful than just a spoof.

Certainly my *Camille* is unique—but it's *Camille*, it's built on something. I think that people who see the play and see a man as a woman feeling what people formerly thought only a woman could feel or do shows that these things are universal and that these roles are artificial, imposed, restrictive. That's one of the reasons I cast against type. Also it's very theatrical to cast against type, because you're seeing more acting than you would if you were casting somebody who is already that way. They don't have to do as much artwork on the part.

What I did was experiment with female impersonation—I put tremendous emphasis on the context. A man or a woman might be better at evoking a specific personality or making a definite point in the play. You get different levels of reality and unreality, and what ultimately happens is that the rigidity with which we look at sexual roles and reversals breaks down.

Finally, the most profound theme of the theatre is role-play—that roles are interchangeable, that personality is an artifice in life, and that it can be changed or interchanged. I believe that is the eternal message of the theatre.

For us I think it wasn't so much that we took on wrong roles because of sexual identification, but that we refused to take on any role—we wouldn't be one or the other sex because we saw that it was artificial; because we didn't make the clear conventional identification.

45

■

One point that is commonly missed in my work by people who have only seen one isolated production is the extremity to which characterization has been driven. Some performers will specialize while others become chameleons. The dexterity with which a highly intuitive and disciplined group of people may transform themselves can only be appreciated by comparing actors in different roles. The tendency of the novice is to assume an unwholesome pathology when what they are in fact seeing is the diagnosis of a physician. Nevertheless, an actor's identification with a character he is playing is a form of hedonism. Its positive or negative effects have never been measured. The performer's greatest accomplishment is the performer's tightrope walk between intuition and dogma. Certainly all forms of drama threaten to depose morals. The comic character is loved for his vices which bring him success; the tragic figure is destroyed by his virtue. Drama is the paradox which causes shock and surprise.

Drama at its greatest is paradox. To ask unanswerable questions is the secret to capturing the imaginations of humanity eternally.

The great work of art asks an unanswerable question. The longer the question remains unanswered the greater the work of art becomes. When the question is finally answered the work of art deflates and becomes worthless. This is more than an argument for obscurantism and novelty, my cynical friends!

6

The theatre must be rescued from pornographers and academics. What do academics have in common with pornographers?—a morbid and voyeuristic exploitation of ready-made content. The academic adopts a cause; the pornographer depicts the sexual act. The offensive thing about them is that they both demand to be taken seriously. Laughter puts them to flight.

This brings us to the birth of comedy. It has been said that tragedies end in death, comedies in marriage. This explains the death of comedy. Marriage can no longer be considered a happy ending.

In a comedy the two opposing forces of the drama must be reconciled. This is the aesthetic problem. The humor is the result of the tension and release as the two seemingly conflicting streams meet with obstacles and delays as they rush toward their resolution in a common sea. This process is morbid when a ready-made resolution is inevitable.

I call my work Ridiculous because the only ideas that interest me are paradoxes. (No, I'm not serious. I'm anti-serious.) It is this state of conscious-mess that I play with at every point of the plot: the seeming impossibility of resolution.

■

Why are audiences packing the Evergreen Theatre to see what is perhaps the least commercial play ever written—*Hot Ice*? This is not unusual in a theatre of paradoxes. The play has aroused critical controversy. Because I am responsible for the play's invention I will try to answer some of the questions that have arisen.

Is the play original and to what degree is it a reworking of the film *White Heat* by Raoul Walsh?

Did a playwright ever borrow a plot before? I saw in *White Heat* a plot device that was totally usable: a certain relationship between a gangster mother and her son. History is cumulative in this respect. Is *Oedipus Rex* off-limits because it was done two thousand years ago? Or is Woody Allen's *Sleeper* up-to-the-last-minute because it is a retelling of *Rip Van Winkle*? I used only one plot device from *White Heat*—the epilepsy. There is not one line of dialogue from *White Heat* in *Hot Ice*. (Not that I didn't like the film's dialogue. It wasn't appropriate. I just couldn't use it.)

■

Several years ago I was living with some friends who were firm believers in euthanasia or mercy killing. As much as I admired many of their ideas on ecology, I never felt comfortable with the idea of mercy killing. Life to me has always seemed sweet if not sacred. Another friend was at that time making arrangements to have himself frozen after his death in the hope that some future age would discover the key to bringing him back to life.

So there it was, a conflict that was not really a conflict—a paradox—the perfect Ridiculous idea. It was at that time that I first saw Raoul Walsh's movie *White Heat*. The next day I drafted a scenario for *Hot Ice* set in the mold of a gangster epic. It wasn't a story of life against death but rather of killers versus those who aspire to immortality. But in *Hot Ice* the killers are police. I put the killers on the side of the law because without the support of the law euthanasia becomes murder.

The Euthanasia Police Force evolved into a very strong image. We weren't sure who they were or what they were going to be like at first. Gradually we added things: we decided they would be sort of S&M macho; we oiled the bodies; we added chains; we put the silly wedgies on them.

The piss scene around the table: this is an image that was wrought.

It was a decision: there'd be a certain kind of lamp; they'd be in a certain kind of lighting; there would be a lot of cigarette smoke; a radio would be playing . . . building it up layer by layer, finding one detail after another.

Images are like symbols. They're consciously wrought, not something that just comes about. I take a raw material that I see and try to intensify it to create a certain impression.

■

We cast against type in many ways. For instance, as Buck Armstrong I'm playing a character who's into a machismo bag—he's affectionate toward other men in camaraderie, but he's not admitting to any homosexual tendencies or anything. This is as much a drag role for me as playing a woman. I'm investing a certain kind of psychology and attitude that is not my own—my own opinion, my own attitude; I'm playing the opposite of what I feel. And it is incredibly liberating for me because it's a rush, it's a thrill to play somebody who is the opposite of myself. One can take on the mannerisms, the behavior of any character, if you're skillful.

Most people learn one language and speak it most of their lives. Some people are exposed to more than one language and they *speak* more than one language. We were exposed to more than one possible sexual identity and we're bisexual in the way other people are bilingual. I like to show that in the theatre.

■

The Cagney film doesn't have a happy ending. The criminal undergoes a total transference when the agent relieves him of his seizure, and actually loves him, but the agent remains the predator to the end and kills him.

I found that extremely disturbing. To me the betrayal of love was so horrible that I couldn't get over it—I couldn't deal with it. The cop betrayed the trust, and I couldn't play that, because I'm playing opposite John Brockmeyer, whom I love.

A cop is sent in disguise to work his way into the confidence of the cryogenists. The man he is hunting comes to love his predator . . .

reversal after reversal as we find ourselves enmeshed in the paradox. To find our way out of the maze we must abandon the intellect which finds itself deceived at every turn. Only feeling and intuition can save us: the reassurance of laughing in a mob; knowing that you are not alone in the labyrinth.

As long as you cling to the intellect and the rational, the paradox has you in its web. Circumstances beyond our control: a simple definition of farce.

Laugh and you are free.

■

Every time I have written a play I chose a classical model upon which to build it. *Big Hotel*, my first play, was based on the movie trailer; hence my reputation as the father of nostalgia.

We did a play called *Stage Blood*, about an actor who is reluctant to play Hamlet, so it was a *Hamlet* within a *Hamlet* within a *Hamlet*. I got to do *Highlights from Hamlet*.

I wanted to write a ghost story/murder mystery. I borrowed a book from a friend called *How to Write a Murder Mystery* and there was a list in it of things you should *never* do in writing a murder mystery. I did them all. It was the only list in the book, so that was the easiest way.

We followed the *Hamlet* plot blow by blow. My father in the play has recently died, and my mother, who plays Gertrude, is marrying the guy who plays Claudius, and so on. After a certain point, it's hard to tell which scenes are from *Hamlet* and which aren't. The actors keep quoting from the play, so it's open-ended.

Such amazing things happened when I was writing it! There's a speech that I did in my dressing room, that I took from Joyce's *Ulysses* and changed around—about the relation between the father and son. "The son unborn mars his mother's beauty; born, he brings pain, divides affection, increases care. He is a male: his growth his father's decline, his youth his father's envy, his friend his father's enemy." And at that moment the ghost of my father appears to me. I'm nude—I'm changing from my street clothes, which are all black leather, into the black Hamlet costume—and my father appears and touches my hand in that gesture of Michelangelo's God in the Sistine Chapel, and he delivers a speech from Kyd's *Spanish Tragedy*. It's the same speech that Joyce was parodying in *Ulysses*. He says,

> My son! and what's a son?
> A thing begot within a pair of minutes, there about . . .
> Methinks a young bacon,
> Or a fine little smooth horse colt,
> Should move a man as much as doth a son;
> For one of these, in very little time,
> Will grow to some good use; whereas a son . . .

And suddenly, when I was writing this, I remembered my own father saying, "Children! I should have raised pigs, I'd be better off!"

The real murderer of the father was me—killing my father in fantasy, working through and finally forgiving him. It was a milestone for me.

Stage Blood ran for three months, but I got a feeling of disappointment from the audience. They'd come expecting something else—expecting a product, something they were used to from me. Nobody was in drag in *Stage Blood*, although the Hamlet character, you feel, turns out in the end to be homosexual. Nobody really *got* the idea that it's a play about an actor who is reluctant to play Hamlet.

■

We always review the art of acting. We created an actors' theatre, an acting troupe. In the long run, you can't get to the roots of conviction in a director's or playwright's point of view that you can when the actors mean it.

It takes years to develop that kind of understanding actors bring to your work, and that is what finally gives the work a base, a depth. Of course each actor has his or her own style, yet it's unified.

I think all forms of acting should be played side by side; I've never tried to codify the acting you see here. Some of my actors do a type of acting that tips the audience, with a stylistic wink, that this or that is supposed to be funny, but others perform deadpan or ambiguous acting that gets a laugh only when they do or say something that is actually funny.

There's a lot of confusion in my audience as to whether something is funny. I savor that because it makes the audience make a judgment, commit themselves. I appear more inscrutable and my work takes on more levels of meaning—it could be taken seriously, it could be ludicrous.

Roles are constructed with careful planning as to what impression they will create. They are not just arbitrarily given out.

When the actor becomes a primary creator, he is totally responsible for who he is on stage, which is terrifying to most actors. It's like having nothing to go on but yourself, an immediate situation and your coworkers.

The actor creates the role in a primary way—from his own imagination, wish fulfillment and fantasy life. It's your creation; it's more daring. This way there's a lot invested in our roles.

■

A lot of times an actor will improvise, and he could never repeat it. But I have total recall when it comes to dialogue, so I go home and write it down word-for-word, as he said it, and hand it back to him the next night. It involves many trips back to the typewriter, dragging the script that was written that morning into rehearsal and hammering it out on stage that evening. It's a very intimate way of working. It makes the plays very organic and personal to us.

The risks are great working this way, though in our company there is virtually no risk because we share this way of working. This makes it possible to be that free.

This relationship we have is very delicate and unique. We didn't set out to have it. It grew out of many years of work, and it requires a special atmosphere. It's really not something an actor can do completely on his own, without sympathetic coworkers who feel that way as well. You're working intuitively, and people are projecting images of what their role will be. When each actor is working to project his idea of what the character he will play will be, we begin to find the "play" in these characters.

An actor is amoral in that he wants to play the role, to live that life for some reason. It may be a life that others will disapprove of.

You can't ask an actor to make a moral judgment about the character he's playing. You *can*—Brecht said you should—but when it comes to getting into the role, there is some reason why you want to play it, and a lot of times it's something that you wouldn't exactly want to admit; a lot of times it goes unspoken. Why would I want to play this nasty character who beats people up? Why play Bluebeard? Why did I want to play this violent, awful person? Am *I* that way?

I read this little pamphlet—the Mao Tse-Tung line on Stanislavski—attacking Stanislavski because he had the "seed" theory, that each person has the seeds of any kind of character in him and all he has to do is find those seeds and cultivate them and become the character. Mao was very upset about that. The party said some people—like the working class—are heroes, and don't have the seeds of being a filthy capitalist or an exploiter, necessarily.

It's idealist theatre. It's a moralistic view. For myself, it is dangerous. We run into it in the group. We talk about "Why have you cast me this way in three plays?" and "Why am I still that person to you?" and what does it mean and why are we doing it that way. It's an ongoing problem. I've been frightened of these relationships for a long time—they're so intense—but I've overcome that in some way. I'm willing to face them or get into them, give myself wholeheartedly in a way.

Actors can more control their destinies, their stage lives, if there's communication, if they're not just passive, and say, "Yeah, I'm willing to play your maid in five plays if you want me to." If you don't want to, why do it? Or if you do want to, do it.

If I play a sexist pig in a play, it doesn't mean that the play is a sexist pig play; it might mean that the play is an attack on that. But I have to take on those characteristics in order to show them, and sometimes there is a lot of confusion about that with audiences. Most professional, commercial productions go out of their way to eliminate that confusion, because they understand that the audience is insecure and try to cater to them, make very clear what they're trying to say.

■

This Ridiculous thing is something that I inherited, in a way, and then I followed my own impulses. I never tried to prove I was Ridiculous. I've done plays that were funny-peculiar but not really funny-ha-ha. I'm the first one who thought the Ridiculous could be comedy. Before that it was an angry, dadaist, surrealist thing.

I feel very fortunate that this is my world—this world of buffoons and clowns and ne'er-do-wells; non sequiturs and great jokes and lousy jokes; the freedom of imagination allowed to do anything I want to try, to be as bad as I want to be or as good as I can be. Ridiculous is the most unpretentious thing you could say.

A satirist always places himself above the thing he is satirizing. He is going to show you how all these other people aren't any good, expose their foibles. But we've never called ourselves the Theatre of the Ridiculous—this is something others call us. The original was the Play-House of the Ridiculous. We call ourselves the Ridiculous Theatrical Company, which means *we* are ridiculous. We are not pointing a finger at others and saying *they're* ridiculous. *We* are the buffoons.

If you oppose seriousness and ridiculousness or humor—if you put them in opposition to each other and say that we are one and somebody else is the other—then it seems it can't be serious. But the fact that we've dedicated seven years of our lives and hard work to something is a kind of seriousness about something. We're serious about humor.

I don't think the two things really conflict per se. It is a question of decorum and temperament with us. We don't want to keep a straight front and try to convince people that this is terribly serious and important and heavy, because this is against the goal of making them laugh and have a good time. We're temperamentally unsuited to it.

But what after all is theatre for? It is a totally didactic art. Evolution is a conscious process. Humanity must take the next step. One set of values must replace another. How about polysexuality and ethical eating instead of immoral eating and strict sexual morality?

∎

Why satire? Laughter is a sign of recognition. Each laugh is a consent on the part of the audience leading them to a conclusion which they cannot escape. Art means finding your way through a tangle of possibilities. It's a closed world, a microcosm.

It's like a karmic debt: anything I take in has to be transmitted out, just like eating. It's got to come out somewhere. It's the same way with mental food.

Decadence is to art what manure is to organic farming. It creates a fertile atmosphere.

In this country, the middle class is groveling for scraps to maintain their facade of uplifting morality. But it's all a lot of hypocrisy and lip service.

Shaw says marriage suits seventy-five percent of the people. Twenty-four percent go along because they haven't got the courage to say what they think, and they get the other seventy-five percent to join them in persecuting the one percent who *won't* go along.

That's the way it is with eroticism and with art. People who do what they want are persecuted by people who don't have the courage to do what they want.

Artaud is a continuing influence. Lately I've been examining the idea of the sensual pleasure of going to the theatre. I've been reading Nietzsche, and that has something to do with it, Wagner and all that.

In 1973 or 1974 we went to Zurich, Geneva and Brussels. In Brussels, we were treated like kings. They thought it was the greatest thing they had ever seen. *Whores of Babylon, The Grand Tarot, Bluebeard* and *Camille.* . . . It was a triumph. One night it was the height of masculinity, and one night the height of femininity. I had Brussels at my feet.

∎

There is nothing so ardent as the love of a young man for an old whore. This has been my relationship to the theatre. This bruised Beatrice has led me from Puritanism to hedonism. And how she made me aspire! To

55

win her from her pimp I would commit murder. Not for nothing *Camille* is the biggest moneymaker in theatrical history and *Oedipus Rex* the greatest tragedy.

The theatre can only be saved from pornography by hedonism. Hedonism is the antidote. Does this sound shockingly eighteenth century? The theatre needs more than restoration—it needs a rebirth. Comedy was born of an impulse toward revelry and song, from the Greek words *komos* meaning revelry and *aedein* meaning song.

I went back to plot, and over the years did many different experiments with it. Eventually I began to use plot in the way a modern uses abstraction. It became a question of distorting the plot. I wrote profoundly influenced by the study of commedia dell'arte and particularly its great champion, Carlo Gozzi, who wrote a book on plot and archetype. He set down the thirty-six archetypal dramatic situations from which all plot is derived.

When I began to look at the plot matrix, I became fascinated by the idea that there were only thirty-six situations. I realized that if, in fact, the worthy subjects for drama are a finite number, and even the situations in which we find ourselves in reality are archetypal, then perhaps the idea of the plot being real and true—the domain of the realist who wanted to make autobiographical sense—was a myopic view of the human condition. An artist who works autobiographically may limit the number of possible plots to fewer than thirty-six.

It is a case of innovate or die. Gertrude Stein said, "Kill the nineteenth century dead." Mission accomplished. We are entering the last quarter of the twentieth century, the "modern" period in which the destruction and reduction of forms has led us full circle: zero. Nothing will come of nothing. We have entered the postmodern period. The avant-garde is dead and we have left it behind. Having a new idea is as gauche as being seen in a new suit (Cocteau). It is time to ransack tradition and embrace all the conventions. It is time to start rendering subject matter.

7

P eople are surprised that I have a head for business, but somehow one lurks there. You have to threaten and haggle, bargain, bargain, bargain. It can be fun.

In one way, it's easier if you have no money. Then everyone is exploited, including yourself.

Those were the years I ran up those enormous debts. I was trying certain experiments for a long time, meeting with success but hard-won success—artistically, I mean, not in terms of box office, God knows.

■

Usually we just rented a theatre for one time. We tried all different theatres. But the generous support of the National Endowment for the Arts and the New York State Council on the Arts allowed us finally to maintain a permanent theatre, the Evergreen Theatre at 55 West 11th Street. The luxury of our own theatre made it possible for us to rehearse in the same place that we would be performing, mount our productions when they were ready, expand our playing schedule to six performances a week, do repertory, develop and expand our audiences, and allow the company to explore a whole new area of theatre: children's theatre.

Professor Bedlam's Educational Punch and Judy Show is an orgy—an acting addict's orgy. It's an illusionary scale, so I feel like a giant.

With hand puppets, it's your hand that's acting. Your hand becomes a metaphor for the whole human body.

The puppet is a purely theatrical creation. It is almost the most pure expression of the performer in the sense that the *mise en scène*, or scenic element, and the performer are one. The puppet has unlimited expressive possibilities.

What we today call special effects is basically puppetry. All special effects in film are based on either double exposure or puppetry. Those techniques really originated in the theatre—not double exposure, of course, but the idea of extending the human being's expressive possibilities through the use of puppets.

That was a study and a fascination of mine. It constantly gets rewoven into the fabric of my work. It's part of my vocabulary as an artist.

Puppets keep their looks forever.

■

The success of the children's show was astounding. I started doing children's theatre because I thought it would be fun. Not having any children of my own—and I won't—it's a very high experience performing for them.

We draw off one another, and I have this wonderful opportunity with *Professor Bedlam's Educational Punch and Judy Show* to give children their first theatrical experience. That's a real trust for me—helping create future audiences.

I did the *Punch* for myself, and it went over so big that the New York State Council on the Arts asked me to accept a commission for another children's show, *Jack and the Beanstalk*. That was an ill-fated production. I have since learned that when you do plays for children, you are really not being judged by the children but by the parents.

Sometimes people who are involved with children's theatre are very, very conservative. If you get too weird, they get nervous. You can do anything you want if you're doing it in your own theatre, but if you accept a fee to go to a school system and perform, suddenly everything is too disturbing for them.

One person insisted on an intermission and it hurt the build-up of the play. Another group said it was five minutes too short and they threatened not to pay us. Another beat us out of the fee.

People in children's theatre are too sordid. People in the porno industry are more honorable.

■

Caprice was about a war between two fashion houses. Bill Vehr and I played rival designers. I was Claude Caprice and he was Twyfford Adamant. I was going to be a homosexual character and I'd never played one before. I had to do some research!

I got the idea from reading *A Rebours* by Huysmans. The character I played was based on the main character in the book. Sometimes it's a plot that I like. In this case it was a character.

Twyfford was more of an S&M type: an asexual who is a voyeur, loves to have other people have sex while he watches. A lot of these characteristics were from people we knew, many celebrities in the art world.

With *Caprice* I was trying to combine five different plots into one play. It was supposed to be a Restoration comedy. It was supposed to be a naughty farce with disturbing ideas being presented, and it met with the fate of plays that do that.

People have preconceptions about what you should be doing. As a parodist it's difficult, because you're making fun of things. In *Caprice* I showed the gay world, and gay people were the ones who were most offended. Some thought it was great and understood it; others thought that we should only be presenting a so-called positive image of gays. I would never stoop to presenting a positive image—of anything.

■

Adela Holzer commissioned me to write a book for a musical about Catherine de Medici and the St. Bartholomew Day massacre. I didn't know anything about Catherine de Medici, so I started doing an enormous amount of research.

I did have the actors in my company in mind. I always wanted to do it when we could afford to give it the full Renaissance production it deserved.

It's a historical drama. Catherine's son Henry III was a homosexual king who had an entourage of minions who were flaming, semi-transvestites as well as expert swordsmen and homicidal maniacs. They were dandies who wore tons of makeup and extremely fancy dress. It was all very decadent. They all vied for Henry's attention, and they used to kill each other regularly in very savage duels. Sudden death was the code. None of them ever lived past thirty. They were always murdered by each other.

I read every play that was ever written on Catherine and thought I could collage all of them. Eventually thinking of plot as an abstract thing led me to take a plot and create a completely original play. I thought, "I could take one of these plots and write out the dialogue and have a perfectly good play."

It's like a recipe where you bake a cake. Everybody comes up with a different cake, but it's basically the same recipe.

I heard that Dumas *père* had written a play with Catherine de Medici in it called *Henri III et sa court*. I found one of those rotten nineteenth-century translations that tries to make everything sound Elizabethan and read it in the library. It dealt mostly with her homosexual son and his honor guard of minions and an intrigue at court that had been mentioned in a number of plays and histories. But the plot was out of this world! It was a real cloak-and-dagger, rip-snortin', nineteenth-century melodramatic plot. I wanted to use it. It was just the structure I needed to create the event.

What I did was abstract plot from this play and adapt the plot structure to my needs. I took the play and said, "First scene: Ruggieri the astrologer and Catherine," and then I read the scene and did this to it, "He says . . . she says . . ." right down the line, just a hint of what happens in the scene and who's in it, until I had virtually a commedia plot-outline of the play. The play itself was unusable.

So I took my outline and wrote out my own dialogue. *My* Catherine said to her astrologer what *I* wanted her to say about the situation. *My* view of the political situation slipped in, and then I used contemporary things plus what I knew of the period from my research. I wrote it out in my own words.

Then I started feeling, "I took this plot. It's such a great play, but I didn't invent it." I compared it to the original and it was absolutely nothing like it. It was absolutely original stuff, but it had the same skeletal structure.

In the play, Protestantism is a radical new sect as viewed by the Catholics. I thought it would be very good for the Moral Majority to remember what it was like when they were considered the *im*moral minority. They were considered an extremely radical, dangerous, perverted group.

·

In 1976, we went to Florence and Nancy. In Nancy it was peculiar, because everyone there was a theatre person, so I was being judged by people who were perhaps more conservative and a little jealous of my freedom. I created a piece especially for Nancy, based on a Turkish shadow-puppet character. They were shocked.

It was very interesting. The day after we played the first time, the papers came out with scathing reviews: look at this demented, deranged, sex-obsessed. . . . The next day the theatre was packed. The Grand Theatre. Every performance sold out after they heard that it was this vile, pornographic, obscene, deranged, worthless. . . . They packed themselves in, but everyone disapproved of us. When we went to that café where everyone would drink at night, everyone was staring at us and looking very shocked, as if we fucked onstage. But the theatre was packed.

·

I want to play every town in *this* country. In New York it is the best theatre, but outside it is the *only* theatre. They are delighted with it. They think it's wonderful. There is more approval, because they don't have so much to choose from. Just the fact that it's theatre is amazing outside of New York.

·

My main problem as a writer now is with language. I love the language. I'm hung up on words.

I enjoy dance myself, but there came a point in the mid-seventies when I wanted the people on stage to stop dancing, stand still and *talk*. Yet there they were, dancing around and making us feel bad that we were so out of shape. Indeed, it got so that I wanted to see people who were in *terrible physical condition* talking for *hours*.

■

In the early plays, there was always a motif, and the language would be a parody of that motif—science fiction, or *Grand Hotel*, or gothic horror story. In *Eunuchs* I tried aiming for an Oscar Wilde sort of headiness, a very elevated diction. In *Corn* I was able to get by on clichés and country dialogue.

The problem is, when you're not parodying a genre anymore, how do people talk? The minimal vocabulary was Beckett's solution—also Racine's. I can see that as a possibility, but I want something richer than that. Passion sings in opera. In the theatre it has to do something else.

It is richness that I want—that panoramic quality, the allusiveness of language.

■

Everyone likes famous works and famous situations. That's why they are famous. Wagner was not the first one to deal with the myth of the *Ring*. It started out as an Icelandic myth, then it was spread down into the *Nibelungenlied* in the Middle Ages. Then Wagner was the *modern*—the nineteenth-century interpretation of that myth. I tried my own version, the Ridiculous version—doing the *Ring* in a night.

Themes are worked and reworked. Basic human themes, throughout the ages, continue to have meaning because the basic human relationships are repeated again and again, so they communicate through history: the father-and-child relationship and conflict; or lover and lover. . . . And people are able to improve on these stories, give them new meaning.

Most contemporary playwrights feel the literature of the theatre oppresses them, but it's there to be used. I feel it is mine. My originality lies in another realm from discursive writing. It's an art of arrangement and allusion. For me, using quotes from other sources gives a verbal richness that I couldn't get otherwise. I like my plays to have a dense texture and resonance because I have to work in them night after night and I don't want to get bored.

Compared with the great ages of the theatre, my plays are really mediocre, but they're better than anything my contemporaries are doing.

∎

I love the incredibly inflated theatricality, the preposterousness of opera. I followed the plot from different libretti of the *Ring*, including Wagner's own libretto, as a scenic structure, used it as an outline. Then I improvised; in a sense, invented the dialogue. I employ a selective attitude, like arranging gems in a setting, using words as objects.

It was influenced by Joyce, but I didn't really invent new words, which he did in *Finnegans Wake*. I felt that each word would be understood, although you might need an expanded vocabulary. *Der Ring Gott Farblonjet* abandoned literal speech and went into a completely abstract poetical language. Because it was about the evolution of man and thought, it was also the evolution of language. People had debates, rational discourse, and the medium of speech suffered through vaudeville and German Yiddish. It struggled out through all these different permutations.

Trying to invent a language of the theatre, I was trying to layer the language so that it wasn't like everyday speech. It was almost another language, a poetic medium. We all have the same vocabulary, ultimately, and the ability to choose words out of that vocabulary. I wanted to play with the idea of showing an evolution of speech. The characters speak different ways, using words that ring of certain periods of history. I gave the characters linguistic leitmotifs: the Nihilumpens speak in potato-German; the Gibichungen speak an elevated revenge-tragedy Elizabethan speech; the Valkyries—chaste, heroic, virgin lesbians—have Gertrude Steinian speech. (My Valkyries were lesbian motorcyclists. Valhalla was Lincoln Center, which we burned down in the last act.) I presented a kind of history of English and German compacted: the Forest Bird speaks in plain English, then Siegfried tastes the dragon's blood and suddenly understands birdsong, so he starts to understand English—at least, that was my justification.

It seems now as if I wrote my way through history.

■

Costume tells a lot about character. It creates the scene. It is the visual aspect of the actor.

Unless the actor is naked, he has to wear something. The actor's visual impact is based on his costumes and his face, whatever is exposed. Great care has to be put into that. It is extremely important that it be right, that it express the character, that the actor work in it and so on. It must be appropriate.

For instance, in *Der Ring* I dressed the Nihilumpen chorus in plastic garbage bags, cutting out the neck and arms. The design became very rich.

The staging was so complex I'd planned not to act in it at all. I wanted it to be heavy—a parody on the heaviness, the ponderousness of Wagner. Like the wedding procession in "Götterdämmerung"—it was funny, but it was also beautiful, intense and pompous, yet rather a joke on pompousness, as the people were wearing garbage bags and carrying plastic swans on their heads. That is the splendor of opera—that kind of corniness.

It was a fabulous work of art. But a lot of people didn't get it. A lot of people loved it as one of the greatest things they had ever seen in their lives, and then there were a lot of people who just didn't like it. They didn't even know Wagner, or they felt it needed Wagner, or you had to understand Wagner to get it. I didn't think so.

They were puzzled by it, disturbed by it. Sometimes the subject matter isn't appealing, or the audience is not interested in the subject. How then can I control them? I don't *have* to control them. I have to follow what interests *me*. Then the audience judges.

■

In the course of the development of our company I always directed from the point of view of an actor in the company, which is internal direction.

Many people made me feel bad and said, "Oh, if you could only see it! You could see all the mistakes. If you could only be an objective eye, the play would develop more quickly. If you could only see it like other directors." I began to feel more and more that I had to try that.

It was the eighth or ninth year of the company. Having directed everything and having always played roles, I began to think, "Yes, something is missing. I've got to see the play." So I directed *Der Ring* and wasn't in it, and I realized something about it: it was the most perfect play I'd ever seen. It was designed for that—I was going to do the play I wanted. If I were to go to the theatre and see a play, what would I want to see?—I created it for myself.

As I sat and watched it, there was something missing in it for me, but I didn't know what. It wasn't really a disappointment, because the aesthetic pleasure of watching it was very great. Later I realized there weren't any loose ends. It was a deck without a joker. It was because I had directed it from the outside. I had worked the way other people work and it had become perfect. You know how easy it is to be perfect, how incredibly easy, and how hard it is to be human and have failings, especially in public—to put that vulnerability into a work of art.

I also didn't know what to do when I wasn't in the play. I figured out that I couldn't sit and watch it night after night because I would go mad. Also, I couldn't see it freshly anymore. Other directors can go off and direct another play, but I have this company.

I knew none of this, at first, when I did the *Ring*. I sat and watched it night after night. I watched it forty times and I couldn't even think of an improvement. Then an actor left and I went into the play to take his role. Immediately *I* was what was wrong. I hadn't been rehearsed, and no one had the objective eye. The whole thing changed. Everyone changed. I would start doing things and they'd say, "Oh! You can do that?" and I'd say, "Well, why not?" They'd say, "Oh! Well! If *you* can do *that*. . . . You wouldn't have let us get away with that!" I said, "You never tried anything," and they said, "We didn't know we were allowed."

It was the difference between having an authority figure outside of the play and being in the play. Suddenly everyone started to take the liberties that I was taking. It didn't change the vision one bit. They didn't compromise the things that were perfect about the play. But a new spirit came over it.

.

I'd been doing *Punch and Judy*, and I realized I'd like to have a different relationship to the figure, one where I'd be a character in relation to him. I'm interested in the mask, what it can do—very objective.

That summer there were a number of ventriloquists working on the street, and I watched them. I suddenly realized that with *Punch and Judy* I was carrying around all these puppets, and there was one figure who could create another person with nothing but his voice. It appealed to me. I thought it would be wonderful if the dummy could be something *portable*.

I was in Philadelphia doing *Punch and Judy* on this stage that had been used in a circus. The set looked very Diane Arbus sitting there; it had this wonderful quality that the Japanese call *suchness*. I imagined myself sitting with this pretty, weird little screen behind me, a ventriloquist's dummy on my lap.

I saw a ventriloquist on the street on a Saturday night and knew I had to do ventriloquism. I became obsessed. The next day I talked about ventriloquism continuously and drove all my friends crazy. I was tortured all day Sunday because there was no place to get a dummy.

Monday morning I got the Yellow Pages and looked up every place that sold them. I found one that had toy dummies and they said, "If you want a professional, hand-carved dummy, you'll have to go to Tannen Magic." So I asked a friend of mine who is a puppeteer—she costumed ventriloquists' dummies—and she said, "They're very expensive." I asked her how much they were, and she said they were three hundred dollars.

I went to my savings account and withdrew every penny I had, hailed a cab, went to Tannen Magic, walked in and looked at a whole case of ventriloquists' dummies. Most were not very appealing. But there was this little child sitting among the dummies, and that was *Walter*. I said, "I'd like to see that one."

They didn't even take me seriously—they don't sell too many of them. They brought him out and I looked at him and asked the price, and they said two hundred fifty dollars. I said "Wrap him up," gave them the cash and that was that.

The box looked like a little coffin. Walter was carved by a ventriloquist in New Jersey. A lot of people said he looked just like me.

I think I looked like that when I was a kid, but maybe I'm just projecting. Maybe dummies come to look like their owners and owners begin to look like their dummies after a while. That would mean I'd be looking younger and younger in this case, so I don't mind.

The day after I bought him, I started going on the street and trying him out. The minute he is out of the box a crowd forms. It's instant theatre.

■

When I was little, my older brother gave me a dummy and I did ventriloquism. Nobody paid any attention to me. I don't remember anyone saying it was particularly good. Recently, when I told my mother I'd got a dummy, she said, "You used to do that so well." I said, "I didn't know that."

I knew I could throw my voice. I was always interested in puppets. Then it all came together. I knew I was going to turn ventriloquism to a new and higher purpose.

I hold these conversations with myself—two parts of myself, divided and always set in opposition. That was really the impulse.

■

I bought a rare book on ventriloquism, *Practical Ventriloquism*, by a man who was in Henry Irving's troupe at the turn of the century. He didn't believe in using dummies—he felt that was a corruption of *pure* ventriloquism, which means vocal performance, exclusively: you imitate the sound of a distant train, a voice coming from the floor. You can throw your voice to create an illusion. The author included a section on working with figures, but basically didn't approve of it, thought it déclassé.

Although we think of the dummy as being terribly important, actually it's not necessary at all. Ventriloquism is very appropriate to radio. Edgar Bergen always used a dummy, though, even on the radio.

I went out, studied it and read every book I could find on it—what the classic terms were, what ventriloquists traditionally did—and I found there was a stock in trade among them. There was a whole list of devices that had to be mastered in order to be a successful ventriloquist.

■

Then I got a job in this whores' bar on Third Avenue called Little Peter's. It had these black transsexuals doing lip-synch, and a friend of mine—Larry Rée, from the Trocadero Ballet—was doing a drag and strip act there as a goof, because it was summer. It was real sleazy and fun—it was like *The Blue Angel*, even to the proprietress, this blonde, chubby woman from Hamburg, mothering all the prostitutes and transsexuals.

I went home to my Bauhaus theatre chart to analyze what form of theatre this was and I came out with *fairground*. So I thought, "That's where I am. I'm in a fairground. That's the nature of this."

I found it very hard, because actually the lip-synch that was being done is *also* ventriloquism—which is very funny. The performers were their own dummies. . . . So I got very turned on. I thought that was where I really belonged, in this very raunchy crowd carrying on with fever and disorder—which I've always romantically thought was the true atmosphere for theatre . . . men and ladies of the evening, and all kinds of people.

It was a wild-and-woolly atmosphere, but I don't think that *they* had the same sentimental attachment to *me* that I had to *them*. They couldn't figure out what the hell I was doing there.

I didn't go over well. Believe me, they didn't like me. When I did slapstick, I captured them, but somehow my mike never worked, or something. They liked a lot of it, but ultimately the place got too crazy and I left.

I finally decided they didn't appreciate me, so I did ventriloquism on the street, on the Staten Island Ferry, on the 42nd Street library steps. Stuart Sherman, who likes to work outdoors, had a grant to do street performances, and I tagged along.

I can take Walter anywhere. Though I've realized since that the dummy is like a guitar or something: you have to *carry* it yourself. You wouldn't dream of carrying puppets or another person. So maybe in the long run it's more of a burden to have Walter.

Then I felt I had created a portable artform, where I could indulge my extra appetite for theatre above and beyond what I could do with my ensemble, beyond what I could afford to do.

■

Ventriloquism is not considered a branch of puppetry. It's part of magic—based on misdirection and illusion. Puppetry is "honest."

A ventriloquist is an authority figure. The dummy is a ne'er-do-well. He's always an antagonist, an unbridled critic, demonically bent on destruction. Dummies have tremendous license—like fools.

Next to Walter, I seem almost normal. Being the straight man is the hardest part. Walter gets the laughs.

It is true that Walter's rather pretty for a demonic dummy. But there's something also about that fear of the beautiful child. . . . Walter scares me a little bit. I don't like gazing at him, because I do get a rather bizarre feeling. I have to get away from him sometimes. He sometimes says unexpected things.

■

Then I decided to write a play mostly in the form of a cabaret entertainment. *The Ventriloquist's Wife* was a nightclub act that was really about magic and other skills.

Jerry Stiller suggested I use Black-Eyed Susan as the dummy. Actually we tried it that way, but it didn't have the right effect. There was something wrong with the scale. We are the same size . . .

The Ventriloquist's Wife is, in a sense, pure theatricality. For years I had wanted to do the story of possession, which is the ventriloquist's story. I like the idea of the ventriloquist who's doing the dummy while the dummy still has a will, an opposing will. Because you have an opposing will within yourself. Mentally.

I catalogued the resources of ventriloquism, of what ventriloquism could do, and I used that as my vocabulary. Susan and I worked together. I taught her ventriloquism—a few of the secrets—and she could do it perfectly.

Susan and I decided to play out this fantasy between us. I wanted to use my own name because that made it more ambiguous, more like *Games People Play* . . .

I was creating a piece for cabaret, so I analyzed the essence of cabaret entertainment, what made something work. I then realized that these things were essentially variety turns, so I deliberately created a narrative out of them for maximum effect.

It changed from night to night. We did have a script, but every performance was different because every audience is different and it evolved that way. I felt that the accomplishment was that I'd done what I set out to do: synthesize a drama, with a plot and characters and a story, with the idea of a nightclub act.

A lot of it was owed to radio, even though the visual impact is very strong. Much was communicated verbally, just by standing still at a microphone.

It was a breakthrough for me—not the ventriloquism as such, but because it opened the door for something in the theatre that I had hit upon earlier in my work . . . why certain moments were more Ludlam, more my own.

8

Along the way we reopened a number of theatres most people didn't even know about, including the 13th Street Theatre. Some of those theatres seated only about sixty people.

Of course we used to have a theatre, the Evergreen. . . . Ah well, change has always been good for us. Keeps us on our toes. My temperament is to rally against obstacles.

I didn't want the company to become an institution. When we left the Evergreen we thought we didn't want to make a commitment, we just wanted to *play*. But we found so much of our time and energy was consumed just finding pieces of real estate, securing them and getting kicked around, we all began to realize it wasn't *practical* to cling to that amateur status we had so loved.

I wanted the Cherry Lane, actually. We put down a deposit on it and waited, because they told us *The Passion of Dracula* would bomb. But I'd wanted this place—One Sheridan Square—for years.

In 1977 we took this theatre on a ten-year lease. I wanted to really work in this theatre and let the audience come to us.

It cost a lot of money to take the theatre, things that never get on a show onstage. We had to buy lighting equipment and put down an enormous security deposit. Then there was the regular rent.

■

I have everything I want. Commercial theatre really just means profit-making theatre, and I can't see any reason why my work should go to make a profit for someone else who invests the money. Then I would become an employee.

I have plenty of seats here. We'll grow into this theatre. I would feel the need for a larger space if the audience couldn't get in, if there were no room; then I would think of a larger theatre. But as long as there are empty seats, I think this is good.

Now I have all this and I can do anything. Of course I am also inhibited now, because then I didn't have to pay anyone. In those days the money was never the reason why it couldn't be done. Now the payment is an obstacle. It means I can't do because I don't have the money.

Part of it is the decision to be professional, to be a professional artist who makes my living at this. It forces me to make certain decisions. If I want to be a professional artist I have to make certain compromises, just as to be an amateur you have to make compromises. You realize that if the play has to go on at a certain date, it's going to go on on that day, whatever happens. You might want to postpone it, but you cannot.

I want to just fill the seats here, so that the actors can live and we can continue to produce. I am not that wildly ambitious about dumping all this and going on to something else. I want to perfect this, that I've devoted so many years to.

.

We have to work out the problems of working in the round like this. Other productions that we did were originally staged for the proscenium. We are really trying to deal with this room and how it works. It *is* an obstacle, but I think it's something we are solving.

I think that it lends itself to epic stage, which is good. For years I worked in an epic flounce, and then kept getting picture-frame stages. Finally I found that melodrama worked much better in a picture-frame, so I started working in a melodramatic form. I longed for a more flexible space, although I liked doing things on a proscenium.

My work became associated with the proscenium, but that was just a phase because I had to work that way. This lends itself to another kind of art, and it's very exciting to explore it. It has a lot of possibilities.

This is the first theatre we have ever had that I really *like* being in, aside from certain very glamorous theatres in Europe, or very beautiful opera houses. Even then, one doesn't want to spend much time in an opera house. You go there to do your job and then leave, whereas in this place I have more the feeling of comfort and enjoyment of the way this room is.

It focuses one's mind somehow. A central area has something very profound in it. I have to figure it out. Maybe it will be a circus.

There is no curtain in here. I can't drop it. I can't *reveal* a scene. I have to *motivate* it, bring it on for a reason. It can't just open and there it is.

For comedians it's very important to have the whole audience see something that's happening, that's funny, all at once. It's very hard here. Here, no matter where you go, you are in somebody's way. You have really to clear the way for the big funny things.

They don't all see the same play. I don't even try to make them see the same picture. The actors have to really change. If you go very far downstage and turn your back on one row, you are still seen by more people than not; you have the sides seeing you in profile. On a proscenium stage you think in parallel, but here you have to think in semicircle.

I've worked in the round before, so it's not new to me. But I think it will definitely change the choice of plays and subjects I'll do, because I'll always pick things that lend themselves to this shape, and they will be more successful here.

■

Utopia, Incorporated was the first new play in the new theatre. I had the idea of writing the entire play in vaudeville gags, and a plot that constantly contradicted itself.

Some plays are very long, like *Der Ring*. It was four hours long. This one wasn't too long, as I realized we had very little time or money for it, because we had just taken the theatre. I wanted to do a project successfully in the amount of time we had and with the amount of money we had. I wanted it to be something complete and beautiful but modest.

I saw this show in Las Vegas called *Hallelujah Hollywood!* Every costume cost ten thousand dollars. They had ostrich feathers and peacock feathers and rhinestones, and it went on for hours, with two million dollars' worth of costumes being paraded around. There was absolutely nothing there, though. Pure spectacle. Everything was worth what the price tag on it said.

If you make a set out of gold, everybody knows it's at least worth its price; whereas, if you sculpture something out of a base material that's entirely worthless, the judgment is on its aesthetic quality exclusively. It can't be interpreted materialistically.

Styrofoam, for example, is expensive, but they throw it away. The design is for very specific purposes—each part is designed to pack something and only that one thing, to fit the shape of it so that it can't be reused—which is a terrible waste, because this stuff doesn't decompose; it stays around forever. Having a superior material like this around is very unfortunate for the ecologists but very good for us. We can create things out of it.

Commercial theatre doesn't have to survive. They can afford to spend a lot of money on each production, and they don't care. They destroy everything after using it. But what I want is incredible richness and variety and spectacularness, which is very expensive if you are going to use everything brand new.

The ability to recycle and transform things with imagination gives me a spectacle at a fraction of the cost. At no cost: these things don't cost anything; they are free. We find them in the streets. It took K.K.'s genius to transform them into art.

■

There is no kitsch in my productions. I don't use it. Kitsch is Broadway theatre. Kitsch is SoHo. Kitsch is the avant-garde. *That's* kitsch.

Kitsch pretends to have a big meaning. That's what kitsch is: pretentious. Meanwhile it is really shitty art. Whereas camp is not that . . . although camp is so prostituted as a concept today, it is impossible to talk about it.

But kitsch has nothing to do with my research and program. Kitsch is made out of very expensive materials. That's part of it. The joke in kitsch is that it's so much expense and work when it's something of so little value. That's the joke.

Here the joke is that nothing expensive is needed to create high art. This is *alchemy*. We take base metals and transform them into gold. Or mental gold.

■

Some of these costumes I designed last year before we even did the play: Susan's costume, Bill's costume, my costume, the grass skirts, the umbrella-hats. The play was only partially written when Bill and I set out to design the costumes. I knew what I wanted it to be, and I was already picking and choosing things.

The playwright in his script may need the set designer's and costume designer's ideas, but the set design and costume design are based on the script's ideas. Suddenly you see something embodying them and realize a whole new ground becomes possible, because of the way something looks or who the actor becomes.

■

Plots generally break down into types. When I am about to write a play I am aware right away of what type of plot it is, and I begin to deal with it that way.

As far as utopian tradition is concerned, I thought the possibilities were either to think of a completely new utopia, with my own program for how to make a perfect society, or to satirize past utopias, or to collage past utopias, taking the best of each one—those which I think to be the possibilities. . . . But I didn't really want to do any of those things. What interested me was the idea that throughout the history of utopian literature there are two conflicting schools of utopian ideas. One is the world perfected by Reason, in which human beings subdue human nature and make it conform to the rational, ideal society. The other is the Garden of Eden idea, that natural man could live in a paradise where the fruits fall off the trees and no one has to work; they can indulge in sexuality to the utmost, and human instinct could be totally fulfilled that way. In *Utopia, Incorporated* I wanted to represent the journey *inward*, into the inside of the earth, which might be the inside of the mind, to show the conflict between these two ideas.

Anarch is like Prospero. But I wasn't so much using *The Tempest* as I was using the same plot Shakespeare used, an Italian plot, from the Andreini commedia dell'arte scenarios, the "Enchanted Arcadia" plot.

■

I like the old conventions of the theatre. Everyone has to reinvent them for their own purposes, but I like them. I think that they are great and that they should be used.

There are two ways of doing classic Italian comedy: you can approach it as a sentimental thing, where you are trying to recreate a sense of what had gone on before; or, you use those discoveries in a collision of techniques, of aesthetics, which creates a new thing that means more to us.

When I do commedia I try to get rid of the picturesqueness. That's the first thing that has to go. The Callot illustrations—out. All that Scala business—out. Just make it about right now.

Commedia is resolved at the end—marriage is a happy ending—but one of the problems for modern comedy is to restore harmony at the end when so many values have been toppled down. Asymmetrical and irregular works have to be produced in order even to begin to evoke reality.

Many conventions of the theatre are outdated or fall into disuse. In some periods certain conventions are more taken for granted than in others. In a sense there's a cultural recycling program going on here: like an archeologist, I unearth these often defunct or forgotten theatrical techniques, and through my own research and by working practically in the theatre, I try to find out how they worked when they were living things, to bring them to life again.

What I like in the commedia dell'arte is that it didn't have that prejudice that the creator of the piece can't act in the play. In all other theatre, the person creating the play isn't supposed to be in the play—it's considered hoggish or hammy of him to do that—whereas in commedia dell'arte the *actors* are creating the play and the leading actor, even if he doesn't have the leading role, is usually considered the "boss" or the "major director." He invents the play. *For the actors.* And the actors do it.

I think that's healthy. The plays are created from the inside out. When the director stands on the outside manipulating his puppets, you get a less vital work.

Art and true experiments always involve a fixed element and a variable, out of which interaction the work is generated. The fixed element is form or conception and the variable element is expression or choice.

The architectural plan of the comedy, the plot, is fixed no matter who may improvise on it. The plot was something agreed upon, and then the detail was worked up by the artists as they staged this play. The detailing—i.e., the dialogue and *lazzi* or gags—was worked up by the actors in the rehearsal period. The plot existed independently of the dialogue. They were able to be topical and didn't preserve the topical stuff, thinking of the dialogue as ephemeral. When Goldoni tried to revolutionize the Italian theatre, Gozzi had him driven out of Italy for writing down the dialogue.

Good clowning is a cooperative artform. In the commedia dell'arte the comedian must share the stage, set up his fellow performers, remember his bits, be prepared to cover for another actor, have spare jokes and dialogue ready for any unforeseen event, ad lib, and keep the plot going while doing acrobatic feats, juggling and prestidigitation. The commedia dell'arte was a bawdy popular form, a celebration of the body, whose tempo is the pulse of wholesome life.

I don't think that the invention of the play in any other period was as much in collaboration with the actors. And the commedia dell'arte actor couldn't be replaced, because he was the only one who knew those lines. To train a new person to take over was an incredible problem. Clowns handed down con-books, with all their jokes and wits written down, to their sons.

As a playwright, I am not conflicted about the old debate between the improvised and scripted drama. They can and should exist side by side.

■

Before studying commedia dell'arte, every time I was reading an Elizabethan play I would be staggered by the cast list. But when you familiarize yourself with the commedia cast list, you realize that all cast lists are essentially the same. When you look through the Salerno book of scenarios you see that each cast has its little variations—the people change, though their basic personalities do not change. So what the characters become is an agent of some psychology; some basic primitive desire is embodied in each character. The plot is yet another way for them to go in and get what they want for their characters. This brings us back to the comic technology of the script.

In finding this I found a technical gold mine, a gold mine of comic situations that had come down to us and which are the archetypal situations of all times. In "The Dentist," for instance, every page of the scenario is full of every device and gimmick in the comedian's bag of tricks that had ever been thought of. I wonder how much has really been added to this.

A return to commedia dell'arte is a search for ancestry for the form of modern comedy—burlesque, vaudeville, mock tragedy. In the commedia I find classical format.

All I'm doing down here is working within a comic tradition, using character types that have been around for centuries. I'm just trying to make them live again in a way that's funny and thought-provoking. If I'm able to do that successfully, then I'm not just somebody *in* the comic tradition, but somebody who's *advancing* it.

■

Here we have, for the first time in dramatic literature, the abstract use of plot. I was pretty set on *Utopia* having a confused plot. It was the first time in a long time where I had a vision of what abstract plot could be.

What if the plot itself, the bare bones of the plot, was used abstractly, could be destroyed, distorted, changed, altered? We acknowledge that archetypal situations happen to everybody. Why do they have to happen in the order in which they originally happened? Why don't they just happen again and again in a sort of abstract way?

Whether Dorothy is swept away by a tornado, explorers find the world time forgot, Ferdinand is shipwrecked in Prospero's domain, Alice falls down the rabbit hole, or we find ourselves in Shangri-la matters little. The new world will be ruled by a magician with a daughter who has never seen a man, and in the end the spell will be broken and the world destroyed, usually by a volcano. The magician foresees the end of his rule.

With a plot that moves with such assurance, with the ease and determination of a river in its bed following its inevitable course, we are freed from both the burdens of consistency and originality of detail. At every turn the play contradicts itself yet the plot advances relentlessly. All of the facts in the plot could conflict with each other at every minute, but *the plot would go on*, in the same way it went on in every version of the story.

Formerly, when the playwright felt that the plot was the result of details, when two details contradicted each other he couldn't have a plot anymore, the plot was immediately destroyed. I can have a plot because I realize that the plot will go on anyway.

The plot is an architectural concept of the play and the architecture of the play holds up the structure of detail. All details can contradict each other. In my play the plot is reinforced by these contradictions, because the plot has its own will, whether or not the details make sense.

Anarch can be fifty years old, but Phyllis can be three thousand years old. They came to Utopia in 1946, but they have always been there. Her mother died, but they don't die. The list is endless. And the more it contradicts itself, the more the play works and the richer it becomes.

The audience was disturbed. They said, "How can this be true if that's true?" But a lot of people recognized that all the stories we used had that one plot.

If I have something from *The Tempest*, something from *Lost Horizon*, something from *Utopia*, something from *Erewhon*, something from Plato's *Republic*—whatever those utopias are—it is only because the plot is that type of plot that it can exist. The characters become agents of the action, agents of the plot. Characters as agents; characters as vehicles; characters as masqueraders; characters without pretense or psychology; characters precisely motivated; characters with composite histories; characters which do not endeavor to be believed . . .

The acting is both a feat and a personal appearance: stand-up comedy and costume parade. The actors model costumes rather than wear clothes. There are no fabrics: everything is made out of garbage.

Anarch: "Why, you could build a Utopia out of the garbage that litters your streets everyday!" We did.

■

The language, a satire on humor itself, is literary, clichéd, surrealist and original in its *arrangement*. The dialogue consists of jokes and puns, aphorisms and platitudes orchestrated and delivered by characters which make no sense whatsoever, if one tries to pin them down to psychological parameters.

I try to select jokes that are *appropriate* for everybody's character, that are *in character*, but sometimes I want the script or the literary aspect to supersede the characters, or the illusion of individual characters, like in the scene where we are all punning. We are all doing the same thing.

If we are going to make a character out of punning, maybe there will be one character who always puns and one who always uses the wrong word in the wrong place and so on. That will be character. But here everyone is punning, which to me was a way of creating the night, that particular night. It's a night on the Happy Island, there is some kind of madness in the air—something like that—and everyone keeps punning. For here it's the *scene*—the *scene* has a unity, just as if everyone were speaking in rhyme. It is creating a style to the scene, to give the scene a fuel. Everyone is into the same thing, and this gives the scene a flavor, its quality.

Those jokes create a way of thinking. They *imply* a psychology after a while. At first they are just jokes, but after a while that joke applies to characters' psychology and creates a world where people think differently than we do. They think crazy, so that you are in a world where people think crazy, and that creates certain stimulations.

An entire scene of twenty-minutes duration is sustained on puns alone, the audience groaning rhythmically after each line, shouting appreciation or derision at the actors. Some audience members explain the puns aloud to the person sitting next to them. Bursts of mad laughter; cries of "Stop it, we can't take any more"; more laughter, boos, hisses. One or two are insulted by the whole thing and walk out. Several puns receive ovations. A woman in the front row clutches her head with a pained expression on her face. Some people think the jokes unbelievably simpleminded, while they go over the heads of others. The power of words has been reaffirmed: they drop and detonate like little grenades. The audience has again become a battleground, the theatre a ring, a forum, a theatre of combat.

■

I think that the play is operating on more than one plane. I think there is a level of reference, but this is not the end in itself. It's like looking at an abstract painting and saying "Ah, Vermeer!" Maybe no one would ever have guessed it was Vermeer. . . . It is the same way with me: where I have learned all this from and what I refer to isn't really the reason for it all. It's the technique that I developed of producing works, but it isn't the reason for it, the justification for it. It's an effect it has to have, but it's not that conscious. At a certain point, when you have acquired a technique, you don't really have to concern yourself with that stuff too much anymore. I don't know if I ever did.

The reference isn't just a reference. It's a literary fragment with an intrinsic value. Does it have to come with credentials? You hear the line, the quote, and it was originally written by John Donne, William Shakespeare, Herman Melville or somebody else. Is it these credentials that give it value?

I don't care whether the audience knows who originally wrote it. I just want them to hear it now. Maybe they give me credit for writing Shakespeare. That's lucky for me. The audience doesn't need to know where the line comes from to get its effect.

I deliberately call attention to the sources as an aesthetic effect, rather than hiding them, which is the strategy of other playwrights. I try to get an allusive quality. People will hear the echo of the other work. It might be a refutation of that work or it might be drawing on that work, but it's an echo. The play becomes bigger that way. You don't need to know any references, but if you do it helps.

Picasso said, "No artist is a bastard. We all have forebears, and we build on the work of others." I don't believe anybody is totally original. It's a fantasy idea. We're able to reuse things without being slaves to them, by using parody, reinvesting them with new meaning.

■

Utopia was going to be corny. Every line was a joke. It took me years to dig up all the jokes and arrange them in such a way that they could advance the plot. It was like slavery. And I got it and it bombed.

It recalled the Italian Futurists, but people weren't ready for it. They thought these were the best jokes I could think of, and that these were new jokes.

■

We have really tried on average to make the theatre an institution, where people could go to the Theatre of the Ridiculous and see a play and be guaranteed that it would be of a certain quality. But in most cases it's luck or timing where you get to see something good. It's not that regularly available.

All the time we were off, people were calling and asking to see the various plays. We have only had this theatre for six months. I think it will become very famous, now that this is its location.

■

We just did six months of repertory. Three plays a week, plus the children's show. Three completely different productions every week. Rotating.

When I first did *Camille*, it was a much simpler play than it is now, because at that time I was younger. Even though I had the feelings, I just wasn't able technically, or maybe I just had to practice. As time passed and I became more experienced, the play got better.

Whenever I revive one of the old plays, it's always very funny to me, because in some ways it might lose something from its original interpretation, but in many ways it gains because I just know more now. I don't make the same mistakes I did when I did it the first time. If the original was still not totally satisfying, if there still are things that I was not happy with, I'll continue in the revival to try to solve these problems. In some plays I thought that the original was so perfect that I tried to reproduce it perfectly.

■

I spent a lot of years keeping a company together of eight or ten people who were skilled in doing this repertoire. But for producing a totally new and original work I had to relieve the actors of that burden of all those performances. So we stopped performing.

Also it is an economic factor: repertory is very expensive. It's much more expensive doing three plays a week than doing one a week. For instance, the crew has to change the set every night. That's a fantastic lot of work, a staggering amount of work.

The actors psychically are much more drained. They have to be always different. They have to keep their characters separate, they have to keep their costumes in repair and find the props and the costumes. Just finding them is difficult.

It's a phenomenal amount of work. No one else has really been able to do it but us. We are the only theatre in New York that's successfully been able to do repertory. Maybe because we do it in an unpretentious way, and because we are a very good company that has developed its plays over the years.

There are lots of plays I can revive. I just say we have to do that play and we do it. Everyone knows it so well. This is a true repertory company.

I want it to be a repertory company. I don't necessarily always do the past works, though.

I want to do shorter runs and more different plays every year. I want to do five or six plays for a couple of months each, rather than keep pulling out the old ones and repeating. It gives you a chance to grow up.

Also I want to take a number of classics and restage them in our own way. I want to do *Salomé*—*Salomé* is perfect here. I think *Salomé* would be better in this kind of theatre than in a proscenium.

I want to do *He Who Gets Slapped*, which is another beautiful play. It takes place in a circus. It'd be fabulous here. It *is* a circus here.

You can become very limited if you keep playing one role long enough, and the way you keep yourself fresher is by doing different things. You're inventing something new, discovering, exploring, taking chances.

Repertory also gives a play time to find its audience, and the audience gets to see that you're really an artist. You're not typed as one thing. They see that these things are creations you've invented.

■

For me, objectivity leads to idealism. The humanness of being in the play leads me to the comic vision somehow. I find that my own failings as an actor lead me to discoveries of the clown in me.

In my *Punch and Judy*, the mistress of ceremonies says, "It evolved from the commedia dell'arte, which is Italian for 'Make it up as you go along!'" In the contract of the commedia troupe reproduced in the Oreglia book, there's a very telling line that says one of the actor's responsibilities was to do the improvisations that the director gave him. This leads us to think, since the scripts are lost, that it wasn't making it up as you go along, that it was something else. It wasn't scripted, either. There was some other technique that was operative, which might be compared to the art of the stand-up comedian. He has a bag of tricks that will fit any occasion. All are precisely worded and seem spontaneous, and everything becomes a cue for one of them.

■

The Ridiculous Theatrical Company is an ensemble repertory theatre working in the modernist tradition. Our productions are avant-garde in the sense that we are interested both in exploring uncharted territory and in perpetuating or reviving theatrical conventions and techniques which we feel have been unwisely abandoned by our peers. In the latter sense our work is also traditional, because we consider the history of the theatre an invaluable resource, which in this age of stultifying conventionalism on the one hand and narrowly based minimalism on the other is being worn thin by the commercial establishment and ceremoniously discarded by its radical counterpart. We believe that tradition has in the past been inspired and, indeed, can only be reinspired through the artful expression and evocation of newly evolved thoughts and feelings within the fabric of original plays which draw liberally from the history of the theatre in its vast entirety.

All ensemble has to share a unified artistic point of view, and that's hard. In a way, the viewpoint is forged by the members of an ensemble: the leader leads because he embodies that viewpoint. He doesn't force his will on the group; he reflects the group's collective will.

Working with an ensemble of actors is a luxury in today's theatre that would have been regarded as a necessity to our forebears. In the great ages of the theatre, the plays that have since come to be considered masterpieces were realized by companies of actors whom the playwright had in mind when he wrote the roles. The ensemble of actors is the instrument on which the dramatist plays. To keep this instrument in tune requires constant practice, an almost year-round playing schedule which includes rest: time for contemplation, evaluation, and inspiration.

This continuity reflects the classical concept behind the company: actors who play in repertory, devoted to new plays created by an artistic director with a strong point of view. We are able to resist the fads and fallacies of the contemporary theatre because we draw on older authorities.

And I've been lucky that the Ridiculous Theatrical Company has afforded me the opportunity to do everything the way you're not supposed to do it. I've had the chance to grow and to learn from my mistakes. By now I've made so many of them that I'd almost have to strain to think of a new mistake to make.

It's ruthless, but it's not evil. I've created a very nice—though not ideal—atmosphere to work in.

■

A work of art can only reflect the person who creates it. If you have a lot of ideas, and you think, and you are a good person, and you are profound, and you care, it shows.

Clowning can be very human, very humanistic, and reflect human values as much as a serious drama can be a bunch of Nazi propaganda. There is nothing inherently superior about seriousness. In fact the Nazis were totally serious. The Nazis were a perfect example of serious, dedicated, intellectual justifying of everything, having lots of good reasons for everything they did.

I think human values will come out in someone's work if they are there. First you cultivate yourself, and you just keep working, keep doing your work. As your mental health and spirit improve, as you accept pain in life, and suffering, and sacrifice, and experience these things, they are bound to be reflected in your work, and improve it, give it depth.

At the present moment the theatre hangs between two pillars of bondage: the minimalist avant-garde and the new realists. These two schools seem to oppose each other but in fact they hold each other up. Their apparent opposition creates a false sense of choice for the audience. In fact, these two stores offer the same merchandise: literalism. Between these pseudo-poles lies a vast untapped reserve of creative possibilities—expression. In this realm, unlike at the polar crusts, the artist dares to make choices. Values assert themselves. These values are constantly in a state of flux; yet, within this realm of the sensible, an order or rank is established. Preference reveals the artist in a way that might even be deemed obscene or erotic were it not all occurring in the intellectual sphere, where only the most chastened spirits dare to tread. What was in younger days referred to as celebration must now be regarded as commitment, a frontier upon which all but the most confident founder.

What then is the appeal of these theatres? They deal in the familiar. And while they offer no challenge they reassure. An old story—but there's more. Proust pointed out that every truly original work of art disappoints us on our first encounter with it. Why? Because it cannot, by its very nature, fulfill our preconceptions. Its very unexpectedness shocks us in an annoying way. Why that? Why not some other way?

An artist has to be free to be irrational and potentially worthless, to do something that at first appears to have no value. Throughout history, modern art appeared at first to be very bad art because it didn't look like the stale academic work that was done before.

If you throw out the existing standards and create something new, there are two possibilities: you're going to have created something great and of lasting value that perhaps will not be understood at first, or you're going to create something that's really lousy and a waste of time. That's the chance. However, if you're following the established order there's no chance that something new and great will come along because you're repeating something that's lost its meaning.

And where the artist's presence is everywhere felt, there is a suspicion that this artist may be secretly enjoying himself—even though he sacrifices and experiences fatigue. The skeptic waits for an unguarded moment, a moment of relaxation, to attack.

And so we come to the petty rebellion against the seeming arbitrariness of choice, the dreaded vice: self-indulgence in the artist. The very element—the signature—that gives the work its value in the long run.

In judging the work of the artists of the past, it is inconceivable that we would want Michelangelo less Michealangelean, Maeterlinck less Maeterlinckian, or even Mondrian less Mondrian.

9

The purpose of the Ridiculous Theatrical Company is to develop original comedies in the modernist tradition, and to sustain a permanent ensemble of actors who, sharing a comic viewpoint and style of acting, give maximum force and conviction to these works.

We're all together every night of our lives. We talk about the upcoming plays constantly. I wouldn't want to be a *writer* because I'd get lonely.

I surround myself with this whole circus of people and motives and life, and it dances around me. The actors are constantly giving me ideas and wanting parts. If there were no company wanting parts, I would never write a play.

It's thrilling to get input from such creative people. Sometimes I'm inspired by the costumes or sets that someone in the company has designed, and sometimes the input is verbal. I don't always agree with everyone's suggestions, naturally, but we certainly do engage in a great deal of talking when we're preparing a show.

I've never written a play where I didn't know who was going to be in it beforehand, and that it was definitely going to be done. I *couldn't* write just hoping somebody would look at the script.

Not too many people have the freedom I do. They have to submit their plays for approval and correction, and they submit them to a bunch of people who beat the life out of them. Often what's wrong with a thing is what's interesting about it. You correct what's wrong and the thing has no interest at all.

Having this theatre is an incredible luxury. We can work and perform here anytime we want.

■

I love New York. I like to visit other places but New York has the theatre—*is* the theatre.

I love this house we have. It's a beautiful, historical house, a famous old space. In the 1920s it was a magic theatre called Shrine of the Orient. It used to be Café Society Downtown. Billie Holiday sang there and Imogene Coca broke in there. It's got great ghosts. I feel they're there. It's the difference between working in an old theatre that's been played in and being in a theatre that's never been used. And it was a sort-of cursed theatre before we took it over. It had a long history of failure. Then we took over and recreated it and I'm very happy with it.

But I feel the whole city is my instrument. I know where there's a store that sells eight thousand different kinds of ribbon. I know where there are certain props. And sound studios. Where film can be developed in twenty-four hours or in a matter of hours.

I work very quickly. I do a lot of preparation and then when I actually work it's very quick—unless it's very slow.

I can work very quickly because I know how to use the city, how to make something happen. When we were in France doing a play, it took two weeks of trying to get foam rubber for a costume. In New York I know a dozen places where I can get a chunk of foam rubber and quickly make something. In France it was: at nine o'clock on Tuesday the 14th you had an appointment, and then it turned out to be little chips of foam rubber—never the right thing. Everything was so difficult because it wasn't New York—it just didn't have the possibilities.

Fabrics are so easy to get here—you can jump in a cab, you can take a train, you can get on your bicycle, you can go and pick up a yard of something that you need to create a prop. New York is a city that's geared to this kind of creativity.

■

The script is up to me. I doubt if the process is unconventional, but a lot of groundwork is already taken for granted since we've been together so long.

Sometimes I write the whole play in advance. It depends on how much time I have. If I have three or four months and I am not working, I can write a play, and we simply mount it.

Often I write a large section of the script, then we just rehearse that section for a while, to see if it's as psychologically true as I thought and to find the answers to the questions I have about it. Then I go back and write some more, and we rehearse that, and I keep writing as we continue with rehearsals, sometimes just a few days ahead of the actors. This is more interesting from the point of view of watching what happens, because it develops slowly.

I bring the pages I've written with me. I stop at the Xerox place on the way. The actors get their parts in installments, but they're used to it. If I have no time and suddenly there has to be a play, they have to wait for their parts. Sometimes I just happen to get lost, sometimes a character doesn't develop until later, and I realize I have stumbled on something in the process, in the development.

I do a lot of dictating. Sometimes I will just tell a person their part verbally, because a lot of this farce business is very difficult for actors. I have to block it first—they have to know where to go. It's too detailed for me to give them a script first.

You—go over by the window! You—hide in the bed! You—leave the stage! You, over by the window—say this! And the guy under the bed—react to that!

Thank God I have one hundred percent recall. Thank God I have lots of assistants.

■

There are an awful lot of things to discuss during the rehearsal period, because the first draft of a play is not what you see on stage. Some people find it hard to edit their own work, but I can be ruthless about making cuts in my plays.

Writing all the dialogue by myself, in solitude . . . my way of operating would still be the same. It's just that I wouldn't have shared it with the actors.

This way of working is hard, because it is influenced by so many people. Sometimes actors contribute ideas, and that is very helpful, but it is not necessary to make all these changes.

Plays should not be rewritten. They should just be written, no matter what will happen. It is hard to behave this way, but it is rewarding.

They're difficult plays. They're very demanding. Many of the roles are difficult to play. What's grand about this kind of acting is that it's so specific. Every single moment is very clear, more clear perhaps than things are in real life.

We're a collection of characters. We're at our best when the characters are extreme or highly colorful or when we have to go out on a limb to create them.

People are rare who are creative on the level of the actors in this company. Most actors don't want the responsibility of putting themselves in such an immediately collaborative relationship with a writer. There is a level of gratification few people can imagine from such repertory. These people know fifteen roles, roles created for them, roles they made famous.

■

The company became a family for us, in a way. Being gay—except for Susan—we needed that tribal sense of belonging. The gayness is a bond. Of course at One Sheridan Square, we have a larger company with a lot of heterosexuals, and that's an even more marvelous blend.

You really get very close to the people you work with. We're practically married to each other. We fight, but they're momentary things that blow over like summer storms.

Farce requires specialists. Strong ensemble acting is the real secret to its success. This is something that the collectives like ourselves have made great sacrifices to maintain, to keep that level of artistic quality.

Our work is *performance* art. Some pantomimic bits are like coloratura passages in opera, that are left up to the singers. In *Stage*

Blood, for instance, I had to make an entrance where I stepped in a wastebasket, my wig got caught on the flypaper, I bumped into a door and couldn't find what I was looking for. . . . I have a penchant for physical comedy, so I was able to work that out. Another actor might not enjoy stepping in the wastebasket and losing his wig. But for me it's one of the great things to do.

The problem is that we can't replace ourselves. In commercial productions, the stars who originally made the play eventually leave, and other vastly inferior people come in and take the roles. In a group like ours, we are the artists. We don't have understudies. People come because we are doing it. We don't replace ourselves and run in commercial situations.

A lot of commercial plays deteriorate in the course of the run. *Commercial theatre lacks freshness.* Our plays get better and better as we play them. We continue to develop our roles as the play runs. It's unfortunate the critics only see us on opening night.

■

After you spend time producing a new work, you want to play it for a while, and I like that. But I find that to continuously repeat the play over and over again. . . . There is a period of a run where the artist has developed the role to the highest. It is complete and whole. But once you develop a role to a certain point, it goes as far as it can go. To really develop as an artist, you have to go on to another more challenging role.

We're met again with the economic problem of how to support ourselves. The money usually runs out about once a year, transforming us overnight into volunteers. The periods where we're at our most creative—our rehearsal periods—are the periods where we're deprived economically. When we're running, we're doing seven performances a week. We don't have time to gestate. We may be gestating new ideas, but we can't really produce anything new.

Any human institution must be expected to change. Actors sometimes depart and new members must be found. But after devoting years of their lives to a dream, performers can become discouraged and leave for less worthy enterprises which offer greater economic rewards. I would like never to lose a superior artist for this reason.

∎

We had just come back from a tour of the West Coast, and frankly, it hadn't gone very well. The critics had been brutal. I don't want to get on their case, but let's face it, they *can* be bitchy.

So it had been a difficult tour. Of course, we trotted out all the usual excuses—we were in the wrong theatre, it was the wrong time of year, and so on.

We toured from 1970 to 1980. It was more or less a conscious decision not to tour anymore.

The way I toured was: I had a successful play, *Bluebeard*. I had eight characters in it and those eight actors became the core of the company. Then I wrote other plays and parts for them and the plays that matched the cast and were also successful, such as *Camille* and *Stage Blood*, we took on tour.

Because that approach made those actors on tour the core of the company, they always had to be accounted for in every production. It became very difficult, because there was always a tendency to think that these tours should really have these eight people—and it made for a closed society. That's not why we go into the theatre—to always act with the same people and always be with the same people.

And touring limits what you can do—for instance, with sets. Someone would bring in lumber and I'd say, "Lumber—my God, we have to tour with this!"

At one point the National Endowment for the Arts had a touring program. They used to subsidize half the company's fee, so a university or an arts group only had to raise half your fee. Touring is incredibly expensive. You have to pay people's hotels. You have to pay them enough so that they can pay their rent at home. So it's double what it costs for a company in town.

If you have *Hello, Dolly!* or *Mame*, you also have the Shuberts and the Nederlanders, who have chains of theatres around the country that they can move these shows to. But if you're a company that only has one house—I mean this is a miracle that we have our own theatre—you have to book into different places and *they* have to raise the money. It's very tricky.

If you're not dealing with big, mass-media stars who draw the public, then you have to sell on artistic merit. And if your vision is new and has to be explained over and over and over again in every new place . . .

∎

It became eight people who always worked together, and at a certain point we began to feel a need to step out of that, which was difficult personally and professionally. It was difficult for the actors and for me because you don't want to let go of each other, you feel you need each other. But it's very important to find out who you are in other relationships.

We were sick and tired of each other. Anyone who has ever been on tour for any length of time will know what I mean.

And the company was $40,000 in debt. Some of the people left to take other jobs. There was a feeling at that time—in 1980—of something having ended. To me that meant it was time for something new to begin.

You're either doing a new play or you're doing a revival, and revivals take just as much time, and they're just as difficult. So the idea was to simplify the operation. Our charter really is for me to develop original plays. That was the original concept.

There are two ways for a theatre to grow: you can find new audiences for your old works, or you can create new works for your old audience. We had been doing the former for a long time. Now it was time for something new. I felt we could no longer be only a company with a past. We had to be a company with a present and a future as well.

I went to Bill Vehr and Susan and asked them if they'd be willing to work "on spec" for a while, and they agreed. I found Charlotte Forbes, who had stopped acting years earlier, and she joined us. With the three of them and myself in mind, I wrote *Reverse Psychology.*

Once you make your own plays, you don't need to go back to the old plays. You don't need the old repertoire. You pick up what was there or what was meaningful about it and you reinvent it for your own time. Which is a different thing from going back and doing a museum version.

■

Basically, I'm a theatricalist. Ridiculousness is important but theatricalism is also very important; that is, using the theatre in a way that is true to its nature—using that which is inherently theatrical, is of the domain of the theatre.

There is this theory in our century that any particular artform comes more and more into its own as itself, its true nature: that paint is paint, paint is not a tree. Painting, the medium, realizes itself when paint comes into its own, has its own aesthetic quality.

The same is true of theatre. The theatre speaks its own language. The more the theatre comes to this self-realization, the higher it becomes and the freer the subject matter.

We communicate in the language of the theatre: theatre that wants to be theatre, rather than theatre that wants to be something else. I think that theatre has to *be* theatre, has to be *about* theatre. Theatre about something else is naturalism, is realism, is a try to imitate something else convincingly, but it's a dead end. You are very limited in what you can represent on the stage.

This way you are free. The Elizabethans, for instance, admitted the theatricality, they admitted it was theatre.

Once you have admitted it is theatre, we all agree to play along. You can be honest. But if it is a trick, if it is supposed to be something else, truthfully represented through the fourth wall and all that, it seems too much like a limited exercise in style: naturalism. You need to prove it can be done, to do a very realistic thing. We know it can be done, but how much can it be done? We can't have a realistic ocean on the stage; we can't have a realistic airplane.

In naturalistic production, though I'm sophisticated enough to see what they're doing, I ask myself how much of it is intended. The moment they begin to use theatrical conventions—and there's no escaping that in theatre—how much of it do they want me to take as real? Whereas in Noh theatre so much more is evoked, even to the extent of bringing convincing ghosts on stage.

That's part of theatre convention: certain issues are settled and agreed upon, and only then can you get to more profound matters.

Once the idea of theatrical event and its conventions are accepted for what they are, and with relish, then everything is open to one.

∎

When people describe a style of theatre, they are describing how it isn't like reality, basically. They never talk about how it evokes reality, which is something we can't explain.

I think my theatre is the most *real*, the most *natural*, but it isn't *realism*, it isn't *naturalism*. It's evoking reality by showing us what isn't real.

If a man can put on makeup, false eyelashes and mascara, all the artifices of being a woman, then obviously all those things are not part of being a woman. So something is created in that negative space, and that's where the mystery of reality is evoked.

Everything about naturalism is, in a sense, a distortion, because they (Zola, et al) were reacting against the theatre of Sarah Bernhardt and others, and it made a mass movement. But finally it became too selective: it set out to prove a point, and proving a point is working from a preconception, and that is academic. Concept and execution is academic; going crazy and committing an atrocity is more modern.

In the case of the Ridiculous, it is the only avant-garde movement that is not academic. It is not creating an academy out of former gestures and looks.

If you look at today's avant-garde, it has an unmistakable look, and it moves more and more towards a vocabulary. It makes the art respectable, but it doesn't give us anywhere to go.

The people who seriously pursued enterprises like inventing a new kind of acting usually ended up defining themselves by what they rejected in order to have a strong position. It's reductivism. It's minimalism. I don't define myself by what I'm against. My work is not defined by what I leave out.

The best way to create style is to eliminate one element. It's the oldest trick in the book. We'll do it all in black and white: that's one of the real easy ones. Or eliminate plot. Or anything. And that creates a style.

In painting it's more obvious because we're so used to it in advertising; for instance, a model reclining, but they've eliminated the background. It's a blue paper but it's just *blue*. She is noplace. They eliminated where. Or you could get a style by having nude people doing everyday functions. Or you could eliminate one sex. Or one race.

I didn't do that. To me it is the difference between art and art direction. Art is expression and art direction is stylish presentation.

I see the theatre as a composite artform. It requires collaboration and interpretation, and I've also arrived at a theory of what I'm doing: that there is a pure narrative tradition.

In modern art there has been a tendency to try to be pure. Each artform wanted to find itself in the modern age because what modernism really is is trying to find a new *raison d'être* once the old religious ideas were chucked out. And the two basic reasons anybody ever managed to come up with in the theatre were that it is a didactic medium whose new secular function is teaching or that it replaces religion with intoxication.

Unlike the avant-garde, I don't feel the need to have a body of theory to back up my work. I'm too much in the process of becoming something else all the time to do that. I'm constantly devouring things, so that no one approach ever quite becomes true for me for very long.

Many theorists are great theorists but their plays are horrible, a terrible bore, because it's all set up to prove a theory. I think the theoretical thinking has to come *after* the work of art is created. First there is creation and then theory is an attempt to understand it. But if you set out to prove a theory, you are in trouble.

I'm afraid of talking things to death. Often we can't be creative because we're using our critical faculties. The creative and the critical processes are opposites.

Brecht, Artaud, Grotowski felt the need to back what they did. Artaud was more a theorist, he didn't produce much work.

Jarry was more to my liking. His is a mocking attitude toward the theory. I like that. A suit of theory. . . . It's like building your own house: you have to have a feeling about living in it.

There are perhaps subliminal effects that the plays have. I do set up situations where the audience accepts A, B and C, and then they are forced to accept D. It's gestalt, and in a way I change the culture by the way I force people to think their way through something. They went through the experience and they can't go back.

But a political theatre can't do *any* topic because it hasn't come to terms with what theatre *is*. That's where the confusion arises—is it political or not, is it true or not?

It doesn't interest me if it's true or not, it is just there. Even my ideas: I just try them on for size, to see if they work or not. I don't care whether they're aesthetic or artistic because anything aesthetic or artistic is true only insofar as we've seen it before and have come to recognize it that way. But if we've never seen it that way before: then it gets to be interesting—when standards and values are no longer applicable.

I don't set out to prove a theory because then you know what you're trying to do before you do it. The adventure of creating something is lost.

You have to go in there like a child, very simplemindedly. If you say what it's got to be before you start, then you become a drudge, slaving to live up to a preconception. Something else along the way—an accident, some marvelous discovery—may change the whole course of it, and you wouldn't allow that to happen because of that looming preconception.

I'm interested in the inconceivable. All my plays are based on trying to make people more tolerant. The problem is that it's hard to make into a slogan. Our view isn't formally expressed, but the bottom line is providing an audience with something good rather than telling them something specific.

The ambiguity of intention is probably just something in me. I don't know me or my work, and I don't want to know. It's revealed to me in flashes—the Dionysian element, if you will; whatever it is that creates it. It isn't a preconception; I don't set out to prove a theory. *Corn* came close to it, where I set out to make a point about eating food along the way, but the irrational, or better yet the intuitive element, must be the guide for me.

You can't make a mistake with intuition. And as one matures artistically, one's instinct improves automatically.

My theatre is about intuition, the madness of experimentation and the irrational. I try to make the most advanced ideas available to the public.

■

No one ever knows where they got the idea. I observe, eavesdrop and take a lot of notes. I have no trouble generating ideas. The hard part is deciding which one I want to do.

Most playwrights work in an autobiographical mode. They're writing about themselves, so it takes them years to come up with new material. I, on the other hand, am like a lens, focusing on a subject. And I have many subjects. Instead of holding a mirror up to nature, I'm holding up a magnifying glass. And then I focus it on different parts of the society.

I'm really not the kind of writer who writes out of his personal emotional experience, the way people write about their mothers or their childhood. I'm really a classical author and I write about the external world. I use mythic subject matter; I use archetypal plots sometimes; I deal with social ideas or currents or intellectual ideas, or I satirize something or I parody a literary form. It isn't really the just personal to me and not really to everyone.

But I still have connections with my subject that are personal. There are reasons. It may be a metaphorical relationship to the subject, or there may be something in the character of the subject that I also identify with, that I feel is important to our time—that this life mattered to our time.

Now I'm working from life, as those in the visual arts would say. Formerly, people would become nervous and say, "You based that on my life, didn't you?" And I'd say, "No, it's all from Euripides, and Proust, and I got this from the Marquis de Sade, it's not your life." Now I want them to think it's their lives, I want everyone to believe that it's their life.

Comedy is a broad field, and we use a lot of different genres. Some of the plays are tragedies treated in a farcical manner, and some are parodies or satires. Sometimes we use different elements on a collision course—forcing together two things that don't usually mix. That's one of my tactics. I love to put two literary or theatrical forms on collision course, even when they don't seem to go together, and even when I can't figure out what their relationship is.

Certainly it's very sophisticated, the whole business. You can *see* that some Elizabethan actor is bumping into some Pacino actor. In the Ridiculous Theatrical Company, a collision of acting styles is an energizing factor, implying by its very diversity an affirmation of the pluralistic society.

■

Some things you were angry about ten years ago don't bother you anymore. There was a lot of rage in *Bluebeard*, which explored surgery as a form of violence. My work now is more focused.

I don't feel like a victim anymore. I don't have the same frustration I had when the plays were dismissed. Still, the critics are damning me with faint praise.

Sentimentality is the key to commercialism, and my plays aren't sentimental. They're not there to make everybody feel everything's all right. They're meant to shake things up a little bit. Theatre has to be an unruly thing—doing the forbidden, the naughty, attacking sacred cows and contradicting every principle.

If you're a bad boy, you have to deal with never being approved of and always stirring up a hornet's nest. I want to be provocative. I want to talk about the unmentionable. That always causes tension. I feel appreciated, although I don't think anyone can ever love me enough.

Every day I try things. But it is not the conscious process. It's an inner process, like the growth of a plant or of any organism. It's a gradual, almost imperceptible progress: an evolution, not a revolution. I could go on expanding endlessly.

I guess it's controversial. It's hard to categorize, *very* hard to categorize. It's the only really sophisticated theatre in New York. It combines the highest and the lowest: wit and slapstick.

Some of the early works were very lewd. This was a big advantage in the early days, because nobody was doing it at the time and we found a public that got a kick out of it. I think it continues to be a keynote in any work that takes the form of popular entertainment. Lewdness still plays a role in our work, but it doesn't have the same impact.

Shock is an extreme form of surprise: an unpleasant surprise is a shock. I think very few people are willing to admit that they are shocked anymore. I certainly haven't tried to shock anyone with *Reverse Psychology*.

The pretentious people who want it to be so hoity-toity are embarrassed by the obscenity and lowness and the infantilism and the doggerel; and the people who'd like it to be just obscene and low don't like the hard parts. But what about the unbelievably sublime writing or acting that occurs? If you have shit in the play and also have sublimity, you have a total panoramic view, like Dante in his *Inferno*, or Shakespeare.

It's okay to say the plays are scatological, sure, but at the same time they do rise to heights of bliss and sublimity. You can't have highs without lows. The thing I'm against is appropriate and inappropriate material in art—it's shallow.

Other artists want to slant the world one way. I love belles-lettres—Ronald Firbank, for instance, a sublime writer, so perfect in creating a small world—but other artists are bigger in a way, they encompass more, they encompass opposites. There's always this attempt to tame the panoramic, to make it smaller. Ultimately I don't see this as an advance.

When we were working in a mode that has to be called epic, we wanted an emotional response from the audience which went against epic theatre, because in a way epic theatre is more Oriental—although we have Shakespeare, we have the Renaissance, which was epic. The construction of epic theatre is not such that it demands an emotional response from the audience. It is an objective kind of form in which the audience sits in judgment of a pageant of events, a large scope of events chronologically. It spans a long period of time. The Greek idea is that it all takes place in twenty-four hours. It's the unities. It's what I call concentric structure as opposed to epic.

There seem to me to be a lot of problems with epic form. Its diversity doesn't lend itself to self-expression, because when you're working in something that's inherently diverse you always have to try and find unity in it, you're always forced to find relationships among the parts; whereas if you're working in a very tight classical form, you're searching for diversity. It's a more expansive way to work. It works in reverse.

The epic drains you. It demands, because the cumulative effect of the plot doesn't pay off. As Brecht said, in the epic each scene stands for itself, one scene makes the next scene. The more you invest in the epic, you're always getting face value back. In a variety show, each thing is exactly the same as the thing that came before it. You always start from scratch with each act. It's very hard to get momentum going. You have to try to have more thrills, more gimmicks, bigger stage effects at the end to keep the interest going.

We found that epic theatre required tremendous feats on the part of the actor, and the shoe bills were so high! Epic acting puts the burden of everything on the actor in terms of audience involvement. You had to bring on jugglers in the fourth act to keep it going.

Concentric structure—like the well-made play, plays that conform to unities, plays with more intricate structure, where the climax is very controlled, contrived—are more supportive of the actor. Since this is actors' theatre, I felt we needed that support from the script. Personally, I find it more satisfying to act in a play where the climax is built very consciously for certain rhythmic effects. It was inevitable, since an actor was writing the scripts, that we would choose the mode that gave us the most support.

In the classic tradition you get a cumulative effect, so what happens is that the actors benefit from the narrative energy. A plotted, narrative play starts out slow, but it gains momentum. The more you invest in it, the more you memorize the characters and the situation; later, everything that happens becomes supercharged with meaning. At first it's slow getting going, but then it takes off like a skyrocket.

I experimented with epic plays, and I still do them periodically, but there's something fabulous about a play that earns its effects, because in the beginning everything is set up and then later the audience knows what came before, and knows the character and what the character thinks of a certain thing. That's a fantastic effect in the theatre. That's what I really go for.

I feel that I did—fortunately, without anybody noticing it—synthesize the epic form with the concentric form. *Reverse Psychology* is a perfect example. There is no way that isn't an epic play, yet people perceive it as a structural whole.

∎

When I first did my plays, I did them in a way no one else did them: I did them at midnight; nobody got paid. I didn't deliberately do it, but we didn't have any money. It was the only way I could do them, and it came out too eccentric. It couldn't reach the public.

Gradually, over the years, I learned about theatre rules and started to do it in a more accessible way. I start my play at eight o'clock? Everybody starts the play at eight o'clock. My play is two hours long? Everybody's play is two hours long. My play has characters and a plot and dialogue? Everybody's play has them.

The more I let those issues be settled—the more I conformed— the more free I became to make a play as eccentric and different as possible. As long as I questioned what a play was, where the play should be, whether there should be plays or not, I never got anywhere. You could never go forward.

It's like shoes. Everyone can have shoes because we all wear basically the same shoes—there are two or three ways the shoes are made. Within that, people express their individuality. You can change the color, you can have the style you want, you can glue things on them, but basically shoes are made available to everybody because there is a certain agreement on what they ought to be.

I think one's individuality is in a philosophical ground, in a ground of creativity that doesn't call for petty egotism. It calls for a higher egotism, a higher confidence in oneself. That is the will and the daring to do something in one's own way. So many artists waste their time questioning the nature of the artform itself. They question it so much that they no longer work. The reason they were originally interested in it, they kill.

Most people wanted to go in the theatre because they like acting, they like stories, they like dialogue, they like scenery, they like cos- tumes, they like the sense of community of the audience coming for the plot. As soon as they get into the theatre, they want to change all that. They don't want a story anymore. There won't be any characters. There won't be dialogue. It'll have no audience. There will be no scenery. No costumes.

Whatever the elements they choose to eliminate, soon it is no longer the artform they loved. Then they wonder why it dries up completely. They don't trust the pleasure, their own pleasure.

Whereas if we agree that it's going to be a play with characters, dialogue, a plot, take place in a theatre or not, then *what* that play will be suddenly becomes totally *free*. It can be any characters in the world, it can be any plot, it can be any dialogue, it can be any costumes, it can be anything.

For example, I use a more heightened diction, sometimes, because of the stage. And it's not not-realistic speech. I don't even do it consciously. That's a sort of intuition.

This idea of having an ear for dialogue, of capturing the way people really talk, is silly. Language can do much more than that—why not use it?

I don't write the way people speak, from that accursed "ear for dialogue." My language is supercharged with meaning—sustained double-entendre, multilevel punning.

Part of what frees me is that I'm a traditionalist. I took the theatre as a medium in a very traditional way. Instead of deciding that I was going to reinvent acting, reinvent stagecraft, reinvent scenery, I took certain conventions at face value. And by accepting such conventions as plot, dialogue and character, I'm free to invent endlessly. I can dare to put in anything.

I want to work within the tradition so that I don't waste my time trying to establish new conventions. Once the conventions are established, then the variations and the developments are original. But you have to have a very rigid framework. Without that, originality and innovation go unnoticed, because there's no way to measure it. It only shows up in a formal structure. If you're doing innovative work, it's important for the audience not to feel that the whole history of drama is being thrown out with each new production.

I don't see why art that has a history and a tradition is regressive. The danger is not so much regression. The danger is the morbid effect of repeating yourself.

I'm afraid of being unique, if that's what I am. The danger is that you may become a disinherited person floating away.

Once the audience has its bearings within the form, there's no limit to where you can take them. The only limitations are my imagination and the physical strength required to execute what I've imagined.

.

A basic misconception among would-be modernists is that plot is old-fashioned. Many theatre people have said, "Get rid of the playwright, get rid of the dialogue (it's too literary) and get rid of the plot (it bogs us down in the muck of realism)."

Modern playwrights wouldn't deal with plot because they felt it meant causality. They felt they had to follow a very banal kind of logic which all the other arts of the twentieth century were able to get rid of.

The concept that the dramatist could be experimental or modern went out the window. Only the idea of working with the *mise en scène* or doing yoga exercises onstage was interesting. The idea that the plot or dialogue could be new and exciting was ignored.

Today we're really in a period in which the avant-garde is down on story and plot, but I've been adamant about keeping them and exploring them even more. After all, plots pay off in the third act. I don't feel that it's my artistic duty to rehash old avant-garde styles, such as dispensing with plot. Agreed, plots rooted in realism can restrict one's range, but instead of dispensing with plot—instead of tossing out the baby with the bathwater—I've tried to use plot in a twentieth-century way, just as some painters learned to use paints and canvas in twentieth-century ways. The plots of my farces are avant-garde in that they are abstract and expressionistic. All those zany, improbable events in these comedies shouldn't be taken literally; they're simply too ridiculous.

In the new play, *Love's Tangled Web*, the audience will not be able to recount the plot. It's like Feydeau—it's very, very complicated. When you take form that seriously, you don't have much time for anything else.

.

My work falls into the classical tradition of comedy. Form and structure will always be very important to me, as they were back when I was doing those rambling four-hour epics. My early plays were more anarchic; my newer works are more classical.

My early works had some classicism in them, but people couldn't perceive it then. It's not that they didn't understand the plays then, but that they didn't or couldn't see what went into creating them. And that's enough to drive anybody crazy: the distance between what you're experiencing while creating it and what the audience feels.

My work is tighter and more economical than it may have been fifteen years ago. I'm more confident in what I'm doing.

The story exists for its own sake because the story is a coded hieroglyph. In the theatre there is a tradition of plot as a convention and as a hieroglyphic use of incident in the classical comedy, starting with Molière, even Shakespeare or Italian commedia dell'arte. These events, which are the devices, are a little alphabet. It's a kind of matrix of unseemly incident: inappropriate or contrary behavior which the clown exhibits; things falling out contrary to expectation, or propriety; things going wrong.

The abstract element in farce makes it the most modern dramatic medium. Its ability to reflect on the human condition is seemingly limitless.

■

Some artists are subtle. I am *not* subtle. I am *against subtlety*. One of the readings of subtlety is dishonesty. I am obvious *but* I have replaced subtlety with complexity. I don't believe in being simple either, you see.

What the audience sees is very clear and obvious. But there is enough of it, and the mechanism is so complex. It's interesting because of its complexity, rather than being interesting because there is something going on you can't get.

Everything is on the surface. Rather than *hiding* anything, I *show* everything. But the *interrelationship* of all the parts is interesting and demanding. And elaborate.

■

A playwright friend of mine said to me recently, "What is your big contribution to the theatre?" So I said, "I never threw out the plot." He said, "Neither did I, so what's so new about *your* not throwing out the plot?"

It is a question of being conscious of the use of the plot or of not being conscious. You may have a playwright who writes the same plot over and over again, and yet he doesn't know it, or he doesn't care, or he doesn't try to change. It's personal obsession. He is writing from his "soul."

I do a play like a shoemaker makes a pair of shoes. I really have a laborer's attitude to work. I don't come in full of theory and then produce a wretched piece of work. That's not interesting and not good. I'm an expert at making plays because I approach them as a craftsman. That's what I have to offer.

Before I'm an actor or a writer or a social commentator, I'm an entertainer. That's always been my credo no matter how crazy my stuff may have been in the past. I really think of myself as an inventor who invents theatrical pieces. I don't think of myself as writing a play and then arranging a performance.

I'm not out to write the Great American Play because if they won't forgive me for my success with *Bluebeard* or *Camille*, what will they do to me for that?

■

We try imitating the great works and in our failure we find our own originality. A friend of mine, Richard Hennessy, said that the nineteenth century got it right—artists perfected art—while modernism is the history of getting it wrong.

One of my recent crises is that all my earlier works were based on an impossible conception to be fulfilled, and in the failure we found the aesthetic margin. How could it not be perfect?

When you aim for something and fail, the failure is originality. If I tried to copy the Mona Lisa, the result wouldn't look anything like the Mona Lisa—believe me!—but it would be something new and original.

The end of that for me was Wagner's *Ring*, where I chose something impossible to do in one evening and succeeded. Now that aesthetic of failure cannot operate for me anymore.

Whereas in the earlier *Turds in Hell*, the concept was to synthesize

Satyricon—and three other plots—to evoke actual demons and to stage a black mass—and it couldn't be done. The resulting mess and debris was the work of art. I was always good at creating extremely original material by failing.

Once you reach a point of succeeding, there is a danger because you realize you have become simply perfect, merely perfect. No progress anymore, and that's the frontier of consciousness.

For me right now my works can no longer be destruct art, an art of failing.

■

Yesterday I was working on a sculpture, and Bill Vehr stood over me and corrected me every time I did something that was in good taste. Admit the world in a way that hasn't been precensored. Good taste is very oral, subjective; not a very profound concept for art.

The Ridiculous theatre was always a concept of high art that came out of an aesthetic which was so advanced it really couldn't be appreciated. It has to do with humor and unhinging the pretensions of serious art. It comes out of the dichotomy between academic and expressive art. It draws its authority from popular art, an art that doesn't need any justification beyond its power to provide pleasure. It takes what is considered worthless and transforms it into high art.

Basically for me, and for twentieth-century art, it's always been a problem of uncovering sources. It proceeds by discoveries.

In my work, the panoramic quality saves it from academicism. It encompasses a much broader world-view, and I've been able to bring more material into my work.

There are different kinds of artists—innovators, masters and journeymen. Some people are very good at uncovering little techniques, discovering fine points, while others—like myself—are able to organize vast amounts of material into a very solid body of work.

The theatre is a madly complex artform. It is not personal. To make it personal one has to alter it or simplify it to some extent. Some people can control it, but it takes a lot of years.

My work pulsates from expansiveness—epiclike panorama—to concentric, precise work. Now I'm on to a new phase. I don't like things to stay the same, and I'm proud that we've changed. You start with a vision, but I feel much closer now to what I want in art, the kind of company devoted to doing my work, my reworkings of the classics. You either flow with the humanity or try to stay the same and reject people when they change.

The irrational and one's right to madness, that's the key. There has to be an element of danger, of risk, for the art to advance.

It's been a natural progression from the beginning. After a few years of freewheeling experiments, we realized we had broken a lot of ground, and it was time to rake it and plant some seed. That's when I passed into my formal period, which has lasted for a decade.

I went against the trend because I saw that in the past decade the avant-garde theatre had taken a materialistic turn—lots of big spectacles with few words, and stagings which were intended to be profound in their own right. While some of these efforts have succeeded, the dominance of the *mise-en-scène* style has created a need for a grounding in emotion and character.

Now I've broken into a new area of expressiveness and intuition. I've broadened my subject matter and approach, and I feel a whole new life and energy.

I think we're in a romantic period. After ten years of repressing emotional content, the emotions of the individual are now going to come forward. In our theatre we're going to see a flowering of emotion and character. This will fill the void that's been left by a lot of experimental theatre.

■

Surprisingly enough, when I'm writing my plays I don't think that much about whether they're funny. Basically, I want to get the story across and make it real. I'm not telegraphing every minute that it's supposed to be funny. But there's something about my approach that makes it funny.

If they don't laugh, then it's a serious play. That's the good thing about doing ambiguous work, because it can be taken either way. I can become a very serious actor if they're not laughing.

Things are only funny in relationship to serious things, and if you do every line funny, which I've done, then *none* of the lines are funny. Either the audience gets tired of it, or there's no contrast.

You really have to lead the audience into a serious moment, and then pull the rug out from under them to get a laugh. You have to make sure the idea isn't one for a skit, or you pull all the stops out very rapidly and it blows apart.

There's a certain kind of comedy where you can go for the big laughs right away, as in a skit. To sustain a whole evening, though, you have to use a little restraint. Each *scene* has to be a skit, but have a different point. You can't go the limit right away.

Punchy lines aren't my thing. Even witty lines—I'm not particularly interested in wit. The trouble with wit is it has to come out of the characters. If the character is witty, okay, but I've read plays where every single character is witty all the time. They all seem to have the same voice and the same mind.

They say comics say funny things and comedians say things funny. I think I'm more of a comedian in that it's how I do it that's funny rather than what I'm saying. What we do has to be fairly straight to be funny.

There are a lot of ways to get what I wouldn't call honest laughs. Camille can fall out of her bed, if you're only doing the death scene, perhaps like Fanny Brice and W. C. Fields might have done it. But if you're doing a whole evening, there has to be a thesis under it, and you can't do anything that's going to sabotage your longer goals. If you go too far in the beginning and you don't keep it credible on a certain level, you break the tension, and the audience will lose interest.

■

I don't like serious plays where people don't laugh. They seem too artificial. Sure, I like melodramas, and I like a good cry. But the greatest works of art incorporate humor.

Today humor is in very low esteem. The whole idea of humorous art is prostituted to such an extent that it can't be taken "seriously"; there can't be "serious humor."

The whole idea of seriousness is awful to me—it sounds like something imposed from without. It doesn't really imply gravity or profundity; it implies decorum, behaving yourself. That's what I don't like about it.

Serious movies, into the sixties, were the New Wave—pretentious European films, like Bergman and all that. There was this American self-loathing of the Hollywood film, the belief that it was utterly terrible. Anyone who liked it liked it because it was "camp"—it was so bad it was good. Then, when people began to judge these things on their own, it wasn't "so-bad-they're-good" anymore. They were good on their own terms, but we had a cultural prejudice against them.

Comedy is serious. I don't like it when the idea of seriousness is applied only to unhappy thoughts. Comedy is just as profound in its view of the human condition as any decorous or depressing work.

Too often, people substitute the depressing and the horrifying for seriousness. They don't have any truly serious ideas, so they try to create a synthetic seriousness—the seriousness of fear, horror, loathing, revulsion, dread or feeling sorry for people. That's very superficial, though. After all, there are plenty of people in the *real* world who are desperately deserving of our sympathy. Why go to a theatre and pay money to indulge your sympathy synthetically, vicariously?

I really don't think there is a dichotomy between the serious and the comic. Something comic can be great and universal, and something serious can be trash.

There's a popular feeling that you're putting something down if you find humor in it. I think parody is also an homage to a thing. If it's a decent parody, it's faithful to the work while making a joke out of it. It's just for the moment. It's for now. Why not laugh now?

Parody is a lost art, a misunderstood genre in this country. It's grand to be able to laugh at yourself enough to do a parody of something you admire; that is, to do an imitation of it for comic purposes, but also to enlighten one about it. By parodying, you can make other points about it and comment on it in a humorous vein.

My plays are not parodic, but they *are* meant to be funny and humorous. Of course there's a strong element of parody in what we do. It's a way of using the past without being enslaved by it.

There is an *element* of parody, for parody is a way of reusing old things. But in order to do parody right, you have to do it as well as the original. Parody and lampooning tends to be against pretentious, high-minded art, but the parodist gains his authority or the right to make fun by going the original one better. If the audience sees that it is unjust—if it is not as good as the original—they resent it. They'll think, "How dare you make fun of it?"

Basically, I'm using these materials not to make fun of them, but because I think they are valuable. That "so-bad-it's-good" theory is a misunderstanding of my cultural recycling program. What that does is limit me. If I only do things that are so bad they're good, it puts it up to the audience to decide whether I was right or not.

Our style is hard to describe. It's sort of a rebellion against literalness. We go for an expanded reality that makes anything possible. We have found we can give life to a lot of old chestnuts through parody. Instead of fighting against certain elements of the script, we exploit them.

The whole movement evolved out of the underground movie scene, which was very big in the sixties. We used Hollywood films as mythological folklore—something we all identified with—and since then we have expanded to broader literature. The productions that came out of that original impulse were sometimes plays straining to be movies. That led us to an epic and narrative format.

It's broadly accessible. We cut across all the snobbish barriers that the theatre often comes up against.

Our basic thrust is to entertain: to move, touch or make an audience laugh and, finally, to provide an intellectual stimulus. But merely moving or trying to stimulate without having fun is sterile.

We have always avoided nostalgia. We feel *these* are the good old days: it's never been any better than this moment, and it may never *be* any better.

During our years of work as parodists, we found new expressive possibilities in theatrical conventions considered oppressive by others. Plots of multiple complexity have become our specialty.

•

Love's Tangled Web was written, produced and directed in six weeks, and I really loved it. I wish it could have run longer, but it just wasn't making enough money to keep the theatre open. I suppose you could call it a critical failure. In other words, the critics failed it.

I don't know how long plays will run and I kind of like that. We do not have a subscription audience. Rather than be locked into a rigid schedule, we try to let each play have a natural life span. We play in repertory or *en suite* depending on audience demand and the creative needs of the moment.

The freedom we have is very threatened by the idea of subscription. What happens with a subscription is you sell the seat and for every show the same person on the same night is in the same seat—so it's an identical audience, all in the exact same seats on that night. It's too surrealistic for me. I don't think I could take it. I like to think that there's a thrust in the moment, that there's a certain element of spontaneity.

■

My own work is really the work of a modernist in the theatre. All modern art is a quest for the primitive in ourselves through reduction, distillation and distortion. In Picasso's work this led to cubism—analyzing the state and shape of things—and to a study of African art, which ultimately looks like the most sophisticated work.

I've written plays that were trying to revalue techniques from various periods. Ultimately, that is an academic approach, and modernism isn't about being academic; it is about being primitive. Becoming primitive isn't easy when you've been overeducated, overcivilized.

I am searching for the primitive not in the African but in myself. I have a great fondness for vulgar art—vulgar not only in the sense of lewd, which I employ, but vulgar in the sense of "of the people," or for mass consumption, something the people understand without having to be primed for it too much.

I want to bring out the primitive child in everyone who comes here. It's hard to find it in yourself and hard not to give it up, but it's priceless because all that stuff between childhood and senescence is just a digression, a drifting off.

10

The company evolved out of the needs of myself and a number of other actors and designers to see the realization on stage of certain non-conformist theatrical tendencies which defied accepted theatrical practice, marshaling the forces of those who were passionate about the theatre—rather than those who considered it to be business or a career opportunity—to create something provocative. In our rejection of literalism (a convention shared by both realists and the minimalist "avant-garde"), we adopted a position of deliberate unfashionableness. We explored the emotional, expressive possibilities of acting and encouraged decorative richness in the *mise en scène*. We affirmed the currently discarded conventions of the theatre; we viewed them as the essence of the theatrical, its language and vocabulary. We used the great traditions of the past as our authority to envision a future diametrically opposed to the one our contemporaries were predicting. We could not accept as avant-garde purely formal experiments which seemed both bloodless and wasteful.

Anyone who defies the narrow limits of fashion and deliberately goes against the current trends runs the risk of appearing ridiculous. And so we decided to strike the first blow and adopt the name, to create a theatre not about ridiculing others but about the risks of appearing ridiculous to them. This was the birth of America's most original contribution to comedy. Our theatre embraced the popular culture, fit it into history and offered it the possibility of a glorious future with a new sense of purpose. We wanted to obviate the American inferiority complex that goes, "Everything European is better."

Our work draws its power from a dual vision. The outward appearance is Ridiculous but the intention is serious. Because we can laugh at ourselves we encourage this salubrious tendency in others. The clown can take risks because he alone can afford to make a fool of himself; indeed, is expected to do so. The special contribution of the Ridiculous is to expand everyone's sense of what is possible.

The greatest danger to a theatre whose credo is recklessness is the tendency to become too conservative. But the theatre cannot remain immune to the social and economic conditions of society. In order to continue to make our works available to our audience on a regular basis we have become an institution. But our artistic goals have remained the same. In order to preserve our integrity we have shaped the organization and the institution to fit the creative process rather than the other way around. Our policy is to make the theatre a stable framework for ventures into the unknown; to give the irrational free play and to mine this source; to create plays in the theatre rather than in the study; to draw on an expanded pool of actors who have worked in this genre in other related theatres, performance works or films; to offer opportunities for young performers to develop; and to focus the Ridiculous as a movement.

The Ridiculous Theatrical Company holds a unique place in the American theatre. It is the only serious comic theatre and a leading avant-garde theatre as well. We mean to rescue the art of the comic drama from commercial prostitution and the low level of esteem to which it has fallen in our day; to give it its rightful place among the great modern theatres; to build on what we perceive as the main line of the development of comic art; not using this art as an end in itself but rather to foster human values which are threatened elsewhere. The Ridiculous Theatrical Company is an ark which carries forth what is valuable from the past into a future for which we entertain hope.

∎

Exquisite Torture was a surrealist romance, "an ecstasy," our first foray into "poststructuralism," a theatre of pure emotion. "An ecstasy" is a new genre, a vehicle for overly emotional acting.

Le Bourgeois Avant-Garde was like *Le Bourgeois gentilhomme*. It was my Molière. It had all the mechanics, the machinery of Molière, but it had a new concept and new meaning. By spoofing people who imagine themselves avant-garde, *Le Bourgeois Avant-Garde* remade Molière's classic into a relevant modern piece of theatre. In it I introduced a new genre, *unnaturalism*, to describe what happens when the avant-garde becomes more conservative than its audience.

I wasn't attacking experimental theatre. I was, rather, criticizing the kind of work that masquerades as avant-garde but is, in reality, merely confusing.

With *Le Bourgeois Avant-Garde*, we put our artistic statement on the stage, gave dramatic form to our criticism of what we saw to be fallacies concerning the artists' responsibility to an audience. It caused an intellectual stir, and made our position clearer both to our public and to ourselves. Consequently, our role in the American theatre became clearer: to take on the issues of our time through the use of established comic techniques; and to explode pretensions and stale platitudes while presenting a viable alternative. *Le Bourgeois Avant-Garde* was regarded as a major piece of art criticism by many critics.

.

Sometimes a costume will give an idea for a scene or a play. For instance, Everett Quinton found a beautiful gown in a thrift shop when we were doing *Le Bourgeois Avant-Garde*, and I said, "Oh!" It was incredible-looking—it looked like a Charles James. He got it because it fit me and you don't always find a woman's things that fit a man. And he said, "This is an amazing gown," and I said, "I really shouldn't play a female role just for this gown." And even though it seems frivolous—and it was in a way—it did get me thinking along the lines of *Galas*. In a sense, I always thought of that gown as having been an inspiration for it, even though I might have done that play anyway.

Based on the life of Maria Callas, including many anecdotes privately recounted to the playwright and never before made public,

Galas was not a satire or a spoof, but an attempt to use nonconformist theatrical techniques developed by the company to lift the biographical material to the level of myth and metaphor. While *Galas* was a tragedy, the pathos was tempered throughout by sophisticated humor. The play did not require a knowledge of opera but was informative about the world of opera.

From the very beginning to the dress rehearsal, it took me about three weeks to write and direct the entire piece. I had to lose thirty pounds for the role. I wanted to play a female role in order to prove that female impersonation could be taken seriously as art in Western theatre.

After *Le Bourgeois Avant-Garde*, I felt it was very important to strike another blow, to give the public an example of the alternative to the kind of theatre we critiqued in our modern Molière. So I decided in favor of a portrait of a modern woman in whose life I saw a narrative of universal relevance. *Galas* broadened the company's range and proved that real feeling and even tragedy could be expressed in a comic theatre. Audiences easily accepted the narrative innovations.

I was fascinated by Callas. Here was a genius who revolutionized her artform, but when she put aside her art, she had nothing to turn to. Although rich, she died alone in her home in Paris.

When she died, *Variety* gave her a vicious pan. I couldn't believe it. Here was a great performer who practically reinvented opera in our time. I wanted to defend Maria Callas, because any great artist who gets a bad obituary in *Variety* needs a champion.

I used her life as a metaphor. I concentrated on the tragic elements, the mechanics of fate. My interest was not gossip. I decided to take someone who was believed to be a bitch and to show the human side, the behind-the-scenes reasons for the outrageous public behavior, and to indicate the extent to which she was really misunderstood.

She was a very controversial character, very fiery and opinionated. She made a lot of enemies and caused a lot of trouble in the world. The obvious take would be to show what a bad girl she was, but I thought the more interesting approach—because it was the way I felt about it—was to explain why on the surface it seemed that way to others, and what the inner reason was behind the external behavior that people condemned; to show what was really going on.

Part of the price of fame is that your image becomes simplified enough that a vast number of people can grasp it easily. You can never really be all of you. You could become a trademark, in a sense, or a quick idea that people think of—often one characteristic in a performer—that they light upon. I wanted to show the more complex background behind it, and why what people saw wasn't quite true, or how a foolish mistake or a slip of the tongue or a complex choice could be misconstrued.

For instance, walking out on a performance is very taboo in the theatre; however, sometimes you might have to, you might be driven to it. It would be seen as a temperamental thing when actually there was no other choice.

Maria Callas walked out on a Rome performance of *Norma*. Actually, she knew for days that she wasn't going to be able to do that performance, and she begged and pleaded and tried to get out of it. People kept telling her, "You'll be all right. Spray your throat, take care of yourself, by the night. . . ." She kept trying to be heroic, but she was constantly saying, "I don't think it's going to work, I don't know what I'm going to do." They kept saying, "You'll be all right. You have to be."

So she kept putting off the decision, and it got to be too late. She got halfway through the performance and she couldn't do it. She left the opera house, and of course this was a "temperamental" walkout, but actually it was heroic that she tried to do one act of it. It may have also been a bit of hubris, because it would have been humiliating to go through the rest of it. She was not willing to do that.

So there are different sides, different ways of looking at it. I was trying to give a more complex view.

■

I once did a cable interview, and I was introduced as the outrageous Charles Ludlam. I don't feel outrageous. I never felt outrageous. It's very hard when you have an image of something that other people consider outrageous and you feel rather unaggressive. I feel very wholesome, not outrageous at all. I feel that what's outrageous is that some of the things I do would not be accepted. I think it's outrageous to have a narrow mind.

Like Maria Callas—I know I'm comparing myself to the great diva—sometimes things you do that seem terribly new and daring and revolutionary are really traditional things. You're restoring a tradition that's been lost, and they think you are doing something very radical because it's flying in the face of a current fashion that has no real roots in any kind of tradition.

Tradition sounds square, but it isn't necessarily square. The earlier thing is often more radical than the later thing. Early Neanderthal man was more advanced than late Neanderthal. Late Neanderthal got more cretinous and bestial; early Neanderthal was more evolved.

Sometimes art slides back from possibilities that it had. Breakthroughs that at a certain moment in history seemed to be revolutionary and fresh and wonderful later become academic, form an academy that represses lots of expressive possibilities.

■

The variety of these plays demonstrated the flexibility of the Ridiculous aesthetic and the broad range of themes and styles which it can encompass. *Galas* was introduced in repertory with *Le Bourgeois Avant-Garde*, and thus helped fulfill our long-term goal of playing in repertory without relying on revivals. In presenting three new plays in one year, we employed a larger number of actors than usual, affording fresh opportunities for longtime company members while allowing established performers with whom we had not previously worked and younger players we discovered through open auditions to share our stage.

One of the problems is that audiences don't always get to the play before it closes, and people are always saying, "Oh, I missed that one." So what I want to do is try to keep the thing alive for as long as I can; but at the same time, the houses have to be decent or you can't afford to do it anymore.

I found with *Le Bourgeois Avant-Garde* that when the Wednesday and Thursday houses started to dwindle I could preview *Galas* on those nights and it would give us a good week, because the business for *Le Bourgeois Avant-Garde* was still strong on the weekend. That's classically what the purpose of repertory was. It still works.

Also this year, we began a work process which may form a pattern for future seasons: opening a play in the fall which had previewed the previous spring and was reworked over the summer, and then developing in a part-time rehearsal period, over an extended period of time, a new work to preview in the spring and be reworked over the summer and opened the following fall. This combination of performance and rehearsal activity is most healthful creatively, since rehearsing and performing are usually not experienced at the same time.

The other advantage of this system is that you can try a play out, take a break, think about it, evaluate it and rework it. Having profited by our mistakes, we open for the press. It also provides our inner audience—those who do not depend on reviews to help them make up their mind—an opportunity to follow the developmental process. Indeed, we find a lot of our patrons like to come again and again, to watch the process as the play changes.

This system's slight *dis*advantage is that it puts extreme demands on the performer, who must rehearse during the day and perform at night. The rehearsal period has to be longer but somewhat less strenuous.

Keeping the theatre closed a certain number of months each year—aside from providing rest and time to take advantage of other career opportunities—gives us time to reflect and evaluate, gives us distance on the work we have created.

■

People talk about great performances, most of which are luck—the right role coming along at the right time for an actor. But I'm seeing to it that I get the role. I've created it, written it, directed it. My immersion is total!

There's something miraculous about the theatrical mask—the mask that is the actor. Through sheer force of will, I can look handsome onstage, or ugly.

When I was in college, I happened to find a copy of *The Art of Acting*, by the French actor Coquelin, who originated the role of Cyrano. Before he even learned a line of a play, he would go to the costume room and dress up as the character, put on the full makeup.

When he looked in the mirror and saw the character staring back at him, he was ready to begin. That impressed me tremendously.

In school, of course, there was all that emphasis on the Method, and feeling your way into the part. It was always sort of schizophrenic for me—there were too many different things to juggle—but now I think I'm a Stanislavski actor par excellence. I go into a sort of trance onstage and believe in my role completely. Of course, I also know I'm onstage and people are watching—I'm admitting I'm acting—but on another plane my belief is total.

I'm the most constantly employed actor in New York. I'm the hardest working man in the American theatre . . . and I'm very vain about myself. Really great artists who know they're the best have trouble remaining tactful. I do my own bravos by ventriloquism.

■

I didn't know that *Galas* was going to be so successful. I knew it would be good, and that people would like it, but I had no idea that it was going to run eight months. Because we had huge deficits, as most theatres do, it paid to run it and pay off those items, which we did.

I've found that the appetite of the audience has quickened over the years since I've made this policy of not touring and not reviving. We used to alternate a new play with a revival; now, every single opening is a world premiere. No one has seen the play, so everyone in the audience is on the same footing. Every play has that freshness. It's quickened audience appetite and the excitement of those openings. I have much more energy, and everything is electric.

11

After the long run of *Galas*, a play with a large ensemble of actors, I felt the need to work intimately with a small production team. Having long thought of using the old vaudeville trick of the quick-change as the basis for a whole play, I knew that if another versatile character actor and I could master the art, we could people a whole play all by ourselves. After some research and months of experimentation, *The Mystery of Irma Vep*, "A Penny Dreadful," became a tour de force for myself and Everett Quinton.

It's a surrealist-mystery-melodrama-adventure story, influenced by Max Ernst's collage novels. Everett and I play all the characters: Lady Enid and Lord Edgar Hillcrest, Nicodemus Underwood, Jane Twisden, Princess Pev Amri and many others.

This time I started with the device and worked back to the play. Usually I start with a sketch or at least an outline, but this time it was just the idea that two people are doing all the parts and they have to do quick changes.

A playwright can usually bring on any character at any time that he wants, but I couldn't because it involved a change—an exit which had to be justified and covered—and then you had to think of where the various characters had gone and where you had left them and how you could get them back on.

It's really a kind of Rubik's Cube effect. Every time you try to change one element, all the other elements go out of whack. It's that precise.

It was very difficult. At one point we even canceled the first preview, which I'd never done before. By the time I'd solved the ending, I realized it involved fifteen more costume changes. Even though it was very compressed, each change had to be rehearsed dozens of times. It's very tedious, but it's the art that conceals the art.

Those costumes had to come off in a matter of seconds. In the Edwardian period, they weren't exactly wearing something loose and easy to get on and off. That was very difficult on Everett as the costume designer: to have to have something that could look good and at the same time break away, rip off or disappear. These costumes were created to have an illusion of being authentic and at the same time to have a trick element.

We only had a few days, so we put off the opening by a week. Not to mention that I got locked in the mummy case at four o'clock in the morning and couldn't get out.

Do you think people want the sleepless nights? Sometimes I wake in the middle of the night screaming: *"How? Why?"*

It can be terrifying the week before you open if you don't have a second act. In *Irma*, for instance, I had no idea who the killer was until the day before the first preview. I think most people would be terrified not to know exactly how something will turn out.

■

But no one is technically better at writing a play than I am. They just aren't. They don't have the technique.

Once you have those rules digested and at your disposal—such things as counterpoint, harmonics, plotting, characterization, a million technical things that are almost lost today—you can do anything.

I developed a technique while other people were having careers and now I can do anything.

■

There are different strains in your thought, in different compartments sort of, and at some point they come together into one idea. Everett and I wanted to do a two-man show; that was one element. Another was that I wanted to try a quick-change act. And another was that I wanted to do a surrealist gothic in which you could use all these elements in a very loose, almost dreamlike structure. Eventually these things constellated into one production.

Quick-change is a branch of magic, and a lot of what happens is based on misdirection. The changes are possible, but they don't seem possible.

When I'm walking offstage at a leisurely pace, I burst into an incredible run the minute I'm out of sight. Everything goes at a much faster tempo backstage. It deceives you, because you see the person exit slowly and you're still hearing the voice.

Ventriloquism creates the illusion that the actor is disappearing into the distance on one side of the stage, while he's actually already on the other side being dressed as a different character.

The three dressers operate balletically, like a Bunraku team, so we almost don't have to look while we're flying through. We worked with a stopwatch when rehearsing the changes. Those were nine-second costume changes! You can't even be handed something from a different side than you're used to.

It's up to the actor to create the illusion that this madness did not just happen, that you're coming from a place where something other than a quick-change occurred. It takes tremendous concentration to avoid coming on looking like you've just been through a car wash. We sweat so profusely, in fact, that we have paper towels—whole rolls—to use as blotters, so that we can enter looking fresh.

∎

I can't do an elaborate makeup when I'm going from Lady Enid to Nicodemus and back again. Lady Enid has pretty little lips, and Nicodemus is this kind of monster servant.

When I realized the trouble I was facing with Enid and Nicodemus, I phoned my dentist, Dr. Cone, and said "Dr. Cone, this is the moment!" and I took him all the pictures I could find of Fredric March in *Dr. Jekyll and Mr. Hyde*, because I always loved the way those teeth were.

He made false teeth for me in the lab. They fit perfectly and look absolutely real.

I pop the teeth in, and they distort my mouth without destroying Lady Enid's makeup. But the whole thing is so complicated and the changes are so fast, I'm sure sooner or later I'll wear them on as Enid.

■

I use just a few special effects. It took millions of dollars for Michael Jackson to turn into a werewolf, but it only cost me forty dollars for costume pieces and props. I have things hidden behind the draperies and I just pull them out. I distract you with my body movements. I stagger, and meanwhile I'm putting on the gloves behind the drapes and the lights are flashing.

■

I've designed a number of the sets. I have been designing on average one play a year. Others I have other designers do—Jack Kelly, most notably, designed *Galas, Exquisite Torture* and *Secret Lives of the Sexists*. I did *Reverse Psychology, Le Bourgeois Avant-Garde* and *The Mystery of Irma Vep*.

I like to design a set once in a while, especially when I have a very clear conception of what I want. When I feel I need input from another person I work with another designer.

Certain plays remind me of certain designers. For instance, Jack is very good at extremely eloquent decor and trompe l'oeil effects. When I have something like *Galas,* which calls for that kind of opulence, an illusion of opulence, he's a great designer for that.

Some people are better at abstractions. Richard Hennessy is a highly abstract set designer. He did eight sets for *Conquest of the Universe*. Fabulous. Spectacular.

I like to use artists as set designers. Give them a chance to think in three dimensions and with people.

■

A leader does not lead people where they do not want to go. A good leader or director is one who shares some sense of purpose with those he leads. It is when these common goals are expressed by a consistent leadership that projects requiring a great deal of cooperation, such as the collaborative efforts of a theatre, can be realized and the individuals therein can find fulfillment within a larger organization.

I think the key to it all is originality. The greatest joy a human being can know is to bring into existence something or someone that did not exist before. This sense of embarking on a great enterprise and seeing it through to completion is certainly the highest expression of what our society is all about.

This sense of excitement and anticipation is something we share with our audience. They have a very real stake in whether something we have attempted will turn out well. The adventure upon which we have embarked—that of continually confronting our audience with something new—has quickened their appetites for our works. The demands they make on us have increased, but then so has the poignancy of what it truly means to be contemporaries.

The commitment to the new is not so much an act of will as it is obedience to an inner necessity. Ultimately an artist does not do what he will but what he must. It is intuition and feeling that lift works of art above the merely mechanical. And the reward for breaking with convention is a wonderful freshness. It is only by embarking for the unknown that the artist can attain that most difficult relation to his audience: famous and yet undiscovered.

■

The audience has grown so much, it's hard to house them in only one hundred forty-three seats. I have to do so many performances, it's almost like entertaining these people privately.

There is something very special about that, though. I do love a small house. All the great theatres were small—the Moscow Art Theatre was one hundred ninety-nine seats, the Living Theatre was probably about one hundred fifty, Antoine's theatre in Paris which began the whole realistic movement was a ninety-nine- or hundred-seat theatre. Many of the great theatres were small, so there's a noble tradition there.

I love it when the tour groups come down, and I hear them

explaining what the theatre has been, and then they say it's mine, and they explain what I do. I love that, because it's like being part of history.

That theatre is immensely important to me. From my earliest days, you see, I always knew just what I wanted to do. I wanted to have a theatre in the Village that did experimental work, and I wanted to produce a new piece every year that people would look forward to seeing.

We had to build up this space. This was all a shambles. It had been a Greek theatre. It had stone benches. When the Loew's Trans-Lux East movie theatre went out of business and they tore it down, they donated these seats to me. They said, "Come up and get them." It was an opening night, but we went up and got the seats during the day and then opened that night. It may have been inadvisable for the play, but at least we got seats.

It was rather terrifying for me to give the order to tear out the other seats because I thought: what if we can't put those in and I have ruined what I have? Because I do try to keep the energy onto producing the play. Most theatre people take over a theatre and immediately start to redecorate. I never do that. I sort of clean it up and then work on the play. Then gradually the theatre is improved.

■

This play represents a further development of our use of magic, stage illusions and performer virtuosity to narrative ends. While the play is perhaps the most exhausting challenge an actor could take on, its demands forced us to tap acting resources whose existence we had only suspected. The run of *The Mystery of Irma Vep*, far from being a repetition, was an exciting period of growth and discovery. We are not the same actors we were when we began work on this piece.

■

When I was younger my plays were more cruel, because I was less sensitive to people's suffering, including my own. Anthony Trollope says, "The difficult thing about satire is that once you have the lash in your hand it's hard to know when enough is enough." You tend to beat the person mercilessly.

I think it's true that there's a little more understanding now than there was then. My early plays were all pain, all cruelty, all victims and predators. Now they're more warm.

I feel more sympathy now for my fellow travelers on the freight train rushing toward death which we're all riding. Some people are just a little further toward the front of the car.

■

Acting, especially in *The Mystery of Irma Vep*, is physically demanding. Changing characters every few minutes, the trickiest part for me is remembering to use the right voice for the right character, not to talk in a falsetto when I'm supposed to be a bass. Because of the quick changes involved, there is always the danger of two characters blurring together. However, once an actor gets a specific role fixed in his head, he can switch back and forth from one to the other. It's a matter of discipline.

Acting is a daily chore I do. It's the physical work of the theatre. It's very satisfying physically and emotionally. It's difficult, it's frustrating and it's very demanding, and it's from this that one must rest because you can get really tired. It's like running a marathon.

In modern times, we've had to deal with something they've never dealt with before: the long run. If you play every day, give or take fifty days, you've got close to three hundred performances a year, even more. This means that actors must perform the same way over and over again. This encourages predictable habits rather than experimentation and growth. A true artist, on the other hand, must dare to try something new.

I feel that, as an artist, as an entertainer, your basic job is to create something of interest for others. But what happens is that you can get so caught up in a part in a play that you never think about whether anything is of interest to your "other," more real self. You're so busy being interesting onstage that you can sometimes forget to be interested in the so-called "real world."

I think artists whose lives are about *being interesting to others* have to take rests, which means time to be boring and not being of any interest to others. This may not have publicity value. It's just something for *you*. You must find the time.

•

If I say I'm conservative and you know my work, you think I'm crazy. What's conservative about me is not my morality—my mores, my view of people, my manners—that's *not* conservative. What's conservative is my belief in tradition, a viable tradition. If you're going to paddle your boat against the stream, nothing can happen to you. If you get into the current, it carries you along. You benefit from all the discoveries of all the artists before you, and you take your boat that much farther along the stream.

The place where I made a breakthrough personally in my work, and which I think is unique about my work in the history of comedy, and what makes it another phase, is that traditionally comedy has been the voice and the tool of the conservative or the status quo. It punished the deviant, it punished the nonconformist, it punished people who deviated from conventions. They were made fun of, and they got back in line because of a fear of being ridiculed. Basically, comedians exhibit contrary behavior. When everyone laughs, you know not to do that.

In my hands, comedy becomes the tool of the deviant and the original, the unique, the forbidden. It punishes the status quo, changes the way they think about things.

Ridiculous makes the normal ridiculous, makes the normal, the conventional and the standard the figure of fun. The deviant, the eccentric and the original minority triumphs over the norm.

Ridiculous is not conservative. When one freed oneself of the need to be serious, one stepped out of the world of what other people thought should be into the world of what one wanted for oneself.

•

If I demand of the audience to take it seriously, I have to do it in their way. If I don't care whether they take it seriously or not, I can do anything I want. I am totally free.

It's the pose of the fool. The fool has a license to say things, to do things that serious people can't do.

One of the greatest weapons that people use on you to get you to conform is ridicule. So you don't dare to do anything that people will laugh at. It's a way that society exerts pressure on you.

However, if you take the position that you are already going to be ridiculous, they are powerless. They ridicule you? They are doing what you want them to do.

If I were doing serious theatre, some people would take me seriously and I'd be very happy. Some intellectuals would take me seriously. But then there would be some who would ridicule me and say I wasn't any good and that was a bunch of shit, and I would be all upset for that.

This way I use reverse psychology. *I* say the play is worthless and ridiculous and meaningless, and then the public, in its perverse refusal to do what I told them to do, insists that it's profound, serious, important and philosophical. Whereas if I said it was serious, profound and philosophical, they would say it wasn't.

Even when I get a bad review, it works perfectly in my favor, because, after all, of the Theatre of the Ridiculous what do they expect? For a while critics even tried to complain that it wasn't ridiculous *enough*, but that didn't work either. "This isn't ridiculous," they said. "This is serious." Already they played into my hands.

This way I can't lose. Whatever I do, it comes out all right.

I am never disappointed when they find deeper meanings. Maintaining one's status as a clown, that unserious attitude, is artistically aristocratic because one is never forced to be serious. That's an incredible luxury. You can be brilliant, if you're capable of it, but you don't have to be serious. Like Rossini: his works are very funny, but musically they're as brilliant as anything that's been composed.

Also, you can do a lot of things about social changes with satiric impact. You have the fun of doing things and condemning them at the same time.

The notion of the Ridiculous implies an inversion of values. What people esteem in a particular time will usually appear ridiculous at a later period. Intellectual fashions are much worse than fashions in clothing.

Ridiculous is a great concept, because it frees one from having to conform.

The conventions of the commercial theatre are very limited. It always comes down to what's polite and what's nice—basically a form of censorship. But once you break down those barriers, there is no limit to what you can explore.

The Ridiculous is a convenient name. Each time you do a play, it expands the definition of Ridiculous. It's been general enough to give me breathing space.

I sometimes think that the Ridiculous is the only serious theatre. After all, everywhere you look in this world there's something that's ridiculous. It's important to help people see that.

I often think all theatre is ridiculous, but we're willing to admit it.

My theatre has not changed that much in its essentials, although I think we do it better now. My goal was always to have a theatre that's popular, but also had extremely high quality. I think I've finally managed to bring those elements together.

Sometimes it's hard not to be obscure. The hardest thing in the world is to be clear—sometimes it's hard to make these things clear to the audience. I may have found the way by now, because *Irma Vep* has been so successful, and everyone understands it.

12

*I*rma Vep was a stretch for us as actors, a feat that left us changed forever and for the better. It also represented a further development of our use of illusionistic stagecraft. By incorporating magic and illusions into our works we heighten the plays' effect and produce new levels of audience involvement, challenging their preconceptions of what is possible by seemingly defying the physical limitations of time and space. While stage magic is generally used for its own sake, we have made of it a tool of expression at the service of a dramatic idea.

While sustaining the run of *The Mystery of Irma Vep* we began the developmental process of *Salammbô*, my dramatization of the novel by Gustave Flaubert. Because of the amount of sheer physical energy required to perform *Irma Vep*, we rehearsed *Salammbô* part-time; that is, three days a week, three hours per day. Rehearsals stretched over a three-month period. *Salammbô* required a large cast. I saw this as an opportunity to discover some new talent. I cast the principal roles with members of my company and held auditions for the rest. For the army of Barbarians I sought athletes. Eventually these roles were cast with champion bodybuilders. Their ability to pose like statues coupled with their refreshingly naive acting proved to be a *coup de théâtre*. Visually, the play recalled the Orientalist paintings of Gérôme and the films of Cecil B. DeMille, while sounding like the proletariat heroes of the

Actors Studio. The production became an uncanny combination of brain and brawn, all in the service of Flaubert.

■

Salammbô is one for the boys, believe me! We decided that we gays have been through enough in the last couple of years. We are going to give them a little something.

In the novel Flaubert describes the veins popping out on the arms of the barbarians. The gods and heroes of antiquity had incredible bodies, but on the stage you always get scrawny actors, who can act. I thought it would be great to give a hot vision of antiquity.

We're using a stage full of the biggest bodybuilders we could find. It's surprising how inspired they really are. Some of them have not acted before and they're really inspirational. There's a lot of talent that's being unleashed.

■

Flaubert's extravagant novel, *Salammbô*, has exerted a certain fascination since it first appeared in 1862. It was both an immediate success and scandal. Mussorgsky attempted to make an opera of it, as did Debussy. Both abandoned the project. Ernest Reyer actually completed an opera based on the novel, with a libretto by De Locle on which Flaubert collaborated, although Flaubert did not live to see it performed. The Bolshoi Ballet did a ballet of it. Oscar Wilde found in it the inspiration for his *Salomé*, as did Mallarmé for his *Herodiad*, a poem which has inspired the mirror scene in my production.

Set in a lost civilization about which we know almost nothing, *Salammbô* is above all a synthesis of archeological research and pure imaginative art. It is a tragedy that is not altogether intended to be taken seriously; and yet, to quote Flaubert, "It was a melancholy task, resurrecting Carthage."

There is something haunting and melancholy, while at the same time exuberant and ridiculous, about the forbidden love of the Barbarian, Matho, for the High Priestess, Salammbô. Like all of Flaubert's work, *Salammbô* tends to manifest a longing for excesses and pleasures of the imagination unattainable in reality by the physical limitations of the body. It was admired by the Parnassan school, a group of artists dedicated to a literature that approximated the plastic quality of painting and sculpture, of jewelry and lapidary art. If the characters in the play are indeed statues, they move through a series of museum tableaux which give the impression of rushing forward and standing still at the same time.

In dramatizing Flaubert's novel, it was necessary to evoke the sense of the extreme within the finite frame of an evening in the theatre. While the play may seem shocking to those unfamiliar with the original, we hope that we have found in essence what Flaubert gave us in such comprehensive detail. But isn't our task, in staging such a work, identical to the dilemma of the play's protagonists? To accomplish in art what is unattainable in life.

■

We're developing a style of performing, not using one that's already established. It's an ongoing process, different from what you see other places because we never start with the same approach. Also, the actors can do things here they might not be able to do elsewhere, such as designing sets or helping with costumes.

Some reviewers come here expecting the kind of mechanical ensemble acting you can get at the Royal Shakespeare Company or anywhere on Broadway. Where does that leave me? Out in the cold, because that stuff is dead as a doornail. They direct all their lines to the audience.

Sometimes a reviewer will call our performances "amateurish," but what he doesn't understand is that our so-called amateurish style has been consciously, purposefully arrived at. We don't want to be slick like Broadway performers because we don't want our acting to belie the effort that goes into a production.

After all, it's the awareness of effort that makes a live production, such as a concert, more exciting than a recording, or a Navaho rug more interesting than a factory-made one. The mistakes in handmade rugs and live productions might show more than they would in slicker, highly edited artforms, but so do the triumphs.

Furthermore, the conventions of commercial acting just aren't broad enough to encompass the variety of human life that you see right here on the streets of New York. At the Ridiculous Theatrical Company we want to create vivid, memorable characters, and the mannerisms used by many commercial actors are simply inadequate to the task. Many Broadway actors tend to shout at moments of high emotional intensity, and they all shout at the same pitch! That drives me up the wall. And there's the habit male actors have of sitting with their legs a mile apart when they want to indicate their masculinity. It has become such a cliché, and not even a valid one—European men don't sit that way. And many commercial actors wander around the stage too much. They walk and turn, walk and turn, for no reason except that they fear the show will be dull if they stand in one place.

■

I'm terribly Geraldine Page and Kim Stanley. Whenever I feel the least bit dried up, I think of them and a whole new life comes over me—those funny little nervous twitches and so forth.

Even if you imitate another actor—unless you are an impressionist—what comes out will be original. Learning from other actors is useful, especially when you use them as a reference for a completely different type—collage them.

I'm very impressionable. I've always absorbed a lot of influences—not so much stylistic as psychological, working with actors in ways which allow them to perform in different styles. I'm known for kinky casting and I discover people—sometimes on the street, sometimes old friends. I also draw on a pool of rather extraordinary actors out of the avant-garde. Certain things I've done have been considered anti-professional. I'll take a person who has nothing to lose and put him in a star-making role.

■

My face is my fortune. I think there are moments of beauty in it and I think there are grotesque moments. From two different angles, sometimes I can't believe it's the same face.

My mother was looking at a picture of me as Salammbô, and she said, "Oh, you look so beautiful in this picture, just like me when I was a girl." Because I do look like her in drag.

■

I will do more female roles in the future, even though it gets more and more taboo.

A friend of mine, Christopher Scott, said he felt for men right now there is an incredible identity problem about masculinity and that drag threatens this. But I think an artist is like a shamanistic figure. It's not what everybody does, it's that the artist is a different beast.

If you have a flare for playing females, it's foolish to let anything hold you back. Artists have to be very androgynous, especially actors. They have to be capable of understanding human feelings in general.

Drag is always in.

Though I was one of the people who predicted the advent of the masculine homosexual, machismo has crested, and I think there will be a rediscovery of the concept of being neutral in the battle of the sexes, or to pass back and forth. It's very unfortunate that when gay men became butch—or appeared to become butch—the drag queens were not admitted to certain bars and gathering places. They were something from an earlier period that nobody wanted to see or deal with, when actually drag queens were the cutting edge of the movement, the revolutionary fire-starters. It was the drag queens who stood up to the police in the Stonewall riots and fought in the streets. It was not the leather people, who are basically masochists.

Drag is a triumphantly dominant image because it is based on the concept of the woman as invincible and all-powerful. Beauty is a weapon that makes one invincible. This idea is at the heart of all Marlene Dietrich's movies. She has the ultimate weapon in those movies. The men have guns but are powerless. She can do anything because she's so beautiful.

My plays let men and women step out of their traditional roles. Theatre is a way of experimenting with life—a kind of research-and-development department for the culture at large.

We're imprisoned in our gender, and the ability to get out of it is very forbidden. Tiresias was turned into a woman, revealed from his experience that women got more pleasure from sex than men, and they blinded him as punishment for the revelation.

So there is that desire to know what it is to be the opposite sex. It's one of the major curiosities, and I think it exists for everybody. For those who *can* cross that barrier, it's a magical act.

Theatre has a magical and religious basis. Many of the things we see strike us in a very primordial way, but these are mysteries. I don't think everything can be explained.

I don't think everything about female impersonation can be explained. The fact that it bothers people is its power to a large extent. The fact that it can disturb or puzzle or confuse or shock is part of its magic.

There's a longer tradition of men playing women than there is of women playing women. So, as my dear friend Professor Leon Katz at Yale says, women playing women needs more justification because it is the newer thing.

Every major comedian in the country does drag. You have to do it. You're not a comedian if you don't. Johnny Carson does it. Abbott and Costello did it.

But to play a *role*, comedic or serious, of the opposite sex, that's different. It's more *Oriental*, it's more in the tradition of the Kabuki or the Elizabethan theatre.

You don't know if you can do it until you try. What's also interesting is that many actors *want* to try it.

I need the variety. I do need to play female roles occasionally. It's like an alter ego. She's in there somewhere, waiting to come out.

Perhaps I have a spirit that's female in me. When that takes over, those thought processes inhabit my whole body and it's as though I were a woman.

I know it's acting. I never think I'm a woman. I'm a woman having a fabulous time in a man's body.

But I like my male roles. I find that that's a side of my personality that absolutely has to be expressed. I would not want to just play female roles.

I think I'm an androgynous being to a certain extent. And that the male characterizations are informed by a recognition—if not on the part of the character, on the part of the artist creating the character—of the feminine side of personality.

Being male in real life, I play a variety of male roles. The female is this actress I find in myself who then in turn plays the role. It's not the actor playing a female role. It's the actor transforming into an actress and then playing a female role.

Becoming this actress is a big change from the male part of me—it's a role just to become this actress. So in a way all the females are one thing—the males are different characters. The female libido comes out and she in turn plays the role of Camille or Galas—two different personalities.

I think there's a difference in our psyches between what male and female are. I think the female represents the intuitive and the irrational. The male represents the rational, law and order and conspicuously trying to do the right thing or the wrong thing.

Some men are irrational and some women are rational. They're not truthful to male and female principles—the great, archetypal concepts. But releasing the female side of my personality is *symbolically* getting in touch with the irrational, subconscious part of my being.

■

Salammbô opened for previews in repertory with *The Mystery of Irma Vep*. It was an immediate sensation. The repertory system once again proved viable as a way of introducing new works. All preview performances of *Salammbô* were sold out. The theatre functioned optimally throughout the season. We seemed to have made a breakthrough and to have reached a new level of success.

It may be that our audience is now greater than our seating capacity.

■

I don't believe in giving all. I don't give all. My work is the tip of the iceberg of what I'm involved in. The theatre is only one aspect of my total personality. It's not my whole existence. Often it's the only part that others see.

I'm always writing or working on a production, but I have hobbies I indulge in as a sort of alternative world, because I think if you share your life with the public as an actor does you have to have some private part of you that is not accessible to the world, that you cannot share.

I draw and paint, do puppets. I'm interested in growing plants. I also breed tropical fish, which is more complicated than the plants—Siamese fighting fish in particular. I keep breeding records and cross colors. I'm working on developing a new strain, a unique strain that's never been seen. At the moment I'm at a genetic dead end, though. They show no interest in sex at all.

I also raise canaries. Some people like to breed horses. I can't in my apartment.

For a while I did mystical paintings based on Puerto Rican santería statues and tropical fish themes, but now I do male erotica. I think it's exciting that paintings can actually arouse one.

In August I think I'm going to rest. I've never taken a vacation in my life.

I don't like to sit—although I do try to keep my mornings very peaceful. That gives me the strength for the day.

We live simply. I hate to be a bore, but it's true.

I like to read and to daydream. To some people, it's very antisocial to sit and just read a book. It's a daily struggle.

I exercise. I do ten chin-ups every day; thirty to fifty situps; fifty pushups, or some days thirty. I have to remain physically fit. After all, my body is how I make my living.

Why do I collect religious statues? I was raised Catholic and I'm fascinated with Catholic imagery. I suppose I've clung to the idolatry element—the reliquaries, the hands, bones, etc.

I do have a home life, but I work terribly hard, too. I have a lot of energy, but I rest. As I've progressed in my career, I've surrounded myself with a company of people who can do their job and waste less of my time because they don't have to be corrected or checked.

It helps to do something you enjoy. It's exhausting, but it doesn't feel like work in the sense that it's an obligation you don't really want to do.

I tend to be anti-fun. I'm not really a fun person. Fun is always a substitute for real pleasure. Where you are not permitted to have real pleasure, you are permitted to have fun.

Real pleasures are things that involve a lot of hard work to attain. Fun seems to be a gift from the outside, but real pleasures are attained through one's own achievements. That is—again—hard work.

■

For me and Everett, what's really interesting is that we might be irritated with each other and play a scene where the lines mean what we're saying, and the audience is absolutely thrilled with this "great acting." Words are filled with meaning nobody knows is real. Then if you're supposed to play sexual desire, you can look at the person and make him a thousand times more attractive, a million times more desirable.

You have to work at it. It can be stressful, but basically it works out. We have a lot of understanding of each other. We have a private life that's quite pleasant. We just do what people do, but we have the theatre, which is so exciting. Sometimes you have to get away.

This apartment is just the very intimate space where we live. It's a wonderful apartment. I like the light, I like the street, it's near the pier, it's near the bank, it's near the theatre . . .

Eventually I know there'll be a change, but I dread it because I hate to uproot. It feels secure here. We've got our things here. It's crowded, it's crazy, it's like living in a ship's cabin.

We work hard. It's a creative life on a very high level.

The kinds of things we think about and have and share are very creative. We're always doing something interesting. It's a nice give-and-take.

If I think of an idea for a play and he knows that I'm thinking about this play, he'll immediately start doing research. There's no formal beginning or end to these things. It's constant, but it's almost like play.

We work terribly hard and we don't have much time for anything else. We go to the opera, to dinner, whatever people do.

Our life together is no more or less boring than that of other people. But we have a fabulous relationship and I guess that's something to be envious of. It's incredible, the influence people can have on each other.

It's the most romantic thing in the world, to find a soul mate as well as just a lover. Someone you have something in common with, so the love is not a rivalry to the career or to the creative aspect of one's life.

It makes things very special: when we have creative differences, the love can pull us back together; and when there are love differences, the creative end of things keeps us talking.

■

I don't have to worry about money right now. You'd never call it riches, but I make a living at my art. To me, that's untold riches.

I wouldn't mind making lots of money. I would adore it.

I've always felt economic success should go with great artistic achievements. But I'll tell you something: I enjoyed the bohemian period.

I didn't enjoy being poor, I didn't enjoy actually not having anything to eat at times, even when soup was twenty-five cents a bowl and I couldn't afford that; but I lived a kind of interesting, amusing life, and when you're young you can do that.

We have struggled, we've been broke, we've starved—we've been through hell. Many, many times we've saved that theatre by starting from scratch and rebuilding it. It's not about self-exploitation, it's about being an artist and making a lasting contribution to the theatre.

That to me is the real greatness. It's because of us and people like us that there are any live plays at all.

■

I love doing *The Artificial Jungle*, playing a nerd. Everybody in the cast is a good friend of mine, and we have a great time backstage. It's a joy to go there.

I was inspired by Camus' *The Stranger*, in a way. I was trying to show how people make an existentialist justification for things, saying the universe is a jungle, and that as human beings we are right to function, to be amoral. I was trying to attack that idea.

What I love is when the play functions on many levels and transcends its sources, goes on not only to be better than its sources but to be more important, to have its own overriding illusion. This happens even when you're sending up suspense.

In this play I am making fun of the devices of frustration which are used to create suspense. The audience really does get upset. They get worried. They go, "Oh. Oh. Oh no! Ack!"

It's working even though it's making fun of how that works.

■

This is a season for the distillation and consolidation of discoveries made over the past twenty years of our existence: clockwork timing, a compelling dramatic situation, and the use of popular American culture as a metaphor for philosophical thought and social satire. In short, we have created a theatre that can be laughed and thought in.

The Ridiculous Theatrical Company is the only ensemble company to emerge from the underground in the sixties to achieve mainstream acceptance by influencing the way theatre is perceived and expanding its expressive means. Because of our emphasis on the creative process, we are always the theatre of the present. Our company is an ark which carries the endangered species of the theatre over the troubled waters of fad and commercialism. It is the essential theatre, because it is about communication. Through the miasmas of media hype and disinformation, an ever-increasing audience has come to seek sanity among the mad and the wisdom of fools. For it is the comic theatre that provides the greatest vehicle for thought and an innocent forum in which to project our deepest aspirations.

I often think of creative artists as importers or smugglers who bring their ideas across the border of reality from the realm of dreams, where things do not exist, into the world of reality, where they can be seen and shared by all.

The comic view, when in the service of a worthy subject, can be a great enhancement to life and an intellectual as well as emotional outlet for the audience. Humor makes it bearable to regard what is great and terrible in life. The Ridiculous is not only a wonderful form of entertainment but a lens through which we gladly contemplate the mystery of existence.

ESSAYS

Colette

The play began with the standard life-affirming song that drives my Aries optimism to despair. The first appearance of the stars on stage was not applauded because Gerald Freedman directs plays the way a policeman directs traffic. But Zoe Caldwell and Mildred Dunnock overcame the plastic mediocrity. They hid behind the piano during this embarrassing ordeal.

The playscript is not an inspired piece of writing. Although the author, Elinor Jones, claims to have based the play on the collection of Colette's autobiographical writings, *Earthly Paradise*, it looked more like the movie *Isadora* to me, complete with poetic young studs and Tarot cards. The formula is too pasty to be intriguing.

Miss Mildred Dunnock plays with reserve and achieves her effects with great economy of means. This is a quality peculiar to older actresses who, rather than endlessly proliferating the mannerisms that made them famous and becoming cruel caricatures of themselves, distill the essence of a gesture through the years until it emerges—a monolith. Miss Dunnock is a stately understatement.

Keene Curtis impersonates a remarkable variety of male characters: THE FATHER, THE CAMPING OLD HOMOSEXUAL and THE TROUPER. Although his powers of observation fall down in his portrayal of the Reporter, I think he teaches a lesson in Character Acting.

Zoe Caldwell gives a virtuoso vocal performance which shows us what words can be and affirms the power of poetry. The incantation, the hypnotic chant and the Alchemy of Abstract sounds need not be sought in the Exotic. They are here in our own English language when that language is spoken well.

The scene between Colette and an elder Sophist will be of particular interest to readers. While working as a pantomime actress in the French Music Hall, she meets an old actress who admires her on having girl lovers. "If one woman acts like a pseudo-man it will cause great trouble," she croaks. "What could be more ridiculous than a woman pretending to be a man?" This overly discreet handling is homosexuality packaged for heterosexuals' consumption. But Zoe Caldwell telegraphs the rest as subtext. The pantomime scene in which she bares a single breast is a jewel because Zoe Caldwell is a jewel. But acting this script she is a jewel in a dung setting.

I asked Lola Pashalinski, "How old is Zoe Caldwell?"

She replied, "Thirty-five or forty."

The bald paunchy gentleman sitting in front of us turned around. "She's thirty," he said.

"Think of that, she's only thirty," I said.

"Think of that," said Lola.

As we were preparing to leave the theatre, I said to Lola, "I hear echoes of Judith Anderson in Zoe Caldwell's voice, and I sometimes think I am seeing Judith Anderson as she must have been when she was young."

"Did you ever see the photograph of Judith Anderson with the Great Dane in *Vanity Fair*?"

The bald paunchy gentleman in front of us was standing and putting on his coat. Suddenly he turned into an EVIL THEATRE FAGGOT. "Judith Anderson masturbates," she snapped, "Zoe Caldwell *acts*." She made her exit hurriedly.

"These Evil Theatre Faggots, tch tch tch," said Lola.

On my way home I wondered to myself why it is that when the new gods appear the old gods must fall into neglect. Because we now know the wrath of the PEYOTE GOD, must we forget the ecstasy of BACCHUS? Could there be a Zoe Caldwell if there had never been a

Judith Anderson? Could there have been a Judith Anderson if there had never been a Sarah Bernhardt? Could there have been a Sarah Bernhardt if there had never been a Rachel?

Oh EVIL THEATRE FAGGOT you are a fool! If there is no tradition there is nothing to camp on. There would be no today if there had never been a yesterday. Where were you twenty, fifty, a hundred, a thousand years before YOU were born?

Mr. T. or El Pato in the Gilded Summer Palace of Czarina-Tatlina

A Fairy Tale

Do you know Mr. T.? Perhaps you have seen him in a doorway on Christopher Street. He is the proprietor of the 266 East 4th Street Gallery. His tenement apartment where he shows his own art. He ran the Miss Teenage Queen of the Arts Contest. Did you vote? He built the Sacristy of the Hamptons with his own hands. Did you see it? He ushered guests into the Sanctum Sanctorum in drag impersonating Ethel Dull the art collector. Were you there? If you missed these art events you were ruined socially and didn't even know it. But redemption is still possible . . . if you dare to visit the Summer Palace of Czarina-Tatlina!

Once upon a time there was a little boy whose mommy made him go to Mass every Sunday and to Catholic School during the week. On Saturdays when the other children were out playing Tag, Hopscotch and Doctor this little boy was on his knees in front of the priest confessing his sins and doing penance. One day the little boy ran away to the Big City. At first he felt very lost and alone. He had no money and no place to stay. But he soon discovered that certain older men in the Port Authority Bus Terminal would give him money if he let them suck on his pee pee. So he did.

One day the little boy, whose name is Mr T., found a home in the ghetto at 266 East 4th Street. Here he met Puerto Rican boys who were Catholics like himself. They peed in the hall and made him get down on his knees in front of them and suck on their pee pees. This reminded him of the confessional. He liked it very much. "I never want to leave the ghetto," said Mr. T. "This is where I live." Then the *junkies* robbed him of the money he had just gotten from the older men in the Port Authority Bus Terminal.

Mr. T. got tired of living on the gratitude of older men ("Besides they're not that grateful," he said), and got welfare. Now he hardly knew how to express *his* gratitude to the City of New York. Yet with all these things—a railroad flat on the fourth floor of a tenement; the companionship of the queens on Christopher Street; and the Welfare Grant— Mr. T. was not happy. He felt a longing in his heart, a nostalgia to hear the Mass prayed in a language he did not understand. The reforms of the Ecumenical Councils made him feel disinherited. If only he could combine his taste for botanicas, gypsy storefronts and Puerto Rican boys with the grandeur that was Rome . . . the grandeur that was St. Petersburg. He prayed to St. Catherine for a sign. And the sign came. He would build the Artorama, a genre more queer than Mexican folk art and a thousand times more detailed than Macy's Christmas windows. The Artorama would be the apotheosis of the Catholic religious holidays—Christmas and Easter rolled into one—an electric train, tinfoil Wonder City where jewel-encrusted rats in ecclesiastical garb murmur novenas in detailed replicas of Fabergé Easter Eggs. The heart of Christ bleeds rubies into a levitating grail. Silver stars hang about the head of a life-sized statue of St. Francis from the painted blue sky above your head. Forgeries of the crown jewels of the Imperial Family of Russia serve as harbingers of the *new* orthodoxy of Queer Catholicism. Rome and the Pope have become too liberal. They are heretics in the sacristy of the Slum Goddess. Mr. T. begins the seventies with an invocation of the muse and a clarion call to return to the tradition of high art. Reincarnate the nineteenth century! The glamour of the Baroque will be revived by renegade Catholics. Fig leaves will fall from the crotches of Roman Statues painted in fashion colors.

Mr. T.'s dream is to build a chapel to the martyred saints in a storefront on East 4th Street. Perhaps he would paint frescoes. But his Public Assistance Grant from the Department of Welfare does not permit the undertaking of so ambitious a project. Attendance at his art exhibits (he shows in his apartment only) has been limited to a small coterie of people in the know and Puerto Rican children in the neighborhood. They love Mr. T. because he has entered their world and crystallized the Puerto Rican Mystique.

Last week Mr. T. gave Mario Montez a large fake leopard handbag which she now carries as Leopard Woman in *Bluebeard*. "She's the first Puerto Rican artist who knew she was Puerto Rican and used it," he said.

Mr. T. is influenced by the Ukrainian religious art around Avenue A, too. "Polish and Ukrainian kids have big dicks, but they're too mean."

"It's a cop-out to fall in love with someone. It's just an attempt to lose yourself. I think it's better to make things. Don't you?"

The things that Mr. T. makes are not made to last. His is a transitory art that creates an illusion and then disappears. For this reason it might be called theatrical. The images seem to dissolve before your eyes. Now it is an exquisite piece of jewelry or a relic of the true cross encased in a richness unmatched outside the Vatican. Then suddenly you realize that it is made of Saran Wrap or Wondafoil, packaging materials symbolic of the octopus that has us in its inky clutches, the present regime. The item appears worthless if seen from behind or from its "bad" side. We turn it and it becomes exquisite again. This is Queen Art transformed by the genius of Mr. T. into a metaphysical mockery. Profanation of the Mother and the sacred religious relics becomes the veneration of the invert. To have a new idea is as gauche as being seen in a new suit. Heresy is for heterosexuals. Says Mr. T., "Heterosexuals can't understand camp because everything they do is camp."

Mr. T.'s new show can be seen at 266 East 4th Street, Apartment 17 (4th floor) Tuesdays, Wednesdays and Thursdays from 2 pm to 4 pm, Saturdays from 1 pm to 5 pm. Wait at the street level until someone opens the door for you.

A Monograph and a
Premature Memoir

Why I Use Female Impersonators
in My Plays

The theatre has always been to me a place where beautiful lies are told, and playwrighting the orchestration of platitudes around a central flaw in logic or a ridiculous idea. Acting—the disguise and impersonation—is an art of deception. The audience are willing victims of fraud for they suspend their disbelief. Reality, weary of its tyranny, is a tyrant willing to be dethroned. Actors liberate us because they facilitate our belief in the unbelievable. The theatre is an amoral place, a magic circle set apart where the bonds of civilization may be broken and alternatives may be explored without danger to the society. In the theatre our imaginations dissolve those fixed conditions of our lives and we freely indulge our fantasies. All lose themselves temporarily. Abandonment of the ego is the element that theatre holds in common with religion and is the key to the theatre's origin. Actors then are the priests of the drama abandoning their own personalities for those types whom they impersonate.

The greatest and most restrictive bond on one's identity is sex. It is fixed biologically or bio*ill*ogically at birth. Anatomy is destiny. When we impersonate the opposite sex we are freed from one prison only to

151

enter another. You must believe in fixed roles to be able to exchange them. The female impersonator is not one who is freed from the rituals of sexual identity. He understands the rituals better and knows the passwords. He can pass back and forth. While others are content with one sexual identity he has two. He is a great actor because he has prepared himself for both roles all his life.

In the great ages of the theatre men have impersonated women. The Greek tragic heroines Medea, Electra and Antigone were played by men as were all roles in those days. Women were forbidden to go on the stage. The Greeks wrote women's roles for men, which explains why so few modern actresses (except Judith Anderson and Katina Paxinou and Maria Callas) have had the balls to play them. In Shakespeare's day young boys played women's roles until their voices changed and their beards came in. Then their apprenticeships ended and they assailed the longer and vocally more demanding male roles. But while women were not permitted on the stage in Renaissance England they were impersonating men on the stage in Spain as they do today in some operas like *La Nozze de Figaro* and *Der Rosenkavalier*. In the wandering, improvisational commedia dell'arte troupes of Italy men played only old or ugly women. To this day it is believed by Kabuki actors in Japan that women are too close to femininity to capture its essence on stage. The *onnagata* or female impersonators are a cult who believe that to play a woman onstage one must also play a woman offstage. In the words of the great Ayame Yoshizawa, "The *onnagata* should continue to have the feelings of an *onnagata* even when in the dressing room. When taking refreshment, too, he should turn away so that people cannot see him. To be alongside a *tachiyaku* playing the lover's part and chew away at one's food without charm and then go straight out on the stage and play a love scene with the same man will lead to failure on both sides, for the *tachiyaku*'s heart will not in reality be ready to fall in love.

"Should an *onnagata* be concealing the fact that he is married, and people talk about his wife, he should feel like blushing, otherwise he should not be performing *onnagata* roles, and will not make his way in the profession. An actor who, no matter how many children he has, still keeps a child's heart is a born genius," said Ayame.

Youth and sexual attractiveness are the most important qualities for an *onnagata* to project. If he has to play a role that calls for him to appear old or unattractive he wears his wig askew or betrays some slight flaw in his dress to show that his heart is not in it.

The twentieth century has carried on the tradition of acting in drag in the Music Hall: Barbette, Marlene Dietrich, Coccinelle, Nel, Jean Fazil, Antonet, Little Tich; Vaudeville: Julian Eltinge, Karyl Norman, Jackie May; the Movies: Garbo, Charlie Chaplin, Fatty Arbuckle, Jack Lemmon, Tony Curtis. And those great comedians who have spanned all the media: Milton Berle, Jack Benny and Bert Lahr. Underground Movies: Mario Montez, Joel Markman, Frankie Francine, Minette, Henry Geldzahler, John Vaccaro, Jackie Curtis, Candy Darling, Holly Woodlawn. On Stage: almost everybody these days, but most notably Ray Burbon, T. C. Jones, Mario Montez, Charles Ludlam, Lola Pashalinski, Jeanne Phillips, Inez "Bunny" Eisenhower, Alexis Del'Lago, Mr. Eleven, Larry Rée, Mary Woronov, Mae Moon, Lohr Wilson.

Mario Montez towers above the others on eleven-inch Fuck Me Pumps. He is the Guru of Drag. Actresses Black-Eyed Susan and Lola Pashalinski have learned the intricacies of makeup and costume from him and now they have something to teach. Lola refers to getting dressed for any part—male or female—as "getting in drag." Black-Eyed Susan has frequently been seen on stage in Montez Creations. Whether he is playing The Wife, The Mother, The Whore or The Virgin, Montez captures the ineffable essence of femininity. I never tire of writing roles for Mario Montez. He has dignity.

As for myself, I am playing Bluebeard now, a male impersonation. Mario appears as Lamia the Leopard Woman and Mr. Eleven plays Mrs. Maggot, the sinister housekeeper based on a lady who talks to herself on East 6th Street.

When his dream of the part calls for playing the opposite sex, the actor must reconcile his sense of truth with his sense of the theatrical. The drag embodies the paradox of acting.

The Seven Levels
of the Theatre

1. Mechanical

The mechanical theatre is run by functionaries. The curtain always goes up on time. The most important quality in the artist is dependability. The play is written well in advance by a playwright, preferably dead. The actors count their lines, which they learn with the aid of a tape recorder. And the director knows that any play can be made to "work" with a little "tightening up."

2. Sentimental

The sentimental theatre is a ravishment to the senses. It caters to the audience's likes and dislikes. The most important quality in the artist is beauty. Actors spend a great deal of time in gyms, under sunlamps and on diets. Food and drinks are served during the performances, which feature music, gorgeous costumes, pleasant fragrances and comfortable seats. This theatre eternally enlists audience sympathy through the theme of love, which depicts two human beings experiencing the same emotion at the same time.

3. Intellectual

The intellectual theatre sets out to prove a theory. Everything is done for a reason. The most important quality in the artist is studiousness. The director adopts the role of a teacher. Performances are living demonstrations of an argument, usually followed by discussion. In fact, the audience can hardly wait for the show to be over so they can go home and think about it.

4. Social

The social theatre provides a meeting place for people with something in common. The actors and audience come from the same community. Some of them come to identify themselves with the familiar themes of the plays. Others come to see and be seen. Theatrical companies are composed of families who pass on roles from father to son. Although this theatre serves to strengthen a movement by clarifying a group's point of view while affirming its values, it is rarely of any interest to outsiders.

5. Economic

The economic theatre means business: bargaining, buying and producing a play for sale. Because this theatre is primarily involved in a struggle for wealth, the plays it produces stress the importance of money in men's lives. Cooperation is achieved by mutual exchange, and the most important talent is to stay employed. When the money runs out, the theatre disappears with it.

6. Moral

The moral theatre is for good and against evil, or for evil and against good. Dissatisfied with the world as it is, producers of moral theatre seek to change things with the plays they do. Whether improving human beings for the sake of uplift or corrupting them through some supremely perverse delight in nastiness, they are always sorting out right from wrong. Between the good accomplished by the one and the evil accomplished by the other there is a perfect balance which results in no change whatsoever in the moral condition of Man.

7. Supreme

The supreme theatre is intuitive. The artists of this theatre have mastered and internalized the first six levels of judgment. They are spontaneous and lucky. At the supreme level there are no ulterior motives, no striving for one thing to the exclusion of others. If there is anything these artists enjoy as much as complete success it is a real fiasco. They get better as they get older, giving all they have. Because they have suffered, they accept their applause with gratitude. Their secret is that of the ancient Chinese marksman whose every arrow was found in the dead center of a chalk circle. They shoot their arrows first and draw the circle afterward.

Afterthought

These theatres do not exist. They are purely imaginary. Every real theatre is a combination of two or more of these imaginary ones. So please do not take them too seriously. They are meant to suggest the seven levels of judgment we use when we work in the theatre. I learned them from my readings of George Ohsawa, macrobiotics and Zen Buddhism. Thank you for reading my article, and may you never fear to take your curtain call to the sound of one hand clapping.

Manifesto:
Ridiculous Theatre,
Scourge of Human Folly

AIM: TO GET BEYOND NIHILISM BY REVALUING COMBAT.

Axioms to a theatre for ridicule:

1. If one is not a living mockery of one's own ideals, one has set one's ideals too low.
2. The things one takes seriously are one's weaknesses.
3. Just as many people who claim a belief in God disprove it with their every act, so too there are those whose every deed, though they say there is no God, is an act of faith.
4. Evolution is a conscious process.
5. Bathos is that which is intended to be sorrowful but because of the extremity of its expression becomes comic. Pathos is that which is meant to be comic but because of the extremity of its expression becomes sorrowful. Some things which seem to be opposites are actually different degrees of the same thing.
6. The comic hero thrives by his vices. The tragic hero is destroyed by his virtue. Moral paradox is the crux of the drama.
7. The theatre is a humble materialist enterprise which seeks to produce riches of the imagination, not the other way around. The theatre is an event and not an object. Theatre workers need not blush and conceal their desperate struggle to pay the landlords their rents. Theatre without the stink of art.

INSTRUCTIONS FOR USE:

This is farce not Sunday school. Illustrate hedonistic calculus. Test out a dangerous idea, a theme that threatens to destroy one's whole value system. Treat the material in a madly farcical manner without losing the seriousness of the theme. Show how paradoxes arrest the mind. Scare yourself a bit along the way.

The Last Shall Be First

In 1967, at the age of twenty-three, I, Charles Ludlam, being of something less than sound mind, sought to write a play on the grandest theme imaginable: The Conquest of the Universe. I was in fact more interested in exploring inner space than outer—that weird terrain of dreams and fantasy, both violent and erotic, would be my theatre of sexual imperialist war. I wanted to create an epic full of futile mock heroics at once arcane and futuristic. This called for an aggressive application of the techniques of modernism (analysis and distortion) to every aspect of the drama: Plot, Dialogue and Character. Could I build an ark to carry the glory of expression across the stagnant waters of creeping chic and sterile minimalism which were threatening to drown the theatre in mere image-making and "architectural" concerns, reducing performers and spectators alike to catatonia? Could the dramatic be modern? Or would the theatre, lagging behind the other arts, continue to consider its modern masters those turn-of-the-century realists Chekhov, Ibsen and Strindberg? Would my own generation continue to waver between didact and delirium in the theories of Brecht and Artaud? Or must we all flee from *Finnegans Wake* down the blind alley of reductionism, like Beckett?

Rather than go to earlier works when I felt the yearning for some richness and complexity in a play, I decided to stick closely to traditional principles and take my chances that the audience needed a change as urgently as I did and would gladly trade threadbare literalism for a more expressive verbal medium, if all the conditions of classical dramaturgy were met. Shouldn't playwrighting take its place among the modern arts? Of what use is a nonverbal theatre when ballet and modern dance have been brought to such heights by geniuses in those fields? Are not the costly pageants of the theatre of images—sets, costumes and scenic effect—a hollow shell without the portrayal of human concerns? Isn't minimalism an inflationary tendency: less art for more money? Should actors be props or agents of will? Ought all the literary talent in the theatre be confined to commentary, creating reviews more quoted than the plays from which they draw their subject matter? The theatre is the last repository of the spoken word, a place where the language, unhindered by mundane pragmatic usage, soars to a higher purpose. Alone among the performing arts, drama can explore the conflict of wills and provide an arena for combat both intellectual and physical.

Twelve years of experimentation with structure and motif have passed since first we staged Tamberlaine's outrageous career of superhuman plunder and debauch. And yet the battle goes on. Year in and year out, under the guise of the Ridiculous, we attempt the Sublime.

Of course I run the risk all moderns run. People might be as confused by a modernist plot as they used to be by modernist paintings. Modernist characters speaking modernist dialogue might seem too easy at one moment and too difficult the next. The whole affair might provoke the classic philistine comment, "My five-year-old child could do as well." To this I can only reply that I myself was all too slick when I was five and have worked these thirty years to become a primitive.

Costume Fetishism

or

Clothes Make the Man

Costume fetishism is based on the idea of role-playing. It is an artform and social code which serves as an "open sesame" to the libido. The costume is a theatrical way of creating in the sexual act the necessary polarity which is biologically or psychologically missing. For this reason it will be necessary to deal with the two opposing schools of costume fetishism: Butch and Drag.

Butch

+ Keep the things you wear authentic. Avoid chichi boutique leather.
+ Remember that some accoutrement, some element of the uniform must be worn at all times.
+ Only a miserable slave or a bourgeois has sex completely naked.
+ Get a leather jockstrap or an industrial steel ring for your cock and balls. Wear one of these even when you are wearing no other piece of equipment, for unexpected meetings.
+ Have an ornament which when worn would permit no other thoughts except those pertaining to the "work." When removed the wearer becomes totally uninitiate.

+ Never wear brown unless you are dressed cowboy western style.
+ Never wear a beard or long hair. A moustache will do. Shaving is an essential ritual. Shave off your slave's pubic hair. Shave your head.
+ Select the subject of your tattoos carefully. Have the tattooing done by an initiate.
+ Ear piercing too should be done by another member of the order and in the presence of others.
+ Decide on which side you will pierce your ear, wear your belt buckle, and hang your meat. Right side: masochist, dexter, mutton, bottom man, bad boy, slave. Left side: sadist, sinister, shepherd, top man, teacher, master.
+ Sweaters are strictly *verboten*.
+ Never mix brass with steel.
+ Keys should be worn on the outside, especially when hunting.
+ According to the Cabala the ultimate sacrament is the sexual act. Therefore it should be performed on a sacrificial altar appropriately degrading for those two channels of Catholic belief which inevitably run into one: mysticism and sadism.
+ Goethe postulated that a touch of the bizarre was essential to supreme beauty.
+ Hunt the human flies, indestructible men, daredevils and crack-up champions.
+ Avoid the average man and cultivate the freak, not because you like abnormal people, but from the scientific attitude that it is from the abnormal that we learn.

Drag

– Be artificial.
– Wear as much underwear as possible.
– Foundation garments, garters and shoes should be tight enough that you are always conscious of them.

– Suggest a captive in some aspect of your dress. If you are wearing them, see to it that your heels are too high to walk or run comfortably.

– Take on yourself the burdens of your womanhood, the seven dolors of the Blessed Virgin Mary. The transvestite "berdache" of the Apache Indians cut themselves on the inside of the thigh and let the blood run down their legs once a month.

– Say in a hoarse whisper or a thin falsetto, "I'm having my period. I'll have to suck you off."

– Let your beard grow a few days before you plan to go out. This gives the skin a rest and a chance to soften. Shave just before doing your makeup. Avoid cuts.

– A friend of mine used to tie a silk cord around his cock and balls and pull them back between his legs before dressing himself as a woman. He liked to feel them hurt when he sat down with his knees drawn daintily together.

– Remember a big head will give you away every time. Wear your hair to make your face look smaller.

– Gold goes with everything.

Salomé

With the danger of risking the ire of the opponents of the ERA amendment (an amendment which seems redundant when we consider the constitution guaranteeing life, liberty and the pursuit of happiness to all Americans—the pursuit, mind you, not the attainment; loophole?). . . . Certainly the feminists who have adulterated our language with chairperson instead of chairman, person-slaughter instead of manslaughter, and personiac for maniac will not quibble with my interpretation of Salomé as person. Indeed we have all been rejected sexually by someone with a holier-than-thou attitude such as the one characteristic of John the Baptist a.k.a. Iokanaan in Oscar Wilde's erotic tragedy. Salomé's press agent might point out that everyone in the Bible is holy. But holiness these days is just a form of stick-in-the-mudishness anyway. Iokanaan rejected her, which led to his decapitation/castration, since the penis like the body has a head, and all penises seem equally intelligent. "How is it that the tongue, that red viper that spat its venom upon me, moves no more?" Against a background of satiric religious discussion, Wilde set the tragedy of woman's sexuality, which in this aspect is synonymous with homosexuality: both risk the possibility of rejection by the male. The tragedy of one who aggresses toward the male. . . . How does one provoke aggression? Woman's secret? Salomé desires and commits herself. Iokanaan talks only of another man whom he loves above all else—Christ, over whose head he has poured water.

Who is Salomé? Her desire toward this unattainable male is ever the theme of those who love men. If a man aggresses, expresses desire toward a woman, he pays homage to her and reenacts the ancient ritual of pursuit of the male for the female, a ritual reenacted in sport—getting the ball in the basket or goal—and a mirror image of the journey we all made primordially when, as a being composed of two different parts of different sexual identities, the male part of us (Sperm) swam the infinitudes to reach the goal (Egg)—female—and became a whole person. Woman waits.

Just as the male or female cells carry within them the sexually determining factors, so too the individuals, regardless of sex, carry within them both sets of sexual characteristics, to pass on to their progeny or for their own use in self-realization. The ability to recognize opposites in ourselves is the basis of art, definitely of drama. It is part of imagining and imitating. Few people dare to enact their fantasies in art; fewer dare to realize them in the flesh—reality, extra-artistic activities.

So Salomé offers herself to the Baptist. He rejects her; he will not even look at her. Nothing she can do will bring him to her. He degrades her, and reprimands her with the soul. She takes revenge and takes possession of his body. The deadness of the head she kisses is as unrewarding as a limp cock. There is a bitter taste (death? urine?) . . . certainly not love, as Salomé suggests at the end of the play.

Love has a bitter taste. The lover can experience love without the consent of the belovéd. Unrequited. Rape is taking the object by force. Salomé rapes Iokanaan.

From Pillar to
Post Modern

There is no avant-garde. Just a dilettantish nostalgia. A sentimental looking back. The very use of the French expression *avant-garde* is quaint and betrays a desire to be picturesque. To be chic, to be avant-garde, is to be loaded with Old World charm. Ah, those Americans in Paris! How they love to window-shop. No they don't buy. They borrow. They reject. But won't this all look daring when we get it back to New York?

While they were away on tour New York changed. The new conservatism baffled them. To whom were they now selling their nude postcards and views of the *Tour Eiffel?* The giant art complexes served them like a special delicacy whose bizarre novelty was intended to shock the guests harmlessly and stimulate conversation before the main course arrived. Thus their works were used as decoys for audience disapproval, leaving the more conventional productions looking even more conventional and reassuring, when in fact they were merely inept and half-hearted. Not only was the "avant-garde" welcome—the new policy became artists with radically different points of view housed under the same roof. Every period and style was now available, as is often the case where imitations are sold. The newly available technology served as consolation for bohemia lost. Or should I say missed?

A new generation of minimalists or postmodernists or what you will grew up within institutional walls. Because it had no bohemian

origins it was totally without nostalgia. Eccentrics tend to weed themselves out of institutional settings, and the lesson learned by those who
stay behind is, "Why bother?" There it is activity for its own sake, self-
perpetuating and ever reducing itself in an attempt to become definable.
With an in-house avant-garde the management never has to go out of
its own buildings to keep abreast of the latest developments. Or so they
think.

Ludlam Versus Critics

CRITIC: Ludlam, your work is plumbing the depths of incomprehensibility. While some artists' work lapses into obscurity, your work dives into it.

LUDLAM: As you say, I'm plumbing the depths.

CRITIC: You can't go on like this forever. Someday you'll hit rock bottom and then you'll have to start coming up again.

LUDLAM: Toward the light?

CRITIC: Yes.

LUDLAM: Still hoping I'll make you a nice play one of these days?

CRITIC: You couldn't make a nice play if you wanted to. Besides that's not what we've come to expect from you. We want a naughty play that's sophisticated. The kind of thing you do so well.

LUDLAM: Then you don't want to be shocked.

CRITIC *(With a twinkle in his eye)*: Nothing shocks me anymore. Not even boredom can drive me out of the theatre. The avant-garde tried that but I've caught on to them! I'll sit through anything nowadays.

LUDLAM: Besides, now you can write the review during the piece and not miss anything.

CRITIC: Yes, which leaves more time for socializing. We critics are lonely people.

LUDLAM: I can imagine.

Hedda Journal

1st meeting with Mel Shapiro and Leon Katz.
I ask, "What's the concept?"
Mel answers, "You are the concept."
I mention her lesbianism.

■

July 1st
Driving to Pittsburgh with Leon Katz. I threaten to do the entire
role with a Norwegian accent.

■

July 2nd
Interview with Dan Isaacs for *The New York Times.*
Hedda tries to kill the future in the form of Lövborg's manu-
script—and the murder of her unborn child and her suicide.
Hedda refuses to become modern—her tragedy. Hedda's suicide
(unlike Werther's) ends the romantic period.

■

Not so much a black comedy but a bedroom farce played for high stakes.

■

"My aim is to torpedo the ark."
Henrik Ibsen

■

Hedda is the great sphinx.

■

The same plot as *The Vikings at Helgeland*.

■

I will not seek to blend, smooth out or reconcile the contradictions in the character so much as accentuate them.

■

Modern acting does not seek to reconcile or blend:

awkwardness

inconsistency

ambiguity

specific and contradictory facets.

■

Leon Katz later tells me, "I have a proprietary interest in Ibsen and I can't stand anyone to have any interpretation that differs from mine."
I reassure that I feel exactly the same way.

■

July 3rd
    We read the play around a table at the Calvary Church. There is an organ playing Bach's high church music in an adjoining room. I feel that everyone is waiting for me to speak my first line. The scene between George Tessman and his Aunt Julie goes on for five pages. Hedda's entrance cue finally comes. The organ stops. I speak.

■

July 4th

We block the first act, the scene with Thea. Lots of business with Tessman unpacking his books. I help him on the line, "But isn't it someone who—isn't that where he—where Eilert Lövborg lives. . . ." I drop the books. At first Mel thinks it might be too much. But later he leaves it in. We even drop them again on Hedda's desperation. Why?

I mention that I think George Tessman is an ideal husband and Hedda doesn't appreciate him.

■

Before rehearsal:

Leon tells me that anything one says about Hedda is true and that the opposite is also true. He recommended me for the role because he felt that I was the only actor who could play the contradictions in turns, thereby imply a human being/motive somewhere behind them. That I would accentuate the contradictions rather than flattening them out. —Attempts at a consistent characterization lose Hedda—

■

July 6th

Hedda angry.
Hedda petulant—Leon says not petulant.
Hedda in despair.
Tomorrow we begin Act II.

OPINIONS

My Career

I'm in the entertainment business.

As a teenager, I wanted to live in Greenwich Village, have a theatre of original works by me, and do a new play every year. Now I'm there, and suddenly there are a million *other* things in the air, giving me another sense of where to go.

■

It's too easy to be successful. I've always liked my failures better than the popular shows. There's no struggle if you just sit around and lap up the praise.

When you're disapproved of or misunderstood, or you can't get something to work, you grow, you become somebody else, and the next play is very different. But it's hard, because people always expect you to repeat what you've just done.

I refused, because it's good to be untypical. It's always refreshing to be *unlike* yourself.

You're never forgiven your successes. When I did *Bluebeard*, some people hated it because they loved what I did just before that, and there were some who loathed my *Camille* at first because it wasn't their *Bluebeard*. That's really why I'm different from the others who come up with new plays every year. I have more variety.

■

I want to make more films. I want to make a lot of them if I can. The films will help me get to towns that can't afford to bring in the company. How many places can you be at once, anyway?

I also want to continue to build a major comic company that could be a National Theatre, on that scale: an incredible repertoire; a big institutional theatre like Bertolt Brecht's. If you try to retain your gypsy status forever, it begins to deteriorate.

I want glamour, too, ultimately. I think it's just a matter of time before this theatre takes its place among the greats.

■

I admire George Balanchine's career very much. I imitate him, and Martha Graham. They created their own theatres with their own works. Graham built a new tradition and Balanchine revitalized an old one.

■

I write my plays for myself initially, but I write them for the theatre in general, including Broadway, TV or movies. I want them done, they're for the ages. I wouldn't even mind if stars did them.

They're very viable. I want to create works to give other companies that kind of repertoire: modern classics; plays of the dimension of a classic that are really works of modernism.

■

My plays are done all the time.

It's hard if you're identified with your own works. People say they can't be done. I think it's a question of the care you're willing to put into them. My plays are rather sophisticated. Although they seem primitive and exaggerated on the surface, a lot of thought goes into them.

What I'd like to do is stuff the repertory companies all across the country with pieces. They'd find my plays very playable.

My plays are preserved. They're not throwaway works. I think my plays will become part of a standard repertoire because they were invented *in* the theatre.

But actors doing them a hundred years from now will have the same trouble that we're having doing plays that were written hundreds of years ago. They don't work somehow. They feel stiff—unnatural. It's very difficult to make them work. You sense great power, but you're not those people and you can never again capture what that was.

■

I'm occasionally offered roles—on stage—which I can never accept. I have to work here. I have a commitment. I signed contracts to do a certain number of productions a year. I can do film work, but I can't do stage work, because obviously at eight o'clock I know where I have to be.

If it were a movie they could shoot in the daytime. But even then, I had a chance to be in a film and I couldn't do it because my play was opening. And the shooting did go over schedule. It went into the night and I would have had to cancel my opening night.

It's difficult. There is a certain moment when you define what you are and you're that and you're not something else.

I chose the high-art route. From what I do, you can do anything. You can always take a week off from high art and do something else, but you can't take a week off from something else and do high art.

■

It's wonderful to have your own theatre and do it your way and keep it very human and very amusing and keep the bullshit to a minimum. I think most people make their jobs into little hells. I try to avoid that. I do what I want—that's the beauty of it—and I'm right. If I wasn't right most of the time, it would have bombed by now.

I think about the road not taken. I was reading an autobiography of John Gielgud the other day, and I had a twinge of regret when he said that at forty he realized he was too old to play Hamlet. I invent my plays, and that's great, but sometimes I do think I might have been a classical actor. I think doing Hedda will be a serious exploration of that play.

■

It's hard to innovate in the theatre because you have to convince so many people of everything: the audiences, the critics, the producers, the backers. You don't have the freedom that a painter has to just do it his way and have posthumous fame. You have to be there, now.

Of course I want mass popularity to happen. That's what I've been working for. But it's a struggle to get attention.

Every time I have a success, people ask me, "Aren't you upset that this is a commercial success?" I don't think people realize you have to get permission to do things. I didn't just walk into New York and get handed the perfect theatre and the perfect company. People fought me tooth and nail every inch of the way. You'd think it was a crime to want to put on a play.

∎

I haven't thought of it ending, no. But you know that everything has to end eventually. At the moment I feel strong.

You can get less perfect.

I think you just keep going and exploring. I feel that this is only a warmup. There is so much to be done.

I have a lot of projects that I want to do. I think I'll continue to grow, because I continue to learn.

Directing

I like to rehearse for three hours. After three hours it becomes rote, it becomes "running through it" mechanically.

The first hour you rev up, you're getting into it, people start to get warmed up and then it peaks. There's a moment where you've given everything, you've had enough ideas and there's a tremendous amount for performers to think about and chew on. Then your mind goes. You're worn out.

■

A lot of directors block before they go to rehearsal, then come in and dictate the movements they visualize. I don't find that interesting. Being an actor myself, I can't see that it's any use in creating an exciting event.

Trying to realize a conception is just frustration. From the beginning you're into one compromise after another, until you're left with something not at all like what you imagined.

I don't bother to imagine. I just go in, see what is there and try to develop that.

I usually find that the best directing I do is when I don't direct. This sounds like a Zen Buddhist approach, but a lot of times you're really tampering with something delicate. It's even dangerous sometimes to tell an actor that something he's doing is good. The next time it's like a blossom that's been touched—you destroy it.

•

The director's work should be invisible. More often the director wants to sacrifice the classic to put his own personality on the stage. I think that's a mistake, because in the theatre it's the actor who provides the personality, not the director. When you see those superstar directors who want you constantly to be aware of their style, their signature, they ruin the thing because they flatten it out and make it monochromatic.

The director should be like God: we feel His presence everywhere but we can't ever see Him or know Him. Unfortunately, too many directors are like Jean-Louis Barrault, who used to monogram the set. Romans would be marching in and you'd see JLB on their standards.

•

I like to exploit all the happy accidents that come up in rehearsal. Often the actors see things in the script that I haven't seen. During our first readings, they begin to invest the characters with all sorts of information, and then I work from that.

One trick I know about staging is to interrupt the scene and start a discussion. Suddenly all the physical relationships change; people start leaning, talking, moving in a way that is totally real. Then you see how the scene would be in real life.

I don't spend much time on my acting. That's the only problem. In rehearsals I don't really have time to think about my acting and perfect it.

•

I don't panic. I throw tantrums and scream very rarely. I'm confident it's going to be great. It's not an accident. People who are nervous at the last minute are pushing, hoping their work will be good. I know my work is good. I don't have to hope.

I've never thrown my script down and threatened to quit like most directors. I've never said, "*I* am the director!" That always brings doubt as to whether you are.

But sometimes you have to insist on a detail. No one knew what I was talking about when I described the fan with the knife in it that Galas kills herself with. I had to get that prop myself.

∎

There's this foolish democracy business which I hate. I can't stand democracy, and I hate it when groups form that are based on democratic ideals, where each person has their voice and they vote on how something's going to be done. I hate it!

The only way is absolute dictatorship. That's the only form of government I can bear, and I must be the dictator.

But it is perhaps that the actors allow me to retain that delusion. I do feel I get what I want.

∎

We thrash things out. I'm a consummately reasonable man, which makes it all bearable, because if someone disagrees with me it's very easy to convince me. I don't think anybody has ever thought strongly about something that I didn't accommodate it.

It's like a husband and wife who have that marvelous relationship: he gets to make all the big decisions and she gets to make all the little decisions. She decides what they're going to have for dinner, what kind of clothes they're going to wear, where they're going to live—all that. He gets to decide who's going to be the next president. He decides in the Watergate hearings whether Nixon should be impeached. He decides if there's a God or not. In other words, he actually is useless to all practical thinking.

I think it's the same way with me. The actors make the little decisions which are everything, and I wander around blindly theorizing.

I am very practical, though. I must give myself credit for that.

∎

Often on a creative project, a lot of people have input, and this creates a certain amount of drift. The pure idea, the original impulse can get lost; or, if there's a strong, leading figure who is directing, an artistic director who knows what he wants, he can marshal these forces and keep their attention focused on a goal, and it can be very clear, and he can find the designers and the performers who share a vision and keep them focused on it.

A lot of theatre drifts. There isn't a person who can be strong enough without being a bully, pushing his weight around, being a pest. A certain kind of authoritarian figure can make a bore of the whole thing and ruin it. That often happens, as we all know.

But if the director can just keep the object in mind and keep the thing going in the right direction, it can have a wonderful integrity. All the parts can really pull together.

■

Still, shows go out of shape when the director leaves. Actors tend to wear out their roles anyway, like clothes. But in theatres where the director appears in the play, the director keeps that play perfect, if he knows what's right.

■

A lot of people want to be in the director's seat, even though they don't deserve it. That's not how I operate. You see, I deserve to have my theatre because I took all the little baby steps up to that point. A lot of people want the results without the drudgery.

■

When you're acting in a play, directing it and writing it, and doing the sets and the business administration, you could die very easily, just pop off. You have to be careful of not freaking out over every little detail.

You can row the boat or carefully angle your sail to the wind and let it carry you. I sail.

The Audience

What are they supposed to get? What does anybody want from the audience? What is there to want? What can you get from an audience?

All the works are not equally successful. Some of my plays are much more successful and popular. Some are very highly approved of and acclaimed. Others have been condemned as failures, miserable failures.

I don't always have the same level of approval from the audience and the critics. But for me it is always the same problem. What I am dealing with doesn't change. Whether they like the results varies, but for me the process of creating a thing is the same.

Even when they don't approve of the play, I don't feel I have compromised my view. I am sorry that people don't get it. Sometimes perhaps the reference is too obscure or the premise of the work doesn't make sense to them.

Everybody in the audience sees a different play. Trying to control what they see is futile. Trying to absolutely nail it down for each person to have the same impression is impossible.

What I do is create what *I* want and then let them come and judge me. The play must be what *I* want it to be, because I can't figure out how to make it what they want.

It's the grand effect the audience responds to. If the overall effect is evoked, the details fall away.

■

It's important to challenge our audience with new works. They're a very mixed group, I must say, but on the whole I don't think they come to us to be lulled or comforted. They're more adventurous than that. They want something that stretches beyond normal limits. They want breakthroughs. They want us to take the next step, to go further and further. That's very conducive to creativity.

Audiences are more sophisticated than the artists in many cases. The audience has seen the best and is no longer patient with anything but the best. This is partially because of mass media, which has made the best available—we see the most successful actors make films.

If you presuppose the audience is on a high level already, the people will rise to your expectations.

■

Sometimes the stage artist is in love with a small vision and the audience can see through it. I think we're in the era of the Emperor's New Clothes. The audience is saying, "There's nothing behind it."

And audiences are gaining the confidence to say that there's nothing there. So artists are going to be reevaluating—especially in the next twenty years. There will be huge changes in the consciousness of the art world.

■

When I am creating something, I imagine an audience—you have to, especially with comedy. But it is an imaginary audience. I imagine it to be a hundred fifty Charles Ludlams sitting there, but it's a projection of my own imagination. I try to do things that would interest me and hope that there are enough people like me that would be interested, too.

We've always had an audience. There's an inner audience and it goes out in concentric circles from there.

Any theatregoing audience in New York is largely gay, and there's wonderful support from the gay community. But the audience has become broader and broader based. More different kinds of people are coming.

I don't like playing to homosexual audiences very much. I prefer a more general audience because my message means more for them, is more pertinent to them. With a homosexual audience there is an element of complicity—true—but it doesn't have the same power.

■

Continuity is important. The same actors appear in play after play. The audiences have a certain expectation; they know that it's going to be familiar actors in a new role.

People come again and again to see the same play. And people want to see *each* play.

We have taken so much trouble to educate the audience—not in a pretentious way, but by doing four plays in a week: a children's play and three adult plays from various phases of our history. You can become an expert of the Ridiculous in a week. You can walk in every night and see a different play. That lends itself to developing an audience, because people come again and again and can see a lot.

■

In 1978, for the first time, we had senior citizens coming. They came from different groups that gave them free tickets. They became fans overnight. And they will not miss.

They saw one play and they want to see them all. They stop me on the street. They run into my restaurants and say, "We have loved everything and oh you kid—that's a naughty play!"

We have tried on many fronts to expand the audience: teaching has brought the students' audience; the senior citizens; the hospital groups, by way of charity that we do; children's audiences that I developed from the children's shows; many, many different types of audiences. . . . The Village and this downtown area have generally been aware of my work. The gay community has been very aware. The bohemian community in the East Village. The artistic groups in SoHo. Manhattan, generally . . . but downtown. Off Broadway. They know me, and that's where our work is most famous.

Expanding it beyond that has been very interesting. We get the outlying boroughs and out-of-towners now, *lots* of out-of-towners.

We have a large, heterogeneous audience. But theatre *is* a local phenomenon. You have to be physically able to get there.

■

It is a breed. There are some people with very broad tastes, and there are some who go to one segment of the theatre only.

Broadway benefits from its location. One lady I invited to the theatre said she couldn't even imagine going to the Village. Not "I couldn't go," but "I couldn't even *imagine* going." To her, Lincoln Center was downtown, and in a bad neighborhood. So there are all these surprises when you realize how other people see you.

There are the adventurous theatregoers who go to Off Broadway. They tend to be better educated. It's an extra-intelligent audience.

This builds in commercial limitations. To hold the audience that we have, at that level of intelligence, means sacrificing a much larger public in the name of quality.

It's not without its rewards. There are lots of bright people, and you can't do a Las Vegas floor show for these people.

■

There are two sides to fame. There are the people who know you and the people who don't, who are just as important because those people are your future. You can be new to them. It's like having a kind of virginity.

Some people associate me with one successful play—often the first one they see—and they won't go beyond that. They don't want me to move. Instead of trying to convince *them*, I'd rather find new people for whom the thing is a new experience. Appreciative audiences are born every minute.

■

The audience loves it. And they need it. It's essential to their lives. They feel it is an important form of communication.

My audience really feels very personal about me. Different people feel they discovered me at different phases of my career. They say, "I remember when he was doing drag," or "I remember when the plays were so crazy that the actors were throwing bananas at the audience and the audience was throwing them back." They remember different wild things and, in some degree, feel that they've shared in my growth, that they grew up with me. I have a lot of responsibility to those people.

■

In *Irma Vep* there were two kinds of audiences. There was the audience that perceived it as a satire, a spoof, a parody of a gothic thriller, and then there were those for whom it *was* a gothic thriller. The parody was so good that it was just as good as the thing itself.

So there were some audiences that laughed all the way through and others that wouldn't laugh but all of a sudden would scream with fright. It's a thin line.

■

The audience is my enemy at a certain level. What they want it to be is not necessarily what I'm doing.

The Critics

I think that Goethe's three principles of criticism are the only valid criteria: "What was the artist trying to do?" "Did he succeed in doing it?" "Was it worth doing?"

"Was it worth doing?" leaves plenty of room for the critic's personal opinion. What's usually left out of the formula is "What was the artist trying to do?" Most critics start with "Was it worth doing?" and never get beyond that.

"What was he trying to do?" is the great question which nobody dares ask anymore. It has gone out of fashion to ask that.

I believe in art. I think a lot of critics don't, which makes their kind of criticism invalid.

The critic may have a valid reason for not believing in art, but that's another thing. If you believe that art has only one function—propaganda, for example—maybe you don't believe in art.

■

There's the philosopher-critic who fits a work into a long world-picture of the art and its development, and then there's the reporter-critic who is just trying to give you a quick sense of what happened and a quick judgment—a blurb writer, almost. One writes in depth, from a longer viewpoint of the artform, and tends to be more insightful. The other is too quick.

Ultimately, the artist decides what the art will be. Whether or not the critics like it will only affect the economics of it.

■

As anybody who has watched my career can tell, I don't really try to please anybody but myself. Usually artists who are immune to the critics are artists who are following the tried and true, however.

We did a lot of work with very little recognition, with very little major critical coverage. It was very difficult, and I was even a little bitter about it at the time, because I thought that the work was very exciting, very innovative and very important.

You're always building sand castles. Either they get kicked down by big bullies—the critics—or taken out by the tide.

Eventually everything will close.

■

There are a few critics who don't like what we're doing, or they're afraid of it. But the majority of the critics are eager to see the next thing. They are respectful of the work and understand what I am doing.

Critics will sometimes say my work is based on nineteenth-century melodramatic acting. That's not exactly so. The nineteenth century and I got it from the same place.

■

What I really fight against is the hit-or-miss school of theatre—that you're going to be judged on one product; that it isn't supposed to be an ongoing creative process.

It is a problem that you produce a product and a group of judges must come and judge it. They taste the dish. They are in the position of being consumers, and things are often dished up just for them.

There are so many things that go into creating a play—the weeks that Daphne Groos worked on the piranhas in *The Artificial Jungle* to create the illusion; the lighting man and the set designer—Richard Currie and Jack Kelly—working on the tank. The amount of work that went into that alone is staggering. There doesn't seem to be much sense of what goes into costumes, or the amount of reading I do.

Salammbô was a kind of gift to the world celebrating my reading of all of Flaubert.

■

People, in any play, latch onto things that are memorable or distracting. In the case of all the beautiful male flesh in *Salammbô*, the eroticism and luxury of the production, it *was* wonderful! But I think the detractors were distracted from its real theme. They couldn't see beyond the surfaces.

I don't blame them—the surface was fantastic. But they never thought about what it might all really mean.

■

It is a narrow and limiting factor in criticism that critics are so involved in their own personal likes and dislikes, which become in print the substitute for what the play means and often distort what the artist was trying to do.

Likes or dislikes are really the least of what's going to happen at the moment. Some people like one food but they don't like another, or they have a favorite color. It's not a profound level of judgment, whether a play fits into your favorite color.

■

What the critics are really trying to say is that the plays were formerly appreciated only by the few and now are appreciated by everybody, which in some way means it's not supposed to be as good as when it was appreciated by the few. I don't happen to think that concept is true. There's nothing middle-aged about having a broad audience, as we know from popular culture—rock culture, teen stars. Menudo—they have a huge audience. So does Mick Jagger.

What I find is odd is that whatever play you're doing at the moment—even if one week ago you did something totally different—you are defined by the play you are now doing.

■

A few months ago we were doing *Salammbô*. There was a lot of moral outrage in some quarters and I was pilloried for obscenity and neofascism by some of the press.

I think it was very interesting with *Salammbô*. We had a very large number of people: we had bodybuilders, and we had Katy Dierlam, who is very fat and belongs to organizations of fat people who are prejudiced against, who are treated badly. And *she* was treated badly in the press by some people who were fat bigots! Then there were other people who said she was very courageous for what she did and that it was fantastic.

I was called a misogynist for casting her. It makes no sense. This is just catchphrases that come out of a certain paranoia.

The article in *The Village Voice*, "The Reaganization of the Ridiculous," was a piece of narcissistic criticism, because when you can't deal with your reaction to something you turn it into its opposite. The play made that critic feel a reactionary conservative. So rather than admit that she had been outclassed politically, she decided to accuse the thing that shocked, the thing that was too daring, of being conservative. Does this make sense?

■

The Village Voice is not the same *Village Voice* it was. It's a different paper. It's under different management, has a different editorial staff. You can sell a logo, but it isn't the same paper.

Critics are changed, move from one paper to another. Public opinion also changes.

■

Theatre is a little industry, this *art* industry, and people are very harsh on theatre when the theatre really needs nurturing and encouragement. I'm not saying they should write good reviews for everything that comes along, but I think they ought to keep on encouraging an involvement in the theatre, rather than discouraging it.

For instance, the TV news programs will review a play at six, seven, or ten in the evening. They are fighting for attention for something that is going on in almost the same time slot. I don't think they can truly be impartial about another medium.

This is very, very hard on the theatre. Then they play a clip of the play, which always sounds terrible. Then the critic talks over the performers, nagging and criticizing it. It's a parasitic and predatory relationship.

■

I'm not against criticism. I believe in intellectual give-and-take. But I think that it's a dangerous, difficult and perhaps impossible field. If we want it as a medium, then we have to allow it the pluralistic vision that we would want in a culture.

If we want all kinds of people of all races and creeds, we should want all kinds of plays of every stripe, variety, race and philosophy to come forth, and not limit it with irrelevant judgments. Is symmetry beauty or is symmetry stagnation and stasis? Is it better to have a symmetrical play rather than a play with a weird twist in the middle of the story that goes off, or is the twist more interesting?

Critics should not be schoolmarms. Critics should be of a philosophically turned mind and interested in seeing culture develop.

■

Some people thought my production of *The English Cat* in Santa Fe was cute; some people thought it was too cute; some people thought I avoided cuteness altogether! It dilutes the effect, reading a whole pile of reviews at once. I read one hundred fifty of them, and the gamut of opinion is unbelievable. What this proves is that you cannot rely on the press. It throws into greater relief the fact that reviews are only opinions and you've got finally to fall back on the only opinion that matters: yours!

The reviews I really don't like are the ones that don't mention me at all.

■

Critics are behind the times, ten years behind, and they rarely champion anything new.

They never erect statues of critics, you know.

Other Theatre Artists

I go to shows selectively. I can't see everything. I try to keep up with the work of my friends. I go to see Richard Foreman. I also see Stuart Sherman's pieces. I see the Hot Peaches. And the Performance Group I like very much.

There is a marvelous puppet theatre called the Little Players. They use little puppets and do serious drama. They are fabulous.

A lot of these people are my friends, so maybe I am prejudiced toward them. I try to keep up with their work.

■

You have to have your hand on the pulse of the theatrical life. There is a lot of little different things. You hear about them, you get the feeling that something exciting is happening, and you rush to see them before they are over.

■

Richard Foreman really *writes* plays. Foreman has characters, plot, dialogue. He has taken a certain approach to those things, but he hasn't eliminated any of those things altogether. He is still working in a classical form. It may be very fragmented, or it may be very minimal, but he is not a conceptual artist at all. He commits himself to producing a work of art.

193

I am very fond of Richard and Kate Manheim as people too, but I think that they are doing very interesting work.

Foreman is very comical, valid in comedy, too. I don't think that Foreman and I are doing opposite things. He is just involved in something else. He made certain discoveries—he discovered a vein of ore—and he is continuing to mine out this field.

I don't see it as opposing my work, particularly. The only thing I have in *common* with Richard Foreman is we both have uncomfortable seats.

■

Robert Wilson I think is interesting, always interesting, although *here* the plot has been eliminated. This isn't *drama* anymore. This is a different field. He is doing *theatre*, but it's not a *dramatic form*. It's somewhere between pantomime and modern dance.

That's not what I do.

■

The Living Theatre were always considered desperadoes, really never got critical support. Even for their triumphant return in '68, the major press was very critical and skeptical of it. That's part of their stance as artists. They're very great, a very great influence on myself.

In the case of their booking at the Joyce: I saw three of the productions. I thought they were superb. Their production of *The Yellow Methuselah* was *brilliant*, unbelievably great.

We always say in the theatre, "Maybe it was the wrong theatre." You always sense there might have been some way to get it to a wider audience, in a different way.

When something is truly avant-garde, the sure sign that it's avant-garde is that people don't approve of it or don't like it. If something is established and accepted as avant-garde it's pretty much finished. Of the pieces the Living Theatre did, the one that was least approved of—*The Yellow Methuselah*—was the real one. That opened a door to a future way of working.

There is a human quality in what they're doing. You're really dealing with human beings who have not armored themselves and protected themselves in the way that a certain kind of slick professionals do. Most of the rest of the theatre world is bourgeois—kind of middlebrow; not too brainy and not too stupid.

Broadway

Sometimes I think I want to model my career on Ibsen's master builder. Somewhere in the play he says he first built public buildings, then homes for people and finally castles in the air. In many ways that's me, and I know you can't survive on Broadway with a philosophy like that.

What's wrong is that Broadway is not the pinnacle of achievement that it should be. It should be something that you *long* for, that you should want to be on. We all should want this, because it represents achievement and accomplishment and is a fair measure of our talents. Unfortunately, it is not that.

But there *should* be a wonderful place where you're crowned with laurels if you achieve something in art. That's not good enough in the commercial theatre. It has to be an idea you're sure you can sell, and sell a lot.

Besides, I can't abide the waiting in the decision process on Broadway. Between the time one of my plays was optioned, cast and finally dropped uptown a few years ago, I finished three different productions down here. The pleasure of doing it fades when it takes so long.

Down here I do everything with a minimum of money, time and people. Broadway annoys me because it is too *slow*. They want to sit around and talk about it forever. They have got to raise the money, they have got to do this and that. By the time it's on it's such an *impersonal* thing. It reminds me of some incredible high school, something that is very clean, very neat, very impersonal.

Rare artists are able to transcend that, and get a bunch of their friends in, and do a play with people they know. But usually it just becomes very cold.

Then the actors leave immediately after the play opens, as soon as they get another job. So the people you have worked with change. And you lose something.

■

A friend of mine did a play on Broadway. He had a set with a metal sheet and on the opening night there were fingerprints all over it. He wanted to go out with a rag and just polish it—fifteen minutes before the curtain went up—because he realized that it had these marks on it and he wanted it to look like a mirror.

The stagehands union would not allow him to go out and do that. And the stagehands wouldn't do it, because it wasn't in their contract.

In order to get anything done with their union, everything has to be planned in advance; everything that they are going to be asked to do has to be in their contract. You can't say: I'm going to have to move that six feet left. . . . They won't do it. They won't change the lighting if you get a sudden inspiration when you are working on Broadway. You can't say: I like it brighter; the lighting on the left should be brighter; take this light back and just put it on the floor, it will be great. . . . No, you can't do that. You have to plan everything months in advance. It tends to lead to very academic-looking works.

Unions regiment the working process to a great extent, so that any kind of fervor is boxed in. They don't really allow for self-sacrifice. It's a terrible thing to say, but if you feel like working extra hours . . .

It would cost them a million dollars a minute to work my way on Broadway. We couldn't do it.

■

On Broadway, they are terribly serious and, I find, moralistic. When I'm talking to a producer, he wants to say something. He wants the audience to leave saying . . . hmmm. That's completely off-the-wall. That means a prefabricated message. That's a commercial requirement.

Comedy is more intellectual than drama. On Broadway they induce tragedy in order to elicit sympathy that blinds the audience emotionally—present a hero who's handicapped, for instance. That's not good for discussion.

The moral tag at the end is, I think, very immoral. It's a cover-up for no real moral feeling.

∎

My theatre is supported by contribution. It's given outright as long as I produce the work of art I say I'm going to produce.

On Broadway, they not only want the work of art, they want to make money back. So they're nervous, and that nervousness does not lend itself to prankishness.

Every work of art has to have some element of the prank in it, a little bit of the hoax. I think a certain negligence in the way things end up in a comedy is not only a sign of real courage, but also true art.

∎

They all want me to write something for Broadway, then produce it down here. Then if it's a hit, they'll take it to Broadway. Fuck that.

I only recently saw that I'm their competition. When people look at the Sunday *Times* they have to decide whether to go to a Shubert show—or me. I think they like me.

When they drop the ball, people go looking for it. As long as they're bad, I'll be pulling them in.

∎

Broadway thinking is based on "machinery" that is so heavy! It's like this big rock (aaarghh) that doesn't want to (rrrghhh) move. Whereas I can do whatever I want in my own theatre.

I want a big commercial success, I do. It's very hard for an artist to make a living. I just wonder if at a certain point we'll have to charge a hundred dollars per ticket. Broadway, with so many more seats, charges so much more than we do. According to supply and demand, they should be charging less.

■

A Broadway show is a one-time thing. It's not a major life decision. You rehearse for four weeks, put it on and then go home. If I did something like that it might infuse some new light.

Some new ideas wouldn't be bad. Broadway is not doing very well.

On Broadway there is a tremendous amount of money at stake and that makes everybody cautious. They tend to do shows which are tried-and-true. Tried-and-true is usually something that was an experiment a few years ago, a fluke that worked. Then they all imitate it, but people get tired of plays that look the same.

And no matter where you still go in the commercial theatre, there's a tendency to exhibit what I call admirable behavior. Everybody wants to be admired there. But why not? Nobody pays to see something they hear they may not like.

As for big Broadway shows, I think pure spectacle is great, but once you see the MGM Grand show in Las Vegas, nothing else ever seems quite up to it. It must be the closest thing to a Roman circus that ever existed in our period.

Once you see it taken to that limit, that extreme, you begin to want to go back to your basic human situation. Then if you can find theatrical devices that are purely theatrical, that are incredibly entertaining, that enhance the scene, or in some way illuminate it, they become very appropriate. But if they exist just for their own sake, I think they're very hollow, and I don't find them that entertaining.

■

More and more people are asking me to do things on Broadway, which may mean that they are coming to see it my way. I could see myself working on Broadway. It's just a venue. I don't think of it as a philosophy—Broadway is just a way of producing something.

Broadway is not a monopoly, but there really are basically two organizations that operate most of the theatres, and they exercise strict quality-control over what goes into their theatres, so there isn't enough competition. If those theatres were individually owned—as they were in the great days: Belasco had his own theatre, and the Lunts; different actor-managers and different companies, all operating separate theatres, competing like mad for the audience—they would all be coming up with more and more fresh ideas—novelties—trying things in order to lure the audience. But where a few people own all the theatres, it tends to become monochromatic.

When things go wrong in theatre, there are always many good reasons for it. Ultimately what we have to fight is the good reasons. It's the reasons that are the enemy, because they're very hard to argue with: perfectly good, sound reasons why the thing isn't going to be the way it should be.

■

It's so funny when people say, "Oh, your theatre's a cult," when it's Broadway that's a cult. It appeals to a very small stratum. Broadway appeals to a middle-class audience that wants to go and hear about husbands and wives who work out their infidelities, which is pretty dull.

My theatre's about the universal destiny of man, why we're here, what's it all about. What do we feel. What are our aspirations. It's theatre about heroes.

I have a special goal in theatre, and it's not *Cats*.

Opera

Opera isn't an obsession. It's a fabulous artform, though. Opera is the artform of the eighties—the passion and the grandeur.

Of artforms, I would say opera is the height of civilization because it requires the cooperation of so many people to bring it together. The more people who are involved, cooperating toward the achievement of one vision, the more civilized the thing really is. That's what I love about drama, and of course with opera you also have the musical elements.

I would like to work on the staging of opera because I feel there is more there than is being gotten out of the material. I'm able to make the grand style living and real and true, so I'm appropriate for opera because of its uniquely grand style of acting.

Attempts to modernize opera and to produce so-called "good acting" are usually attempts to water the opera down to a kind of realism. As in Peter Brook's *Carmen*—it's really like Actors Studio; not even as interesting as Actors Studio. It's a Protestant version of *Carmen*. Instead of wearing a red dress and having roses in her teeth, and blood, you have a very tasteful navy-blue dress and no rose and no makeup and very toned-down acting.

In the lobby a whole bunch of people came to me and said, "Oh, you should play Carmen," and I said, "I would wear a great dress and have a rose in my teeth, and she doesn't."

Mine would be that: more Carmen than *Carmen*. But that would be the final blow, beating the poor girl to death.

Spike Jones had a version set in a bubblegum factory. But, no . . . I would need a cigarette.

■

I like the absurdities in operas.

When I saw Tebaldi sing *Tosca* at the old Met, she and Scarpia were gigantically fat. He was chasing her around the room, and when she went to throw herself off the parapet, she stepped behind a flat and screamed, and you could see her hand coming out, pulling her gown after her.

It's so delicious.

Or *Lucia* with Sutherland. She comes down to the wedding guests covered in blood, carrying a dagger—and the guests don't bat an eye. They are perfectly polite, eating.

■

Opera performances are very generalized. They go for a basic attitude toward the character, rather than imply the character from a lot of specific actions that add up to something.

I don't think they need to be. But I'm not one of those wretched reformers intent on destroying everything that makes opera great: its grandeur, its passion, its shameless theatricality.

■

A lot of the things that I do have been influenced by opera. It's time for opera to be influenced by me.

I think everyone in the opera world must have seen *Galas*. After *Galas* the offers came pouring in.

There were offers before that: one from St. Louis, another from Long Beach. But they came at the last minute, and I was involved in other projects of my own that I couldn't abandon. I was going to do *La Grande Duchesse* at Long Beach, but I couldn't fit it in. Then there was an Offenbach at the Washington Opera I couldn't do.

John Crosby's offer to direct at the Santa Fe Opera came at the right time. I had lots of notice, two years ahead.

Crosby is a visionary. He has to be, to create an opera company in the desert! And with such daring repertory.

■

When I arrived in Santa Fe, I heard the town was mad at the opera company. Apparently Henze's opera the year before was so disliked by the merchants that they were afraid the Santa Fe Opera would ruin the tourist trade.

I went around and talked to the merchants. There was a lot of pressure on the theatre not to do any more Henze, but Crosby is one of the few who remain dedicated to new works.

■

I have directed two operas—actually one of them was an operetta, the *Fledermaus*, and one was *Die Englische Katze.*

Do you know that one? It is by Hans Werner Henze, the contemporary German, and that was very interesting. At first I felt that *The English Cat* was too misanthropic, but by the time we were finished in Santa Fe, I had come to love the work.

Crosby asked me to adapt *Die Fledermaus.* I didn't change the lyrics, just rewrote the dialogue to tighten it and make it spicy, more sophisticated and delicious. Acts I and III were streamlined. The characters were more vivid and had a reality for the modern listener.

The *Fledermaus* designs were marvelous. They were updated nineties—enlightened and modern, evoking the period but not slavish to it, somewhat like Cecil Beaton. They did not look moldy.

■

I approach opera much as I would a play. But creating an opera, dealing with hundreds of people, there are constraints that I have to accept.

I've done a lot of summer stock, where you are working so fast and the rehearsal time is so little that you are forced to turn to conventional solutions. Every actor must have them in his bag of tricks. But at Santa

Fe we had plenty of time—four weeks—to work out something *un*conventional, something simple, with the ring of truth about it.

I expected more acting from the singers than they were used to. I expected a high standard of acting. Henze's music itself is difficult, and some singers probably felt that conquering it was enough—but eventually they found that the staging helped the singing and made the music more understandable.

The opera was well cast. Everyone was just right for his or her part, and that made it easier. Inga Nielsen, who played Minette, knew the ropes, because she had played the role twice in Europe. She contributed a great deal of expertise to her role. Then Scott Reeve, who played Tom the alley cat, was really wonderful. At one point I wanted him to jump over Minette, who was in a sack, and I felt sure he wouldn't do it, but he did. The effect was like an animated cartoon. Henze came to our rehearsals and saw the commedia dell'arte style I was using and approved.

The composer spent most of his time with the singers, the musicians and the conductor, George Manahan, working on the music—the singers couldn't get the hint of a pitch from the orchestral score. But Henze did help me with his support, particularly when I wanted less movement onstage to allow the music full sway. I don't like busy opera staging.

He seemed to have set to music every thought he had for these characters. Some of the singers suggested we have a pantomime during a night scene on the roof, when there were no lyrics, but Henze agreed with me there should be no people onstage during the postlude—just let the stars and the moon have the stage, along with his music. That created great suspense.

There's a beautiful duet between Minette and her sister Babette in which the two—one rich and the other poor—sing of their different lives while standing with their backs to each other. At the end there is a lot of music. A singer might want to fill that with generalities or conventional stage actions. I didn't want that. I had them stand perfectly still, listening to the music. It was hypnotic. Then, at the last moment, the two women turned and embraced quickly. It was electric.

A movement is not an action. Action must display a will being expressed. You can wander all over the stage, but there can still be no action.

Take the recent Met production of Handel's *Samson*. There you have evidence of movement with no purpose. In fact the movement is a distraction from the beauty of the music. The flicking of fans and the dancing were not needed.

■

What you often get in the larger setting of grand opera is an averaging out of quality. So many are involved in collaboration on a grand opera that it begins to lack a point of view. The number of people who have to agree militates against a fresh or new approach. The best is pulled down, and the mediocre is brought up, and what you get are productions in black and white and beige.

There's a tendency today in all the opera houses to want to go with neutral colors. They're not called neutral for nothing, you know.

I'm a *fauve*—a wild beast, like in painting. Fauvists were wild in their use of color.

■

My talent is not toward static pageantry. I'm interested in shock and countershock. These don't come up in minimalist music.

Minimalism seems to me to be influenced by exotic, Oriental music. It attempts to avoid conflict and restore harmony. To me, drama is about conflict.

I'm not against the music of the trance. Much of it is beautiful in its way, but it's not right for me. I'm a "warrior artist," not a pacifist in the world of ideas. That is the proper battleground, and drama is about that, and musical drama is particularly about that.

How could you express the conflicts in *Tosca*, or the events of the Nazi era, or a repressive political regime, with minimalist music? It has beauty, but beauty is suspect—it is often granted without effort or right, and is seldom earned.

■

People think of me to direct comic operas, but I think I would be good at tragedy. I ought to direct *La Traviata*, having played Camille so many times. I would be good at tragedy, since it is comedy with another face.

Otello is the same plot as a French bedroom farce—husband mistakenly thinks wife is committing adultery. One ends in disaster, the other in laughing at people's foibles. The basic human situation is the same. Both are deeply tragic in their way.

What could be more tragic than the Count making love to his disguised wife in *The Marriage of Figaro*, as he woos her like a lover? Perhaps some company will ask me to do that.

■

Verdi and Wagner are both great. They are, in a way, polar opposites. I would love to stage *Falstaff*. I have done a parody of the *Ring*.

Verdi wrote a lot of stiff political things, but Wagner also erred in this direction. Sometimes in the Verdi there is a lot of flag-waving patriotism I can't relate to. In Wagner, too—that's why I can't stand it.

It's the nineteenth century. It's where they were politically. They were in upheaval, and they were trying to unify. It has always been a problem in Europe with all those different factions, all those different nations fighting and killing each other. It was really a mess.

It might be easier to stage Wagner because it is only one gesture per hour—it just goes on and on, and then the singer makes one gesture. With Verdi there is more complex action, because a Verdi is more psychological. You need a more realistic stage action in Verdi than you do in Wagner. It requires a lot more motivation. Verdi would be probably more interesting to stage. Wagner tends to add static stage action.

But, as I said, I'd love to do *Falstaff*, I'd love to do *La Traviata*, and what I'd really love to do is Weber. I'd love to do his *Oberon*, because it needs a new libretto all the time. The libretto doesn't make much sense.

There is so much beautiful music there to be challenged to, but then I don't think it should be a *songspiel*. It's jarring when they speak and when they sing. It's very hard to unify that.

I think we did it in *Fledermaus*, but it's such a funny piece, and I did my own adaptation. This is a difficult aesthetic problem.

■

In the opera experiences I have had, I was interpreting existing work and had to lend myself and my imagination in service of bringing it to life. At the Ridiculous Theatrical Company, I create the whole work, so it's more exciting, because I can change anything. There is always a limit when you work with a classic. You can change, but there are more limitations.

I find it very creative anyway. But in classic work, it has been done so many times that there are certain paths through it, everyone has discovered it. No matter what you think of, someone did it before.

Here I go on living with the play. After it's created I can still change it, I can make a discovery. It's not frozen, so it can get better; whereas in opera, once you've staged it it goes on for whatever time, but you can't really keep changing it.

■

The opera world, and Broadway for that matter, lack entrepreneurs who are willing to take risks. We need new operas, new commissions. No opera season should be complete without a new work.

Let the living create operas! They should be hired and forced to meet the deadline. Don't be afraid to disappoint anyone.

I've thought of commissioning an opera for my theatre. I've got an idea for it, which I cannot tell.

■

There has been some talk about my creating an opera with Peter Golub, who is our composer. With him I could create an original opera and then, perhaps, I could play with it more.

Peter Golub and I have already done one twenty-minute opera, *The Production of Mysteries*, an excerpt from my play *Houdini*, but I think we should do a full-length opera for an intimate setting.

The most exciting part of it is doing opera without singers: the idea of the popular, untrained voice. I also like what a trained voice can do; it's sheer delight to hear those sounds. But the audience loves it when *we* sing.

Film

I've always been very interested in film, very involved in it. It has a tremendous influence on my theatre work. Many of the great masters of stagecraft went into film, especially in the early days of film, where they were drawing on the theatre.

You see in early films what the stage acting was. You see how fantastic it was, its expressive possibilities and the prowess of those actors. It's just extraordinary.

I've always used film as a way to study the theatre of the past.

∎

I always wanted to make movies. I had always kept a list of possible movie scenarios with my puppets. I always saw cinema as a kind of puppetry.

I made two little films early on, a version of *The Bacchae* and a soft-core takeoff of porno films, a garter-and-stocking kind of thing. I can never allow that film to be shown. A lot of famous people are in it.

I like being in other people's movies when they have the responsibility and I just act. But if I could make movies my way it might be interesting. I just wonder whether my way isn't too slow: without money.

∎

Mark Rappaport sent me the script to *Impostors*. I thought it was a superb piece of writing and I wanted to do it. He wrote the role for me. He saw something about my acting, was sensitive to an aspect of it that I had not seen too many people be that clear about, which is the ability to slip in and out of characters and make an amalgamation of a character out of pieces of other characters and impressions.

Because this character was a vaudevillian and a kind of a schizophrenic, he slipped in and out of personalities. This made a fascinating thing to play. I really enjoyed it immensely.

■

Then a patron of my theatre gave me a box of 16-millimeter equipment which I didn't even understand at the time. Now I realize it had everything you need to make movies.

I decided to make a film. *The Sorrows of Dolores* is like the *Perils of Pauline* or *The Creeping Hand*, starring Everett Quinton as Dolores. As in *Exquisite Torture*, he performs his role in drag.

Dolores goes through all kinds of adventures and traumas and hell. Everyone does terrible things to her. She's the heroine.

Since it's very episodic, I just exploit things. I was at the San Gennaro festival, and there was this incredible act in a tent where a girl turned into a gorilla. Outside the tent there was a banner with a giant, hand-painted gorilla face and a three-shot panel with a girl, a half girl/half gorilla, and the final gorilla. I had to have that in the movie.

Dolores goes in to see the magic trick. They let me film the outside of it and I used a double for Dolores. Then we built the inside of the tent on a set and filmed the rest of it.

One day it was snowing, so I woke people up and said, "It's snowing! We have to do the snow sequence!"

Taking advantage of the Ridiculous Theatrical Company's tour schedules, we've been able to shoot scenes on both coasts, in snow, in jungles and so on. A *major* motion picture.

We shot the fortuneteller scene at a friend's storefront in SoHo. My friend studied real gypsy storefronts, painted a most convincing palmist's sign, and decorated the window with religious statues from my collection. My friend created such an authentic-looking set that the people on the block got extremely upset: they thought gypsies were moving into the neighborhood.

I'm always with Everett anyway, and we were able to take the camera and the wig and the costume wherever we traveled and create episodes whenever anything was very interesting, exploiting—the way they did in the days of Mack Sennett—a fair or an auto race or a snowstorm. Ev would say, "Oh! Let's think of an idea for an episode that would go with that event!"

Movies are involved with time, like theatre is, but the relationship is different. In my film there are no unities. You can be in New York, go through a door, and come out on the other side of the world.

Obviously you can use more people in a film than you can in a stage company, which is the real appeal for me. I can have actors who couldn't commit themselves to performing all the time, who could make a guest appearance in the film and the performance is there forever. So *The Sorrows of Dolores* has many, many stars in it, lots of performers doing cameos, people whom Dolores meets along the way. There's a lot of brilliant acting.

There isn't really a cohesive plot except that Dolores goes from pillar to post, from one sorrow to another and one peril to the next, without much reason behind it. But you realize after a while that it begins to take on a life of its own.

The whole thing is quite a learning experience. The first day, the scenery was ready and the actors were in costume, and I had to figure out how to load the camera.

I felt I had no right to direct a film until I knew the technical stuff. Instead of announcing I wanted to be a film director, I approached it through the camera.

There's no such thing as Santa Claus (don't print that!) and nobody is going to come down your chimney with the technical knowledge you need.

Gradually, I've been embroidering on the story. I keep thinking of more ideas. The film could go on forever.

■

I like working at movies. It's great because I can fix something. And the actor doesn't have to repeat it. You record it and then you go on to something else.

But film isn't alive. *Theatre* is alive. With the film you are creating an object, and once you do it you have done with it. While the theatre requires nurture and continuous growth and daily development. That's why film actors don't stay as healthy.

I rehearse a film scene very roughly. When you are working in a film—in the film I am making now—you are usually working with a fragment of acting, a brief scene or a part of that scene.

You are working with the fragments of an action, so you don't need practice to sustain it. You can try several ways. When working before an audience, you have got to be perfect.

■

I have a number of film ideas. The way my career evolved on stage, I perfected the mechanism for doing plays. The mechanism for doing films is *not* perfected. All my energy goes into the theatre. I have to steal time for film.

If I'm working on a stage project, usually there's some rivalry with film. The film is in some way taking my attention away from the theatre. That's why I think the episodic quality is very good for *The Sorrows of Dolores.*

■

My outfit—Shadowgraph Photoplays—is basically a silent-movie company. We learned a lot as we were making the movie, and since we've been working on it over a period of years, I can tell where we've gotten more mastery of the technique. In the course of the film it washes out because the film isn't really in the sequence that we shot it. I don't think you can tell that in that scene we knew less, but *we* know.

Everett began to know the camera *so* well! I was behind the camera, as a cameraman, but Everett knew so much about the scale of the frame and the gesture after a while that he could say to me, "Not with that lens!" It became an interesting collaboration, working intensively with one other person.

It's really an underground movie. It's very simple. It's very home-made. But we use fabulous locations, and the ideas carry it, as they did in early silent movies. The idea of the action is what's really critical.

I'd love to show *The Sorrows of Dolores* in the Ridiculous Company's theatre at One Sheridan Square. It is in a rough-cut version now, so I'm involved in fine cut. It's been a pet project that we do on the side. One of the reasons that it has so many fabulous production values is that we did take all these years, and so much work went into each scene. But again, every time a play comes up I have to put that aside.

The filming has been going on for about eight years now. It's an art-house piece, and people who have seen the rough cut feel it's very good in what it does.

I'm working on the script for another one, a horror film based on the classic French surrealists' stuff.

■

The other one is a horror movie that we shot in the wax museum of Coney Island for a benefit for Lillie Santangelo, who had been running that wax museum since 1929. *Museum of Wax* was shot in about three or four days. I tried to use everything I knew from *The Sorrows of Dolores* to do it quickly and efficiently.

Museum of Wax is much more controlled. It was shot in a very short span of time, so the overall concept is very unified.

■

I find that I've bogged down on the postproduction, because what I'm good at is shooting and creating the thing. But the postproduction parts, the mechanical stuff—making soundtracks and editing—is not as interesting for me. It's fascinating, but I'm better at diving in, being on the location and marshaling the forces, which is the theatrical part of it.

■

I thought of an interesting movie. It would be very long and we would all be driving. People would drive for twenty minutes, stop the car at the house, have a brief scene, then get back into the car and drive and drive and drive. It would be just driving.

That's what Hollywood movies look like to me. They are all in cars all the time. I think this is very odd, not having a car myself. It all seems very bizarre.

∎

I would like to gradually have my film studio expanded to a major enterprise. I want them to be very high-quality movies. My plays are influenced by films more than they are by plays, so it seems making movies is logical, inevitable. I think it will help to expand the audience, because films can be sent out.

I'll continue to work with theatre, of course, but I want to make movies all the time.

Television

I love radio. I love TV too—it's the feeling of the twentieth century. It's the twenty-first century, because it's a cross between communication and an artform. It's like the telephone. *That* could be an artform—imagine!

I laugh at some things on TV. There's a lot of horsing around that is considered humor. They don't set up enough premises to make the whole thing credible. It takes the sting out of humor, or the bite or the real zap.

For that reason I don't think it's on the high level of comedy or satire. It is usually broad buffooning, a cross between buffoonery and horsing around which is really a degenerate form of slapstick, mixed with the idea of the epigram, which came from the Restoration. So critics want funny lines. They're not willing—they don't have the perspective—to see that it is the situation that is humorous, the way that events are falling out.

We're more like farceurs. We're involved in improbable situations which build and mount with many reversals and counter-shots of action, people caught in embarrassing situations, things that reflect on what it's like to be alive today in this social milieu.

∎

I don't think theatre is in a degenerative stage. I think we're at a stage of regeneration.

Theatre is a handcrafted article. Television is a mass-produced item. It's like the difference between having real cotton or rayon acetate on your body.

In all the great ages of theatre, theatre was special, an occasion, and it still has that quality. People are disturbed by it because they want it to compete with mass media—they want to make it *less* an occasion. They want people to go to the theatre much much more than they do.

I don't think that makes sense. You don't go to the theatre every night like you turn on the TV. You go to the theatre on rare occasions. You get dressed, you go out and have dinner, it's a whole big deal.

The habit of theatregoing is good, but the idea that there should be tons of repertory, with everybody going to the theatre every day—I just don't think it makes sense in a life. How often can you go out in that way, unless you're really a leisured person?

In that way theatre is aristocratic. It can be popular in its appeal, but even in Shakespeare's day, when the theatre was very popular, there was a whole movement—a lobby—to close the theatres. Theatre played in the afternoon then because there was no electric light—it was played out in the daylight—and people were leaving their jobs, closing their shops to go to the theatre. It was considered a threat to the economic well-being of London.

■

What TV has done, in order to make something possible that they can do day in and day out and that you would turn on and watch day after day, is take away the feeling of a satisfying experience.

When you go to the theatre and it's a good play, it should be enough to hold you for a while. You shouldn't have to go to a play the next day or feel that you have to see two plays that night the way it is with TV, where you have to watch program after program after program.

It's built into the form of television that there is something unresolved about the experience, so that even if it's funny—or whatever it is—you feel you have to watch more of it. It keeps making you want more and more. It's like cigarette smoking or nonnutritional food—you keep needing it. Whereas theatre at its highest should be so satisfying that you've had a total fulfillment from that experience.

It's that quality of theatre right now that's at odds with capitalist society, because what we always run into as a problem with theatre is merchandising, the economics of it: how to get the audience to come; will they come back again and again; how do we get the kind of economic support we need? If we do our job as a theatre and satisfy their need, we kill off our public.

If we really satisfy them they say, "I *saw* a play, and I don't want to see another play for six months!" Then we're starving ourselves. This is why theatre has to be subsidized and *should* be subsidized.

It develops taste in people. When it's good theatre, it's an antidote to vulgarity, it develops the audience's sensibilities, makes them better people.

TV deteriorates the mind, shortens the attention span, gives you less and less a wholeness of thinking that a problem is presented, worked out, concluded and solved in some way for you. TV doesn't want to solve anything, it wants to keep you hooked.

Theatre should be subsidized, and the way to subsidize it is dollar per dollar. The government should match the box office.

■

The most hideous effect of TV is that it induces passivity in the viewer. The theatre demands activity. It demands that you laugh, that you applaud, that you boo and hiss, that you get up and go to the damned thing, that you leave, that you go out during the intermission and smoke, that you buy a drink.

TV makes people passive. You can tell when you play to an audience that is dominated by TV. TV laughs for you—canned laughter. It's disturbing for the performer.

One night we did a performance of *Hot Ice* and there weren't laughs—this was extraordinary. We'd been getting audiences that were roaring with laughter and suddenly there was an audience that wasn't laughing. I looked at them and they were holding in their laughter. They were smiling and covering their mouths with their hands.

■

No one's ever asked me to do TV. John Belushi did ask me to direct the last Lampoon show just before they became "Saturday Night Live." That wasn't really a TV offer, it was Off Broadway.

The Theatre of the Ridiculous can't fit into "Saturday Night Live" because that show functions in five-minute segments. The idea of sustaining a thought, a theme, for longer than three or four minutes is out of the realm of "Saturday Night Live." They could not sustain a two-and-a-half-hour show. In fact, the whole show is not as long as one act of one of my plays.

When they're willing to give me a two-and-a-half-hour slot every week to do another play. . . . But I can't really be on "Saturday Night Live" because I'm *live* onstage every Saturday night. You can't be two places at once. I could be on tape, canned, but if you are committed to legitimate theatre, then on Saturday night there's only one place you're alive, and for me that's onstage.

■

Television is a different matter. I'm too wild. TV isn't ready.

A perfect example is the "Gong Show." A dandy idea: each act is more outrageously demented than the other, and you have people who gong them.

The failure of the "Gong Show" is that the worst act doesn't win. They always have one really sappy person come out and sing a heart-rending ballad—straight. *They* would win. The person with the paper bag over his head or the woman with one breast out or the transvestite—whatever—would lose.

What is the new vision here? An incredibly great gospel singer comes out. Everybody already agrees that that's what's established as being great and moving and important in life. I think what is worthless should win.

What I pose is an anarchist threat to what we suppose has value. That's the reason they don't have me on television. Because I threaten values. That's my taste.

I'm really outraged when the good and the warm and the sentimental and the meaningful and the right-headed and the reassuring
win. *That* should be gonged.

The woman who's eating the chicken's foot while the chicken is
still alive should win the contest. That's a Gong Show!

■

Madeline Kahn came to see *Galas* and said she thought we'd have the
right chemistry together on "Oh, Madeline." I played a romance writer
who's a cross between Joan Collins and Barbara Cartland, but I was a
much more modern and foxy type. Actually, I was a man who, in order
to be taken seriously as a romance writer, lives in drag.

I looked unbelievably good in it. I wore twenty thousand dollars'
worth of fox furs.

They really played dolly with me. Of course *I* taught them little
drag tricks, like filling the brassiere with birdseed to give it the movement of a real breast.

■

"Miami Vice" was fun, but I was also directing at the Santa Fe Opera at
the time and I had had a tech the night before.

Originally the producers of "Vice" were supposed to shoot New
York people who were *hot* at the moment, and they wanted us—Everett
and me—to do a guest-star appearance. They were supposed to shoot it
in New York, but they never got to it. They went over schedule. By
then, I thought it was all over, so I took off for Santa Fe to direct *The
English Cat*.

Anyway, I was up all night with this opera tech, which was over at
2:30 am, and I had been up very early that morning. Then we had to be
driven to Albuquerque—an hour and a half away—for a 5:30 flight into
Miami through Dallas, which got us into Miami at 12:30 pm.

By the time we did this "Miami Vice" thing, Everett and I had
been up almost forty-eight hours. Then they didn't have our costumes
ready, so we had to go out with the designer and shop and find
appropriate outfits. Suddenly the Teamsters went on strike and this

location they wanted for the nightclub scene couldn't be used, so they had to build a complete set from scratch. We didn't really start shooting until about 7:30 at night.

When we got on the set, they said, "Let's rehearse." I said, "Rehearse what?" They shouted, "You mean no one gave you a script?" I said, "No!"

They're on a very high-pressure kind of schedule, with a lot of people all hyped up into hysterics.

They finally got us some scripts. We were so zonked and bleary-eyed! However, Everett and I are quick studies, so it wasn't too bad. It wasn't a very long scene, anyway.

Later, we went out and ate in an incredibly expensive Cuban restaurant. At long last we collapsed in bed in the hotel. At six in the morning, there was a car to take us to the airport, and we flew back to Santa Fe. That afternoon, I was back at the opera rehearsal.

So "Miami Vice" had a dreamlike quality as an experience for me. It all seems like a hallucination now.

■

I resist videotape in a way, but I think it's really a great medium. I would like to do something for videotape, I suppose.

One would have to sign away too many years of one's life to do a series. But then, I hope nobody offers me one, because I might not have the moral strength to refuse!

The Avant-Garde

I hate minimal art. I hate conceptual art. I am for *execution*. I am for *maximal* art. Minimal art is inflationary art: less for your money.

Minimalism takes inflation to its logical conclusion in art. You just get the *idea*, you don't get any *execution*. It is not embodiment.

Art is for the body. It has a soul but it has also a body. Playscript is its soul, but its physical production is its body. It seems to me that minimal artists are a terrible bankruptcy.

I am a modernist. But I am a virtuoso. I believe in the whole panoply of creativity. Minimal artists are afraid of that. They are afraid of making decisions and choices.

They don't want to be in their art. They don't want their own taste to be part of it. They don't want it.

I am considered avant-garde but I don't consider myself avant-garde. The avant-garde is ahead of its times and I am of my time, of the perfect moment.

■

Take a great modernist writer like James Joyce—*Finnegans Wake*. The man walked through the door. He opened the door for all of us. Very few people have dared to pass through it. Was he just a madman, crazy, self-indulgent? Beckett, who was his secretary, looked through the door at this maze, this labyrinth, turned tail and *fled* into minimalism. He put his tail between his legs.

You have to surpass your teacher or you're a failure, we all know that. So if you can't surpass your teacher, beat him at his own game, you've got to change the rules of the game.

For Beckett it became some question of minimalism. Joyce himself wrote a play and he did it like Ibsen, but more restrained, much more simple. He didn't believe that what he did in *Finnegans Wake* applied to the drama.

We are ready for a major onslaught on the language of the theatre. Shakespeare did it. He had a new language, a newly fused language. He invented a couple of ideas, knew euphuism, from Marlowe he got a nice, handy verse structure, and he went at it. He took commedia scenarios and started ranting and raving with this new language. That's what I would like to be. I would like to take classical structures and take that step into something maximal.

What happens with someone like Beckett is he leaves me nowhere to go. I can admire his art some, but I can't do anything with it. He went all the way. He made it as little as it could be. I can't do any less. Certain people have—look at my contemporaries. People my own age have done plays that have even less or as little as Beckett.

Paul Foster did a play called *Balls*—two balls swinging back and forth on stage with whispered dialogue. As an actor, where does it leave you? What do you do? You do Beckett and then you run to earlier works when you want to play a part, when you want to do something a little more complex?

Basically the catch phrase for my movement would be "virtuoso maximalism," enemy of minimalism.

■

I have a story to tell. And storytelling is universal, a universal function of the theatre. Everyone can understand that aspect of the theatre. They come to this story. If I tell it in a different way, that is just more delightful.

The avant-garde has trouble communicating. When they have no plot, people can't understand what is going on, which is their limit.

The avant-garde is wrong and the audience is right. The audience is supposed to know what is going on. If artists fail to communicate, it's their fault, not the audience's.

■

I believe that every day is an experimental process of change. But there is a difference between experimentation and creating a style, a synthetic style.

Every artist has the right to do what he wants. I have my own view of how it should be done. It's not a question of whether it is avant-garde or not. It's a question of what the work is. If it's getting rid of something, then I don't think it's a very interesting experiment. If it's finding something or discovering something appropriate to the subject matter, then I think it's valid.

Many Americans don't know what it means to be truly *avant-garde*. They look at what the European modernists were doing in the early twentieth century, such as Artaud's theatre with its emphasis on the irrational and its orgiastic screams, and they conclude that anything that's done in that style today is *avant-garde*. They're wrong, for *avant-garde* and experimental theatre must, by definition, be *new*.

■

Paintings begin to look alike in most galleries. They cater to people's need for the mass-produced, the reassurance you have when you go to a grocery store and you see a brand name.

All of a painter's works today are supposed to look alike. This to me is insane tyranny. It is absolutely sterile, and that is more of a crisis to me than the problem of diversity. Artists should dare to have an edge, to put one color against another in a bold way.

There's a kind of artist who likes to blur the edges, softening, softening. I think sometimes actors do that. They think if they're less definitive they can't be faulted for being definitely this or definitely that.

That weakens individuality, and character is about individuality, what's striking, strikingly unique, the personal quirk.

■

I feel that the whole concept of originality is spurious anyway. Everything new isn't necessarily better.

Camp

Camp has a number of different origins. It's a slang term. I think it originated in the theatre as an actor's word for another actor who was carrying on in excess of a role or who may have been overdoing it just enough to make a sly comment. Sometimes camping is just taking a hopeless piece of drivel, something terribly serious, and playing it for laughs to save it.

Camp had a homosexual usage that came from a special view of things. Proust explains it very clearly. In the C. K. Scott-Moncrieff translation, *Remembrance of Things Past*, there's a long section where Proust describes camp as an outsider's view of things other people take totally for granted. Because of the inversion, everything that everyone else has taken for granted isn't true for you. Suddenly things become funny because you're seeing it as through a mirror, a reverse image. Camp became a sly or secret sense of humor that could only exist to a group that had been through something together; in this case, the gay world.

Then it became popularly known as a word and, as it left the theatre and the homosexual underground, it started to take on a popular meaning. It gained a bad reputation, mainly because it had been hanging out with all those homosexuals, who had a bad reputation anyway.

In the hands of the critics who wanted to define it and tie it down, it started to become very special things. Susan Sontag really did a number on camp by saying it was specific things—a Tiffany lampshade is camp, a Ronald Firbank novel is camp, a Hollywood movie with a Busby Berkeley number in it is camp.

What's wrong with that is camp ceases to be an attitude toward something and loses all of its relativity. It nails it to the wall and makes it very literal. Therefore something becomes definitely camp, which is absurd. Values change. The value of camp, the ability to perceive things in this unique way, is that it turns values upside down.

I think the whole keynote of the Ridiculous and camp is a rigorous revaluing of everything. What people think is valuable ain't valuable. Admiring what people hold in contempt, holding in contempt things other people think are so valuable—it's a fantastic standard.

For one thing, you can get a great art collection going, because you buy the paintings at the time when people won't sniff at the artist, and they become worth a million dollars in a few years. A Tiffany lampshade in the fifties couldn't be given away, now they're $25,000 minimum.

Most people will only value what is obviously already valued. If you were going to start an art collection, you wouldn't go out and try to buy a Picasso. You couldn't. It's museum quality. It's not for us anymore. It's too late.

The same with stocks and bonds. If you use the rule of camp and Theatre of the Ridiculous in the stock market, you could make a fortune. You buy when it's low and nobody wants it, and then it goes up. If you buy it when it's high, you know it's only going to go down.

■

The worst thing that happened to camp was that the straight world took this cult word and decided they were going to do camp. Then you get something that has nothing to do with camp. There's no vision. The perfect example—let's say I was going to camp on Hitchcock. I would get some editors—everything about Hitchcock is the way the movie looks, the incredible editing; the juxtaposition is highly synthetic and artificial, yet it's so compelling. That should've been the look of *High Anxiety*. Instead, *High Anxiety* was a totally flaccid movie. Everything that's so great about Hitchcock was not there, except that it made reference to one of his movies occasionally. There was no essence in it.

The thing that's really horrible is heterosexual camp, a kind of winking at you saying, "I don't really mean it."

■

I don't think camp can be defined. The word had a value once, in that private language a group enjoys among themselves—doctors; lawyers; theatre people above all, I suppose. Now it has been taken over by everyone, gotten lost in the world, become a meaningless cliché. Anything different these days is "camp." It's as bad as all those great old films and "nostalgia."

■

Camp is all about something in the action or the dialogue or the dress— even in the sets—which in itself is not necessarily unbelonging, but which in relationship to everything else is out of line, on its own. Camp is a way of looking at things, never what's looked at.

I think camp is great. The more people have told me that I had to get away from the word "camp," that it's terrible that people would call my work "camp," the more I decided to embrace it. If nobody wants it, come to me! Bring me your poor, your tired, your yearning to be free! Let my theatre be the repository of all forbidden theatrical conventions!

Gay Theatre

In the theatre there has always been a high percentage of homosexuals because—for one thing—to pursue a life in the theatre it's better not to have a family. Gay people have always found a refuge in the arts, and the Ridiculous theatre is notable for admitting it. The people in it—and it is a very sophisticated theatre, culturally—never dream of hiding anything about themselves that they feel is honest and true and the best part of themselves. *Nothing* is concealed in the Ridiculous.

But proselytizing lifestyles is a Brechtian thing—in the tradition of advertising and propaganda work—which doesn't have anything to do with the absolutely rigorous individualism that goes into our work.

When people were saying there was gay theatre, I think a lot of that was about me, because my theatre was being taken that way, as it should have been. There was nothing wrong with that. However, later, people wanted gay theatre to be a political theatre that catered to gay people's needs for group reinforcement and self-respect, dignifying the gay image. My theatre is terrible for dignifying anybody's image.

The people who wanted to show the respectable gay image—La Coste shorts and pleats—were horrified that in my plays they were always disreputable drag queens, and that monstrosities were being committed. In my plays, people exhibit terrible behavior because it's showing the ridiculous side of life.

My art is not based on showing a positive image for any one group. I think that would be a terrible cop-out. That kind of theatre, the preachy type, has less to do with the gay sensibility than with showing how gay people could be just like straight people.

Once I was on a panel of gay artists at the Old Firehouse of the Gay Activists Alliance with Jill Johnston, Merle Miller and a bunch of others. They were saying that gay people could be just as straight as straight people and I said, "No. Gay people should be more *queer*. We shouldn't give up our difference. We're a different force."

I think the real liberating effect is to have something that dares to be defiant, not to show that we can be normal and married with joint bank accounts and holding down respectable jobs. I know for a lot of people that's very important, but I'm an artist. I can be more bohemian. I don't have to pass for anything. It's not that way in computer programming and teaching grammar school, but my value is to throw things open, let air in on forbidden subject matter. Rather than saying, "Oh, it's all so respectable," I say, "What's so respectable about being respectable?"

My work is very much for people who might not approve of the gayness. I take them over the bumps, make them draw certain conclusions about sexism through parody, hold sexism up to ridicule. The same techniques that other playwrights use to maneuver their audience into a sexist position can also be used to make them accept something they wouldn't ordinarily accept.

In a sense, I think I had a big influence on there being such a thing as gay theatre, but at the same time I wouldn't play at all the way they wanted me to. The rage that might have been in some of my plays could never be transmuted into that kind of comfy-cozy thing.

When we played in San Francisco in 1980, everyone thought, "This is going to be the biggest smash in history." But the gays did not come out, the gay papers panned us, people were saying to me, "Nobody says this to your face, but they don't think you're good for their image."

I felt let down in a way. But I also realized that the straight press was misrepresenting the plays as being more gay even than they were in an attempt to discredit them, and the gay people were playing right into their hands by wanting to be so straight about it.

Also, I think it's very dangerous to create an all-gay community because there's no influence from the outside world.

Everybody but a couple of people in my company are gay, but what we do is political in a different way from gay theatre. It's just entertainment, not agit-prop. It isn't preachy and it's for everybody. Politics is a subsidiary function. My own natural, liberated nature has made it that on a very high level.

I think the distinction between gay theatre and what I do, which some people call "queer theatre," is that gay theatre is really a political movement to show that gay people can be admirable, responsible members of the community. It shows their problems. I don't do that. "Queer theatre" embraces more variation, and the possibility of something being odd or peculiar rather than just simply homosexuality.

Homosexuals, just as women, are not politically one group. They are communists and they are extreme right wing, they are fascists, there is every kind of opinion. Gay becomes an ineffective category, whereas "queer" is a little more of a splash of cold water. There is more room for more people in the queer category.

It's the theatre that is queer. This theatre is weird, it is odd, it's peculiar, it's eccentric, it's different. That is also implied, you see, aside from the slightly smarmy little sexual reference in it.

•

I've written plays that have had gay characters. When I did *Caprice*, I portrayed a gay character. But I got the feeling they wanted Richard Chamberlain playing that particular gay guy. They didn't want to see me as representing gay.

Not that I was representing gay politically in that work. What I was trying to do was to explain the relationship between a homosexual artist—in this case, a fashion designer—and his view of the world.

Because I'm a satirist and inherently try to show what's wrong with the world, some groups become picky, overly sensitive. These people feel that you're being negative and critical to them, which may not be so.

I think that it's ghettoization. It's the same as black theatre.

My theatre does use certain elements of this deviant, deserted point of view to interpret to the world, but it's not gay writing about gay.

Because I am homosexual, it becomes significant to homosexuals, I suppose. But I don't think it's me trying to prove that gay people are these remarkable members of society who are going to be bourgeois, because I don't think that's necessarily right. If they want to, fine. I don't doubt that they can be teachers and office workers who are reliable, but maybe depicting them as dangerous characters would be more interesting. Maybe we're not as housebroken as those plays want to make it seem.

Plays have to be archetypical human situations that everybody's involved in. The weakness of gay plays is that because the character is gay everybody isn't involved, so the gay person, to make it universal, has to be involved in something that could happen to anybody.

It comes down to the question of, "Is it gay theatre if gay people do it?"

We all know that there are a lot of gay people who write, direct, act, produce plays, and are hush-hush about their sexual identity. Their works aren't particularly gay. Some even pretend to be heterosexual.

The avant-garde is largely dominated by gays who are more or less in the closet, whose abstract works and concepts don't relate to their sexuality. Is that gay theatre or is it just abstract?

■

Should a play proselytize, try to preach a lesson about gay liberation? For me, my sexuality has always been right out there—sometimes in question and sometimes *the* issue.

Some artists I know are gay writers writing so-called "normal" plays, year in and year out, and nobody ever mentions what their sexuality is. Nobody cares. Major choreographers, dance theatre, theatre of images, abstract conceptual artists—no one ever brings up *their* sexuality. But from the first day I set foot onstage, my sexuality was a major subject of discussion. It always comes up. I may be exuding my own brand of sexuality, thus making a statement about it, but it's always been there as an issue.

If homosexuality has had an influence on me, it has made me feel a greater understanding of both sexes rather than a limitation.

It's a crazy situation. I think it is an invalid artistic judgment to try to oppress art and turn it into an advertisement tool for a political point of view, which is not even a profound point of view, because a political point of view could change like that! Meanwhile they want you to devote your life to putting out slogans, which is what they do in the press to a large extent. The critics—I think—are very slogan oriented.

Their prejudice creeps in. They're dealing with the fact that to them there's something disreputable about it.

■

They call you female impersonator if you play a woman. But why don't they call the heterosexual men who play gay characters homosexual impersonators? Or heterosexual impersonators. Or male impersonators.

They don't write about it as gay theatre though! They have never, really. A few have tried. But now they have code words. They say that it is camp or put it into a different category I don't think really applies.

Being pigeonholed or put into a category, you can be dismissed, rendered less effective in your interaction with culture. Because what they are really trying to say is, "This is for one audience—a small segment—and it is not for everybody," thereby depriving the majority of people of this work which I think they need!

■

A company that was all male or female would immediately lower the level of artistic consciousness. It would turn into a social club, become political. Women are essential in Ridiculous theatre. If they weren't here, it would be a partial view of the world.

Women fare very well in my plays—they come out on top. Women have traditionally been considered sacred. That's something that had to go out the window if women were to become people.

Obviously, in a Ridiculous play everything is ridiculous, but the women in my company feel that they get a fair shake. Homosexuality is not a sexist phenomenon—so it's not homosexuals against women. It's not so much being against women as being skeptical of them and not taking a kind of blanket sentimental attitude towards them.

Just the idea that women are equal to men doesn't mean anything.

Specific women have to be compared to specific men, and even then—how can you compare two people?

Even the idea of liberating women makes no sense to great women. It only appeals to women who have accepted rather conventional and erroneous ideas about their own existence because of economic factors and the like.

■

My work has something to say for everybody that has nothing to do with sexuality. And I think the company, by not being exclusively a homosexual or a heterosexual company, is a model for social organization, enables people to work together in harmony. They don't have to work with people that have just their own predilections.

The conversations are much more interesting having people of different sexualities call each other on certain preconceptions. There is a lot of that in this theatre, which you wouldn't get in a theatre where everybody is the same.

In theatre where everyone is different, where there are gay men and gay women, heterosexual men, heterosexual women, and other permutations, you find them calling each other on things. It's much the same with race: with racial mix in a company—it becomes much clearer.

■

At some point you have to embrace the terms of oppression. The Ridiculous is a theatre that is not ashamed. It doesn't try to conceal the homosexuality of some of its actors, as others do.

What's happened really is that we reach a much wider audience. What we are doing isn't considered gay art.

I never thought of it as gay art.

Sexuality

Our homosexuality gives us a certain view of the world. All our lives we're taught that certain institutions are sacred—marriage, child-rearing, the family unit—primarily those institutions which we rejected. Once we've thrown that out, it's very hard to behave in a serious manner and make these things terribly important to ourselves. They can never be meaningful to us in that way.

This makes us satirical, because we saw how those things didn't work, as outsiders. We have a more objective view, and objectivity always leads to humor.

Comedy is really more intellectual than tragedy. A humorous attitude is a more intellectual way of looking at something.

They say life is a comedy to those who think and a tragedy to those who feel. I think we're thinkers. We're intellectual in our view of things. We cut off feeling—probably because there's been a tremendous amount of pain in growing up—and look at it cerebrally, and then we become satiric.

Whereas if you're very serious, you're bathing in the emotion of it, allowing for those feelings. I don't think we're people who have allowed for those feelings. We've protected ourselves, in a way, with humor.

We wouldn't look at ourselves as neurotics. That was the problem, part of rejecting psychology. It's only recently that the American Psychiatric Association has declared homosexuality *not* a neurosis. We rejected psychology because psychology rejected us.

Another thing about rejecting psychology was that naturalism and psychology went hand in hand, and naturalism was a very stylized way of looking at life, a stereotyped way of saying that the conditions of your life determined who you were. Anatomy was destiny, Freud said, plus your home, your environment. We rejected that.

But I don't think our theatre *isn't* a psychological theatre. It's very, very psychological because it's working with intuition.

I think we come the closest to having real psychology in the plays because of the way we work. The characters are really true to us and we invest the characters with our own psychology.

There are psychologists—Skinner and so forth—who feel that we are not all that individual, but rather archetypal. People fall into giant patterns, and the specifics are worked out in different ways. For example, in *Hot Ice* there's a very strong Oedipal thing: the gangster's mother brings him out of epileptic seizures through a kind of masturbatory massage. It's very sexual, and the audience is aware of it, yet the characters aren't that much aware that it's sexual. The characters care— it's a problem—but I think it's that way with many people: you see them doing something and they're not totally aware of all its implications.

We deal with these psychological archetypes rather than investing each individual with a tremendous uniqueness. We deal in generic types. People fall into these.

Shakespeare used them, depending on social class, age and experience. People fall into broad types, and you can make them more individual within that context. We work that way, rather than claiming that a character is totally unique, yet everyone sees something of themselves in it. I don't know the mechanism.

With psychological drama, the playwright writes the play and the actor has to figure out the psychology of the character. Here the actors are inventing the roles—I mean, I'm inventing the roles, but it's a give-and-take process. I get an idea, I invent the roles on one level, but I'm constantly being surprised by the actor and changing the idea to go with the stream of the creative process.

It's making a creative situation where you, as you actually are, can work and produce. People look at new art and say, "For God sakes, why can't they be painting a picture like Goya? Why is the ear in the middle of the forehead?" What they don't always understand is that the artist has to innovate. He has to do what it is possible for him to do at his time in history.

Perverted *hetero*sexuality has become the standard mode of behavior in our day. I think a lot of so-called heterosexuality is actually *pseudo*-heterosexuality. For instance, Playboy bunnies and *Playboy* magazine and all that kind of thing: I don't believe it's heterosexual. I don't think it's *homo*sexual. I don't think it's *anything* in particular.

It's some kind of perversion that hasn't been named, that doesn't have a label, because it immediately coopted the name "heterosexuality"—red-blooded "heterosexuality." It is, in fact, a *lie*. It isn't really that at all. It's something else, something akin to the pod people. It's something quite gruesome.

We're told this is *healthy*! It's the *sickest*, most *depraved* thing that possibly exits! It's so *exclusive* in its viewpoint as to what is *erotic*—it's so *specialized* and narrow!

I'm talking about the choice of women in a *Playboy* magazine. If only that teeny one-millionth of one percent of the women that look like that—or *are* that—are erotic, what *is* the human race? What's eroticism?

Do all human beings not have the right to eroticism? Or is it limited to a kind of cloned droid, this abnormally developed, perversely uninteresting kind of woman depicted in those magazine spreads? It's almost as though there's this conspiracy to believe that *older* people can't get it up or don't have any sexual drive anymore. There is no really *lewd* older woman.

Whenever homosexuals are depicted, it's always the *old* homosexual that is so horrifying to everybody. A young homosexual is still attractive and sweet and lovable—maybe misguided . . .—but the old homosexual is the evil monster.

The idea that sex is not merely visual but *tactile* doesn't make any money for media people, because major media are visual media: they're doing photographs, they're doing movies, they're doing TV. It doesn't pay for them to capitalize on the idea that sex is very much a question of touch and how a person *feels*. The tactile is played down because they can't make money on the tactile.

The tactile is the realm of the private. Privacy is negated totally. The idea of someone *looking* attractive becomes so important that it's a complete perversion.

That males of any age, or females of any age, would be interested in each *other* seems to me to be an inalienable human right. You have the right to be erotic with whomever you please. I don't think it's so much a question of heterosexual versus homosexual, any more than civil rights could be black versus white. By focusing on homosexuality as a "perversion," the purveyors of the true perversions cloak their real skullduggery. What they're trying to do by making homosexuality so *unusual* is create a smokescreen to mask their true motives.

I don't *believe* the heterosexuals that homosexuality is something *I* experience and they *don't*. I don't believe it because I know that *heterosexuality* is something that I experience. It may not be my main focus or my strongest interest, but it is something I can experience, appreciate and understand.

But the heterosexuals claim they have *absolutely no* understanding of homosexuality. They don't feel it at all. It never even *occurs* to them— it's *so* different.

I don't believe that they're straight any more than I believe that heterosexuality is so alien to me that I couldn't understand it. People couldn't be artists if such things were true. You couldn't be an actor— *definitely*—if you didn't have every possibility within you. You couldn't act, because you simply couldn't understand it.

I would not believe for a minute that we don't have all the possibilities within us. Because acting, theatre—*art*—would be impossible. There would be no common ground where you could communicate, with images or anything, with other people.

■

What we're really talking about when we talk about gayness is exclusive homosexuality. That's a lot to ask, and I think it's very separatist. There are a lot of people who are bisexual, though it's very hard to maintain your status because you have to keep changing partners every five minutes to prove you still go both ways.

I think it's alienating to people to be forced to decide what they are sexually. Sometimes they might be able to relate to gay people because they've had certain experiences or friends, but it's like you have to be a card-carrying gay, like the Communist Party or a union. As a result, you force people's politics into it. The libido doesn't fit into a political category.

I was on a campus once where some kids were talking about being gay. This guy said he was gay and I said, "Are you seeing anyone?" And he said, "Oh no, I'm not gay sexually, I'm gay politically." I was so dumbfounded I just said, "Oh."

It's difficult to demand that people be that decisive about it. I would rather see people come together on other terms, rather than their sexuality.

I always assume everyone is straight. It's more fun that way.

■

Sexism is a phenomenon that has always interested me. Bedroom farce is the perfect medium for a satire on sexism and people's prejudices based on sexual preferences. Of course, sex is *all* preference. So it's all prejudice.

Where sex is concerned, people tend to put themselves into little mental boxes. In a farce, what makes it fun is that you can reveal these things in strokes, one after the other, very rapidly. And it's a theme dear to all our hearts.

Sex will always be a problem. It can never be a tool for advancing anything.

We have to acknowledge our sexuality, but we also have to laugh at it and put it in its proper place—the way we housebreak animals, the way we subject human instincts to law—and then go on to the next level.

■

In *Torch Song Trilogy*, the central character is a female impersonator and he's in love with a bisexual man. He doesn't play in drag that much, but he is in a sense a woman.

He may mentally be a woman, and then he's in love with a bisexual man, which validates his womanhood. Because this guy is bisexual, he's good enough for this guy. It translates something new into something old.

It's a very moving piece, but it repudiates promiscuity. It just seems to be saying, "I'm a good boy and I don't do that." Well, there are a lot of other boys that do.

To make a moral issue of that I thought was rather odd. I thought the sexual liberation was the interesting part about it. Homosexuality is, after all, sexuality.

Sex is very appealing to those who are against it. Even the Catholic Church says it's okay to be homosexual as long as you don't have sex. So repudiating the promiscuity is almost repudiating the homosexuality. How are you homosexual if you don't actually practice it?

■

It's a moronic concept that men should have exclusive rights to masculinity and women should have exclusive rights to femininity. Proust is a perfect case in point. There was this convention in literature called the Victorian Mask, in which you said one thing but you really meant another. You can decipher these things. Proust's great loves were Albertine and . . . they're all male names transmuted into female ones. In the book, which has a hundred characters, practically all of the hundred characters are homosexual, except Proust himself. He reveals that every woman is a lesbian and every man is homosexual, but Proust himself remains straight. Ha ha.

He wrote an earlier version of the book in which he talked about Marcel as *he*. Then the great breakthrough was that he made it *I*. If it had been a later period, he could have lifted the other veils and masks and been more clearly and directly homosexual.

■

The thing that created the biggest furor at Oscar Wilde's trial was that he had taken this boy who was a very low-class kid and bought him the uniform of Eton, dressed him in the best colors of this aristocratic school, and was walking around with him. That's what they were mostly angry about—that he was trying to pass off this ragamuffin as an aristocrat of birth.

You also find it in *Edward II*, the Marlowe play. They didn't care that the king was committing sodomy with Gaston, but that he was starting to give him titles. Gay has a revolutionary aspect in this creation of a spectacular upward mobility that is inexplicable to the outside world and is rather frightening.

That's part of the power of *Camille* too—the idea of trying to legitimize a courtesan as a respectable woman. Class warfare.

I think this is very interesting, and it isn't being dealt with in *La Cage Aux Folles* and other things like it. I think those things have to be explored. A Proust can do it.

Proust goes into what the subculture was in the gay world and why suddenly there could be spectacular upward mobility. In Proust, there's the Baron de Charlut: no one can know him. He's such a high aristocrat, the bourgeoisie doesn't even get to see him, they can only imagine what his life is like. But he and the stable boy are on a first-name basis.

How does this little nobody know all these important people suddenly? I even find that in my own life. You know somebody because you either had an affair or you were best friends with somebody who had an affair.

I think that's basically what's threatening about homosexuality. It's very forbidden in the armed forces because it would break down discipline, break down authority and create favoritism. Obviously, if some private is the lover of a general, the private will start deciding what wars will be fought and what won't—*or else.*

Politics

I think my theatre is political, but what is political is perhaps misunderstood. Politics is about spheres of influence, and in that sense it is political.

If a man plays Camille, for instance, you begin to think it's horrible, but in the end you are either moved or won over. You believe in the character beyond the gender of the actor, and no one who has experienced that can go back.

In such cases, this theatre is political in the highest sense of influence. But as far as pushing for political upheaval goes, it's not true to the nature of art. Art is not meant to tear society down, it is meant to enhance it.

■

The world outside of the theatre is reflected in the theatre. But *how?* I would be very pretentious if I had a theory about how it works.

All these questions are easy to answer if you have a political justification for theatre. But if your justification isn't political, then it's not so obvious.

Part of the reason for political theatre is that it makes it easier to do art. You'll have a ready-made content. All you have to do is do your work of art to prove it.

That's a lot easier than all the millions of intuitions and choices and selections that go toward finding the solid interrelationship between the parts as they are in themselves.

I don't think art has to be socially important. In fact, one of the great tyrannies over artists is that we are called upon to justify our existence by being socially important. In order to be socially important you have to do something that's *already considered important*, which means serving the ends of someone who already has the power.

■

What commitment do I need to go on living and to create this work? The minute theatre has to justify itself outside of itself you have a political message.

The world outside of the theatre is changing and you reflect it. One does act upon the world when the work has an incredible impact on the lives of the people who see the play. One sets an example. One's endurance, one's ability to pursue excellence, the consistency of top high quality—this gives courage and heart to people. It assures them.

The public feels a certain confidence in me. They know that I will do this, that I will continue to do this. It makes an example for them to pursue *their* careers or the things that *they* do.

And they identify my developments with their own personal problems. I am sure, from the people I have talked to, it becomes very important for them. It marks a moment of their lives when they saw that play, when one of my plays was running. It's a measurement of time.

■

As far as politics is concerned, I think this is something that has to be induced. It's a question of *establishing* a political system, but it is also a question of *using* a political system—to make a life.

Most people are so involved with studying something new that they aren't really involved in the working out of the details of it once it's established. Revolutionaries are never concerned with how to make a new system work once they get rid of the old one. They don't really have to face that problem, so they are able to just be destructive. They are able to tear a building down, but they don't have to build a new building. They have no concepts. They are not architects.

Clearing the way is part of the process, but I think there is the element of enhancing society, making it better, improving it and building new structures. Just tearing down old structures is not enough.

There are rewards for architects, we honor architects. But how many architects are honored for tearing down a building?

Revolution is the opposite of the function of art. With revolution you can't really have art, because it's a change, a shifting away from the structure. Artists are trying to make the best of the situation *now* and improve it from *within*. They are not assaulting it from the outside, trying to batter it down.

The more you oppose something, the more you strengthen it. If you are able to change it from inside, you can make it what you want it to be. Banging away from the outside just strengthens the defenses against the attack.

■

Instead of making utopia a faraway place, I make it in this place, now. Instead of having to wait for utopia, we can make utopia right now, right away, start working on it now.

"Utopia" is Greek for "nowhere"; that means "not possible," to begin with. What I am saying is that the impossible can be possible. The impossible is constructed of fragments of the possible—in a new arrangement.

What can be imagined is only what is experienced. Imagination is the process of taking many little things that you experience and piecing them together in a new arrangement.

I am trying to make it clear that the process of rearranging them is a practical process that everyone can immediately get involved in. Make the dream into reality by simply rearranging the pieces.

■

New York is the super-society that is, at the same time, the jungle. They both exist in man. It is not that the outside world doesn't work, it is that we *are* this. And we are also dreamers and philosophers. They exist side by side in us.

The more you accept the rules of society, the freer you are as an individual. The more you are able to conform on the small issues, the unimportant things, the more you are able to be wild or eccentric. That's been my solution.

■

I've never done sixties-style agitprop theatre. I've seen a few other companies do some good political productions, but I've also seen too many instances in which the actors were preaching to audiences who knew more about politics than the people onstage.

I saw this gay political theatre company do a piece for an audience that was full of transsexuals, drag queens and people in full-tilt leather with pierced nipples and tattoos on their faces. The performers came out onstage and confronted the audience with lines like, "You—with your button-down collars and your business suits—you ought to be. . . ." Yet there was nobody in the theatre to whom that applied! Everyone there was as wild and as freaked-out and as sexually liberated as you could get, so what the actors were saying was absurd!

In order to really be political you have to get people thinking, and you can't do that by just going onstage and repeating the same old catch phrases. Much of what passed for political theatre in the sixties was just a fashion, like wearing khakis.

■

The left is in a shambles because there is a lot of conflict about which special-interest group will be helped and how much. The left is divided into a lot of factions, which gives it excitement, but at the same time they are not able to present a coordinated or a united front. Because the left has failed to present a united front, there is, unfortunately, a lot of infighting. I think eventually the left will reemerge as a concept, but at the moment it's all a mess.

The right on the other hand is united by one burning desire—*greed.*

■

Since Reagan got in, there are more people in the street. I see the wreckage. You see one who sits next to a puddle and floats little boats, throws flowers into the puddle. Do you know the one who paints her face blue? And the one who juggles with glass bottles? She talks to herself, just throwing one bottle up in the air and catching it. All around her is broken glass and she's standing there in bare feet. But . . . how . . . weird!

■

I'm not taking drugs anymore, for personal reasons. But probably if they had legalized all these drugs years ago, we wouldn't be having this current problem.

Let's say if there were really high-quality hashish available in the dime store and at the tobacconist, or if people who are now heroin addicts could smoke opium in an official opium den and the government could somehow control it, rather than Mafia gangsters, maybe there wouldn't be as much blood on the streets.

Death. I mean, some people are going to kill themselves anyway. People smoke cigarettes, drink alcohol. These are legal means of suicide.

But I think the Nancy/Ronnie drug investigations are medieval witch-hunting, looking for people with drugs in their systems. But are they looking to find antibodies?

I honestly don't feel that our political figures are honest with us about their own practices, do you? We certainly can't believe anything the Republicans say. It's just come out that they spread all those lies about Kaddafi. Who can believe anything?

You can be sure there's much more going on just beneath the surface. This has been true in most every administration except for Jimmy Carter's.

I think we should have Carter back. Carter was good. If only he could have gotten over his born-again religion.

■

The fear of inflation, the nonissues that drove Carter out of office. . . .
One was the hostage crisis. The hostages were freed the moment
Reagan took his vow of office. But *he* had done nothing to free them.
That was the political gesture on the part of the Iranians.

When asked, Reagan said, "I would have handled this differently."
Finally, he was asked, "How would you have handled it?" and he said he
would have done nothing and now that's what he does do. Nothing.

He will not negotiate. What he means is *take those hostages and kill
them, I don't care!* No negotiating! This is what people would prefer to
the attempts to negotiate. That's one thing.

The other thing is the fear of inflation. Inflation is a good thing.
People don't realize that there's only one cure for inflation and that is
depression.

Reagan had the courage in his first days of office to induce a mild
depression and also to induce a realignment of wealth in the country,
letting a lot of people have no money so fewer people could have more.
Since the people who will have less don't have much power . . .

However, there's no reason why money shouldn't have an expira-
tion date on it. Why doesn't the dollar bill become worthless, like a
quart of milk? *As of January 29th, this dollar bill will no longer be any
good!* You have to spend, you have to keep that money moving. Isn't that
a good idea?

■

Now we're in a period where the people are obsessed with the economy
and ignoring culture. What they're going to find is that it doesn't matter
if you have a wild stock market, money in the bank and a lot of earthly
goods if the culture you are living in is debased. The quality of life
suffers. Is it going to matter whether you are wealthy if the air is
polluted? Is it going to matter whether you are well off if there is no
fresh produce without contamination? Is it going to be worth living in a
world where you are not allowed to commit sodomy, which is one of the
joys of life for heterosexuals as well as homosexuals?

To stray from the missionary position is simply a question of
applying a little imagination to sexual life. Sex has just been put on the

books as illegal. This Supreme Court ruling means *do not use your imagination* and it is therefore a form of fascism.

How can we talk about going to a summit and discussing human rights when we are proffering judges who have opposed human rights, from the simplest idea that blacks should vote to the freedom to express your love for another human being willingly, in private, any way you choose?

You now feel this fascism moving into art, too. How dare you express that? How dare you play the role of a woman? How dare you elevate women from the position they're in? How dare you be sexual? That's next!

■

Everything changes. The Village has to change too, I guess.

When I first came to the Village in the sixties, people were complaining, "Oh, it's ruined, it was great in the thirties." So it goes on.

Bohemia is a state of mind, too, and it may not necessarily be a good thing to be a bohemian. I think there is a problem of ghettoizing yourself and not having an impact on the culture at large. To resist that confrontation, to hide out with people who also believe as you do and spend endless hours drinking cups of black coffee, telling each other how great each one is, is a kind of mutual admiration society.

Sometimes it's important to get out there and really interact with the culture, awful as it may be, and not allow yourself to be ghettoized. *Salammbô* was about that, and it was one of the reasons people were outraged.

I certainly couldn't have called it an AIDS play; it had nothing to do with that. But it was about *the official religion*, which was a state religion, a fascist state that stated, "All who touch the veil must die!" Then you had to die to prove that they were right—in the play—that society always has to be right, even if they're dead wrong in actuality.

■

I'm not sure that I'm prepared to talk about the AIDS question. We all know that people have had to change the way they live.

I think there are combinations of things that make for change. For instance, the real-estate profiteering in this city, which has created a dangerous, almost pathological situation.

Organized society decided that it might be fun to be conservative, and they have to roll in that shit for a while before they find out what shit is. And believe me, it's now sticking to them, and they stink.

The right wing won in a fair open election by a landslide. That means the same people who just a few years previous to this were totally disillusioned with the Republican Party through the corruption of the Nixon administration forgot, or changed their minds, or decided to go back to it with an even greater belief than before. So the American public has what they want. All I can say is they have to experience the pits to find out the truth.

Unfortunately, American society, and maybe all societies, can't cope with real problems, like the AIDS pandemic, until it becomes a crisis. Nobody wants to listen. Then all of a sudden it's a disaster situation and everyone is forced to deal with it. But then it can be too late to prevent it in a simple way.

■

Even in the period of so-called "promiscuity"—which means being indiscriminate—there wasn't anything indiscriminate. People were being very choosy, but they were still having multiple partners. There may have been a few who just put on a blindfold.

It's sad that we've had to go back to the nineteenth century, when syphilis was the deadly disease and people couldn't be as free as they once had been. But even at the height of sexual looseness and license and libertinism, many people did have permanent primary relationships that they returned to. They all went out and fooled around and came back. This is something that heterosexuals do, too.

Heterosexuals gave up the right to moralize when they accepted the pill and abortion.

Assorted Maxims
and Epigrams

1. From time immemorial, music from within has inspired slaves to dance. It is in this way that joy and relief make themselves felt. But theatre is more than the casting off of shackles. We must find harmony with the order of the universe. The celebrations of sacrificial feasts and sacred rites are the means employed by great rulers to unite men. They give expression to the interrelation of the family and its social articulation in the state. Sacred music and splendid ceremony arouse a tide of emotion shared by all hearts in unison. The spectacle must go down to the very foundations of life, awakening a consciousness of the common origin of all creatures.

2. Theatre is the supreme art. It's life itself—you give people two hours of your life, onstage. Time is all we have, and sharing that with people is different from just creating an object.

   It gives people a sense of time, that life begins and life ends. It gives an intensification of life, for several hours—heightened experience, or much more distilled experience than perhaps you would get just sitting around and having a cup of coffee. Something you can't get from the bodily functions.

   You can't get it from sex, you can't get it from food, you can't get it from breathing. You can only get it from the theatre.

3. Ridiculous theatre is celebrant art. The Universe is nothing conceived as illusory pairs of contradictions. Each existent (existing

thing) stands as a peculiarly eloquent hieroglyph for the meaning of all things. Implied is an emphasis on the art of *living*. This nondiscriminatory state of innocence—which I call simplemind-edness, which is at the heart of the creative act—is indistinguish-able from idiocy or insanity. Hence the name Ridiculous Theatre.

4. A theatre that gives a forum to widely varied kinds of people can express unpopular nonconformist points of view, thereby preserv-ing a spirit of independence and the importance of the individual, as opposed to the utility and sacrifice of the individual to the general good.

5. To expand the subject matter permissible in the theatre, from the purely domestic problems to those of a more metaphysical and universal relevance.

6. Man's place in the universe, rather than in the family or a political system.

7. Psychology must be banished from the theatre.

8. Theatre mustn't just ape our daily, literal existence. It should provide us with a vicarious emotional life, for many things that we might like to explore as human beings are really too dangerous to explore firsthand. Theatre is a place where we can try out danger-ous ideas in a relatively harmless way.

9. As I get older, I find I prefer the Three Stooges to the Marx Brothers—that insane sadism. I find it very refreshing.

10. There are some things that might disturb people, but sometimes it's what you want. You just reach the point where you know what you're doing and you do it deliberately, and make it the way you want it.

11. At the heart of the dramatic event lies the spirit of masochism. In the boxing ring or at a tragedy it is the delight in conflict and the illusion of opposition that enthralls. The primary desire of the audience is to witness suffering. The actor willingly undergoes the ordeal of passing through various states of physical and mental torture. Could the theatre ever become a place of profound serenity?

12. The thing that Artaud finally contributed and that dominates our work and that we don't always say is the idea of there being a level of

consciousness that's above morality. It is impossible to operate on this level that Nietzsche called master morality. It opposes Christian morality. It's a pagan idea.

13. The theatre takes on a religious quality because it has to be circumscribed by some kind of control. The mystic act at the core of most religions is usually a terribly dangerous act, always circumscribed by a ritual and convention in order to control something basically dangerous.

14. Theatre is a place set aside to do things that are amoral and dangerous in an experimental way. We enact fearful things or things that we couldn't enact in our everyday lives as a kind of experiment to see what it would be like, how it is.

15. Do you want to be a tragedian or do you want to be a tragic hero in your real life? Do you want to actually live through a tragedy or experience it vicariously? A vicarious experience of something that would be suicidal in real life can be experienced in the theatre with some safety.

16. Heroes are undemocratic characters. It's undemocratic for one character to be that much better. It's sort of *unfair*.

17. Originally, in Greece, there was the festival of Dionysus. Dionysus was the embodiment of an amoral god, primordial, libidinous.

18. Onstage we go beyond ourselves, not limited by morality. That is really the contribution of Artaud. Most people took it on a very superficial level. It ended up being fancy dress.

19. So many artists and critics want to be avant-garde—that is, they imagine doing a play that is painting because they have been taught to recognize the avant-garde in painting and in music. But they are incapable of doing an avant-garde play. When confronted with a "true play" that is avant-garde, they reveal the paucity of their understanding, their thick conservatism. Slaves of their own preconceptions, they miss every moment where the medium has been stretched to the inconceivable and complain as slaves complain. Indeed, the dull ache of incomprehension causes suffering, where the truly fresh audience—not hampered by a conflict of interests— exalts in originality, the quality most desired and most rarely contained in a work of art.

20. To cultivate innovation where there is dramatic necessity, a refreshing alternative to the avant-garde academy, whose formal experiments and minimalist esthetics provide no outlet for skill, virtuosity and passion.

21. Any artist experiments, but all experimenting should be over by the time the audience comes in.

22. One of the problems with accepting a tag like avant-garde or gay theatre or neo-post-infra-realism is that you're a bit like an Indian on a reservation selling trinkets to the tourists. You have no real interaction with the culture, and whatever impact you may have had on that culture is nullified.

    That's why I'll always refuse to be typed as this or that. If people take the trouble to come here more than once, they see I don't have an axe to grind, even though I do have a mission. That mission is to have a theatre that can offer possibilities that aren't being explored elsewhere.

    If you ask me why I've lasted so long, maybe that's the answer: I'm here because I keep coming up with possibilities.

23. I don't think in years, I think in productions. The period that it takes to get a show together is like a year in your mind, so my time sense is based on that.

24. Even when I wasn't being appreciated, I was being appreciated by people who mattered to me.

25. The early plays were a progression of images, small leitmotifs. The progress in our work, especially my work as a director, has been gaining mastery of the whole canvas. All the parts fit together in a very intricate way now. In the early plays sometimes I lost the forest for the trees. Individual images would be very striking, but I didn't always have them all interrelated as clearly as they are now. Now it's all very much a whole.

26. I remember when it was rough and tumble and wild and sleazy. It was sort of a poetic, romantic thing. First there were strip shows and then there were these immortal masterworks being done, so arty and aesthetic and gorgeous and sumptuous and poetic, right next to all that riffraff. It really felt good.

27. There is a fantastic voyeuristic pornography on 42nd Street, where

there are little booths in a circle, with naked women writhing in the center. Men stand in the booths and look through little peepholes that have a curtain that goes up when they pay a quarter, and after a few minutes comes down.

I can see some kind of incredible event going on inside such a circle, where people would get their theatre twenty-five cents at a time. The curtain would go up and come down. You'd have to keep putting another quarter in if you wanted to find out what happened.

28. I regard my contemporary culture as culture; it doesn't have to be European. An evening at the Metropolitan Opera can be claptrap and trash while you could go to a cheap zombie movie and there could be art there. It's completely possible.

The ambiance and the amount of money and who goes and who doesn't go: these things don't guarantee that a creative experience is going to be had, because it's all being done by human beings, and they err or they triumph. Those prejudices don't hold up.

29. That's the battle: to make theatre great when you think it isn't, when you're in a period of commercial prostitution and banalization.

30. The difference between the commercial theatre where you have investors and the art theatre which is supported by the government is that government money is given with no strings attached. The New York State Council on the Arts, for example, buys performances, services. It's a good way to do it. Because government money is buying services, you must come up with what you promised to do.

It's a question of having working capital. If you take it from investors, you have to answer to their artistic demands. Fortunately, since the government money is allocated by experts, they only give it to people with high artistic standards.

31. There are all kinds of cuckoo ways of making money in show business. Doing nonprofit is a small way of doing something very fine.

32. We're always in terrible debt, but that just means we have good credit.

33. You can be much less responsible without government subsidy. With the funding, you have to meet certain standards. You have to start bookkeeping. Everything has to be in order. Every penny you spend has to be accounted for.

34. It requires a certain amount of structure and discipline and order to be able to handle government funds, to receive them and to serve the taxpayer. Anyone who is able to muster this much discipline can get funding if they have some artistic merit and they've found some form of audience. It's very fair. It's just incredibly difficult to make that transition.

35. Hits in the theatre are a problem.

36. In the theatre, free seats hiss first.

37. I'm just glad to be alive and have an audience.

38. "Bohemianism": a milieu to which most artists and poets have been reduced throughout the capitalist epoch.

39. Sell advertising space on the front curtain.

40. People in New York have only seen me work in a small theatre. However, all my training is in large theatres. When we toured Europe, we always played large theatres. But here, because of real estate and all that, we play a small theatre.

41. Theatre is not a decorous place where people go on their good behavior. It's a place where human values, shared by all, supersede those of divisive political factions.

42. I don't like theatre that tries to proselytize, that always tries to reprimand people or reform them. It assumes that the audience is dumber than they are.

43. How could people who celebrated the irrational—the surrealists— ally themselves with revolution, which is based on the concept of man's perfectibility?

44. Gay theatre encourages those who may not have the strength to stand alone against cultural traditions which seek to denigrate and trivialize their profound human needs.

45. Camp is motivated by rage.

46. Homosexuality is a consequence of machismo. One reaches the point at which women become too effeminate for one.

47. Character is that which reveals moral purpose, showing what kinds

of things a man chooses or avoids. Speeches, therefore, which do not make this manifest, or in which the speaker does not choose or avoid anything whatever, are not expressive of character.

48. The actor is a person who can believe anything.

49. With Maria Montez, as with pornography or anything held in low esteem, it's really a cultural prejudice, it's not inherently low. Those films were meant for children. They were meant to be comedies and she gave her all. She gave the films a conviction, which was a fabulous quality to impose on something that most people wouldn't care for.

   The thing those movies don't have that today's movies do is actors sort of winking at you from behind their masks, telling you they don't mean it. I prefer actors not protecting themselves, not afraid to look foolish, not afraid to be thought mad. If actors then could seem to be possessed by their roles, they could justify any kind of theatrics, because the conviction of motivation was there to fill out this bigger form. Not everyone has that much life to fill a bigger form, and those who do become great performers.

50. Actors who come upon the Stanislavski system a little on in their careers are more "theatrical," not because of any fault in the method as it was taught by the master, but taking into account the myriad misinterpretations of that method as it is taught in the United States. Actors should know the system, though. It is essential to any fruitful work in the modern theatre.

51. Artaud was a springing-off point for me, the idea that actors could be hieroglyphic symbols. A character is an embodiment of a concept made of flesh and blood. That gives tremendous strength.

52. The theatre has been held in a kind of death grip during the last seventy years of naturalism. It has evolved into pornography—a peephole on life. Actors are not supposed to know they're being watched. The lie is that what we're seeing is not supposed to be a performance.

   I wanted a theatre where the actor admits to the presence of an audience, where he is free of that pall of reality. I'm trying to liberate the theatre and myself from that—deliberately and consciously.

53. We try to break each other up a lot. Breaking up is an indication that the thing is working, that it's funny. It's part of the atmosphere of rehearsal—enjoyment.

54. Something that gets a laugh once in rehearsal may never get a laugh again because the surprise is gone, or people have seen you do it so many times. There's a tendency to drop it before opening night, forgetting how funny it was the first time. That's a problem—keeping things in: instinct reminding the actor that something was good, that it worked; to trust that it will be funny again for people who haven't seen it yet.

55. Sometimes the greatest effect comes from treating a comic situation seriously.

56. I act better when I forget that I wrote and directed the play.

57. There should be a balance of elements. Even a balance between successful scenes and unsuccessful, a balance between good acting and bad.

58. I would not do anything to impress the audience favorably or unfavorably. I am no performing dog. And yet, if I can do something that will get a laugh, why not?

59. I personally become alarmed if a performer tries to involve me in a play. I find it terrifying. And I'm an actor.

60. Certain qualities considered vices in other people are actually virtues in actors: their talent for lying and their contrariness.

61. If you're going to do drag, you have to specialize in it. You drive yourself crazy if you keep switching back and forth.

62. I want to be taken seriously as an actress.

63. One thing I've been lucky about in my career is that I've had the sense to play characters and do themes that were the right age for me. Great themes require great maturity.

64. All actors, you'll notice, wanted to be marine biologists.

65. People send me scripts and say, "This is for you." It's in drag and it has dwarves and it isn't for me. They don't understand that it's not for me. It doesn't have anything to do with what I'm doing.

66. Acting, directing, staging the play and writing it are all one act for me. I conceive of them all together.

67. You learn from one thing to another. Playwrighting is improved by

acting because you can develop a feel for the dialogue. Yet I think you make slower progress in some ways when you have to do everything yourself.

68. The immediacy of comedy and its audience rapport has served as a touchstone for our wildest experiments. After being subjected to a Darwinian process of selection, we have evolved into a hardy perennial.

69. I think of myself as part of a viable tradition in theatre. The romance of the theatre gives me energy and inspiration: Molière acting in his own plays, with his wife and his two brothers-in-law; Shakespeare playing a lead in Ben Jonson's *Every Man in His Humour*; Marlowe and Kyd sharing a room in London. I feel a part of all that.

70. Most plays never turned out the way I imagined them, so it began to make sense to write them myself.

71. I devote myself to unearthing literary oddities which I savor the way a pig savors truffles.

72. Sometimes men invent great ideas. Other times they are just diction.

73. That's what happened to modern playwrighting . . . no more servants or slaves for color. The only plus today is the telephone, but it's still not the same.

74. I embrace Aristotle. I kiss his sexy Greek feet.

75. My work is eclectic, not ethnocentric. It is a Rosetta Stone of theatrical conventions.

76. The unifying theme in my work is the thrall of Scheherazade. The spinning of a new tale. The thousand and one nights divided by the thirty-six plots of Gozzi.

77. You don't want to do the same thing forever, but you do. It's just little discoveries that keep you going.

78. As you get better at plotting skeletal structures you find all kinds of plays that don't seem to have anything to do with each other are the same thing. A friend of mine is reading *Our Town* and I'm adapting *A Christmas Carol*. They're the same thing. She comes back from the grave; he sees beyond his death and sees the past. It's the same phenomenon. That thing of her coming back from the grave and

seeing the people going about their lives and having more information than they have just kills you. The same thing happens to Scrooge when he sees himself as a child, and he starts weeping for this child.

79. I don't think about immortality. I do think about my work as an ongoing stream of development.

80. Life is so short. We are travelers in the universe. We come from the infinite and we are journeying towards the infinite. What is there to do but amuse ourselves as much as possible?

81. My supreme dictum of art is self-indulgence. If you're not indulging yourself, then you're pandering . . . "to thine own self be true," and so on.

It's the hardest thing in the world to be truly self-indulgent. It has such a bad reputation. The first thing you need is a self to indulge. And you have to know what that self is, and then you have to develop a technique to realize what you imagine, which isn't that easy either.

82. I've taught playwrighting. I've taught directing. I do commedia dell'arte workshops where we use a scenario and create our own modern play out of it. The students make up their own lines.

It's extremely draining, because I take it very seriously. It takes all my energy, all my imagination, all my creativity during that period, and with all that I could have staged a play, I could have done a whole production.

Basically I try to impart the idea that it can be done, so the students feel they can do a play the same way I do. In a very unpretentious way, I try to guide them, but I also try to accept what's there.

Students who take a class with me usually know my work and esteem it. They come because they like what I do already and want some insight into how I go about it. But I can't give them the meaning of life, or salvation. I can only give them a mode of working.

Sometimes the students think they know more than I do, and they either get over that or else I let them go on thinking it. My view is that if they think they know more than I do, they are wasting their money and their time.

It's not going to do me any good to try to convince them. I don't have a cause. I offer myself to them and if they don't want me, there's nothing I can do.

83. When I teach I become very conservative, because what you're trying to give students is a technique. I am a craftsman as much as an artist. And that's the important thing, the craft. They think they're going to get some kind of wild thing because I'm wild, but you have to have a concrete technique before you can express anything.

That's the problem with teaching—it automatically makes you conservative, because you're trying to conserve something: the accumulated knowledge about this artform that's worth passing on.

84. Since *my* technique is totally digested and second nature to me, I can do all sorts of things—I can do things wrong, so to speak, deliberately, to get an effect. Whereas if you teach someone else to do it wrong, they're just doing it wrong.

85. I don't believe in limits.

86. The creator develops the need to cease to exist. And the comedian develops the need to be a tragic hero.

87. It is important that people be exposed to the past through repertory houses, but it is a form of snobbery not to be interested in the minor works of minor artists. That leaves no space for the small virtues, the byways of the arts.

88. It seems vulgar to me always to want only the grandest and best of the past. It shows a lack of confidence in ourselves. And it is wrong to think the masterpieces of the past cannot be matched.

89. There is theatre where it doesn't matter whether it is good or bad. It matters that it is interesting or not interesting. Even bad theatre can be sometimes interesting.

90. In opera staging it is not so much a question of having the right idea or the wrong idea but to avoid the appearance of having had any idea at all.

91. As the Living Theatre moved to sheer physical theatre, I began to back away. It didn't suit my temperament, my abilities, to do that, although I was very impressed with it. I wanted a theatre of illusion

in which I could break illusions if I wanted to. That was too de-illusionistic for me. It really went with no illusion, and the sheer physicality. . . . I didn't think it was a theatre you could grow old in, because it was too athletic! It is also a problem I had with dance.

92. Why is it so good to be young? Is life so bad that the less one has lived it the better? Being young never got me anywhere. I just had a miserable time trying to prove that what I wanted to do made sense.

93. I don't blame people for what they are, but only for seeming to be what they are not.

94. So often it happens that with possession the vast poetry of desire must end, and the thing possessed is seldom the thing that we dreamed of.

95. There are three mirrors in my dressing room: one in which I look unbelievably gorgeous. One in which I look unbelievably ugly. And one I never look in. I never know which one to believe.

96. Artistic temperament is seldom recognized until it is too old to spank.

97. If you tell people the truth you'd better make them laugh or they'll kill you.

98. If I dance I want to get paid for it.

99. I tiptoed down the hall to the mirrored study door so as not to wake the birds—I took this notebook. Closed the door. Sounds of rain against the windowpane. The description of . . . nothing useful. With so many secrets locked in my heart—must cross out that line—something every day—

ENVOI

CHARLES: You must continue the theatre.

EVERETT: But I can't write. I don't know how.

CHARLES: Steal lines. Orchestrate platitudes. Hang them on some plot you found somewhere else.

EVERETT: But I don't know how to make it funny.

CHARLES: You don't have to worry about that. Funny is in the eye of the beholder. You know yourself from doing the same play every night. Some audiences are solemn and others laugh. Let the audience be the judge of what is funny.

The art of playwrighting can be passed on from father to son. Stefan Brecht should have continued in his father's footsteps. Remember Dumas *père et fils*.

EVERETT: But I'm not related. I don't come from the same gene pool as you.

CHARLES: It's not genetic. It's technology. And you don't have to do everything yourself. Delegate responsibility. There are plenty of talented people around.

EVERETT: But they won't do what I tell them.

CHARLES: They will if you pay them.

EVERETT: But the audiences want *you*.

CHARLES: They'll like some plays and they won't like others. It was ever so.